AMERICA'S
TAIWAN DILEMMA

AMERICA'S
TAIWAN DILEMMA

Allies' Reactions and the Stakes for US Reputation

Michael A. Hunzeker and Mark A. Christopher

Rapid Communications in Conflict and Security Series
General Editor: Thomas G. Mahnken
Founding Editor: Geoffrey R. H. Burn

CAMBRIA
PRESS

Amherst, New York

*To our wives,
for not leaving us the moment we said,
"We want to write a book."*

Library of Congress Cataloging-in-Publication Data

Names: Hunzeker, Michael A. author | Christopher, Mark A. author

Title: America's Taiwan dilemma : allies' reactions and the stakes
for US reputation / Michael A. Hunzeker and Mark A. Christopher.

Description: Amherst : Cambria Press, [2025] |
Series: Rapid communications in conflict and security |
Includes bibliographical references and index. |
Summary: "America's Taiwan Dilemma: Allies' Reactions and the Stakes for US Reputation
offers a rigorous open-source analysis of how America's key allies-Japan, South Korea, and
Australia-would respond to US intervention or inaction in a Taiwan conflict. Drawing on
over 100 interviews with experts from Japan, South Korea, Australia, Taiwan, and the United
States, it examines how domestic politics, threat perceptions, and regional dynamics shape
allied expectations of Washington. The study explores the implications for US credibility,
alliances, and deterrence strategies across the Indo-Pacific. By analyzing allies' perspectives-
sometimes contradictory but pragmatic-the book identifies both shared concerns and
divergent interests. It assesses how US policy choices toward Taiwan may strengthen or
strain alliances amid rising tensions with China. Providing critical insights into East Asian
security and alliance management, this study addresses the future of US reputation and
regional stability in a rapidly evolving strategic environment"-- Provided by publisher.

Identifiers: LCCN 2025018632 (print) | LCCN 2025018633 (ebook) |
ISBN 9781638573395 library binding | ISBN 9781638573531 paperback
ISBN 9781638573562 epub | ISBN 9781638573579 pdf

Subjects: LCSH: United States--Foreign relations--Taiwan | Taiwan--
Foreign relations--United States | Alliances | Security, International--Taiwan
| United States--Foreign relations--21st century | Taiwan--Foreign relations |
Deterrence (Strategy)--United States | United States--Military relations--Taiwan

Classification: LCC E183.8.T3 H86 2025 (print) | LCC E183.8.T3 (ebook) |
DDC 327.73051249--dc23/eng/20250626

LC record available at https://lccn.loc.gov/2025018632

LC ebook record available at https://lccn.loc.gov/2025018633

TABLE OF CONTENTS

ACKNOWLEDGMENTS

We would like to thank the following distinguished experts—as well as those who preferred to remain anonymous—for generously taking the time to meet with us. This book would not have been possible without their insights. We nevertheless take full and sole responsibility for the representations and analysis that follows, along with any errors, inaccuracies and/or omissions. These individuals are Chris Bassler, Richard C. Bush, Sungmin Cho, W. Brent Christensen, In-Bum Chun, Elbridge Colby, Zack Cooper, Andrew Chubb, James Curran, Rorry Daniels, Michéle Flournoy, Michael Fonte, Aaron L. Friedberg, Stephan Früling, Madoka Fukuda, John Garnaut, Bonnie S. Glaser, Michael J. Green, Allan Gyngell, Jerad Harper, Harry B. Harris, Mark Harrison, Iain D. Henry, Jeffrey W. Hornung, Chris Hughes, George Hutchinson, Shigeru Iwasaki, Craig Kafura, Nobukatsu Kanehara, Natasha Kassam, Katsutoshi Kawano, Patricia M. Kim, Youngjun Kim, Yoji Koda, Raymond Kuo, David M. Lampton, David Landon, Hsi-min Lee, Nan Li, Darren J. Lim, Bonny Lin, Chen-wei Lin, Oriano Skylar Mastro, Yoshiro Matsuda, Futoshi Matsumoto, Michael J. Mazarr, Kunihiko Miyake, Satoru Mori, James F. Moriarty, Sadamasa Oue, Jaehan Park, Patrick Porter, Matthew Pottinger, Evan J.R. Revere, Sam Roggeveen, Mick Ryan, Ryo Sahashi, Brendan Sargeant, In-Hyo Seol, Ming-shih Shen, Michael Studeman,

Tzu-yun (Hans) Su, Huruyoki Sugai, Yun Sun, Kharis Templeman, Yuki Tatsumi, Ayumi Teraoka, Drew Thompson, Tsuneo Watanabe, Lu-chung (Dennis) Weng, Hugh White, Enoch Wu, Yao-yuan Yeh, Toshi Yoshihara, Tong Zhao, and Weifeng Zhong.

It is perhaps only fitting that a book about alliances and what it takes to sustain them in times of crisis was itself the result of an intense, multi-year collaboration undertaken during a pandemic between two colleagues living 1,500 miles apart. As is so often the case with any alliance, neither of us really knew what we were getting ourselves into when we set off to explore how US decision-making in response to an attack on Taiwan might—or might not—reshape allied perceptions of its credibility. The impetus came from a pair of simulations we ran in 2019. In one, we asked US experts to fill the shoes of American, Australian, Chinese, Japanese, South Korean, and Taiwanese leaders in the wake of a cross-Strait war in which the United States successfully defended Taiwan. In the other, we challenged those same experts to fill those same shoes (sans Taiwan's) in the wake of a cross-Strait war in which the United States remained on the sidelines. Before the exercises, we expected that America's simulated allies would act in a profoundly different way when faced with evidence of American abandonment. We were surprised (to say the least) that this was not the case. The yawning gap between our intuitive expectations and what we observed in our experimental simulation seemed sufficiently puzzling to warrant deeper and more rigorous exploration.

Little did we know that it would take another four years to reach the conclusion of this journey, the results of which we present in the following pages. While those findings will hopefully speak for themselves, we also want to take a moment to recognize and thank those who offered invaluable assistance along the way. There is no question our intellectual alliance would have faltered were it not for this latticework of supportive partnerships. Early on, Kenneth Allen provided crucial insight and advice from his own Day After project. We owe an intellectual debt of gratitude to Iain Henry, whose interview, *International Security* article, and Cornell

University Press book really helped us make sense of what we were hearing in our dozens upon dozens of interviews. We likewise owe an enormous mental and emotional health debt of gratitude to Michael Sweeney and Sophia Lutz, both of whom toiled away at the Sisyphean task of trying to keep us on track and on time as lead graduate research assistants. Joseph Ross, Brian Davis, Carter Plemmons, Clarisa Mclaney, Caitlin Harrington, and Tayyaba Malik also provided vital research assistance in the project's critical first year. Sam George and Maciej Kisilowski provided extremely valuable comments and feedback on the manuscript. And we would be remiss if we didn't thank our children for their unflagging encouragement. (Representative sample: "Good luck on your book, Dad. It sounds BORING!")

Finally, we want to thank the American Academy of Strategic Education for allowing us to run the simulations that inspired this book; the Canadian Forces College, the Center for Security Policy Studies (Arlington) and the Center for Security Policy Studies (Korea) for providing feedback on our preliminary findings; George Mason University's Schar School of Policy and Government for providing undergraduate and graduate research assistants to work on the project; our anonymous reviewers, Thomas Mahnken, and the entire editorial team at Cambria Press for their invaluable assistance with preparing this book for publication; and the Smith Richardson Foundation for its generous financial support.

AMERICA'S
TAIWAN DILEMMA

INTRODUCTION

Is Taiwan a Bellwether for American Credibility in East Asia?

Cross-Strait relations are on a perilous trajectory. War might not be inevitable, but the risk of an armed conflict over Taiwan's status is real and growing. If China attacks Taiwan, the United States will find itself in a difficult position, forced to choose between defending the island nation or leaving it to its fate. Intervention puts American lives on the line and risks turning a regional conflict into a global—and perhaps even thermonuclear—one. Abandonment endangers America's reputation while sealing the fate of a linchpin in the global economy and flourishing liberal democracy of 23 million people.[1]

It is a veritable Sophie's choice, and any American president forced into making it will want to take into consideration a complex array of military, economic, and political factors.[2] Among these, one question will weigh heavy in the calculus: What will America's key allies in the region expect the United States to do? The president will almost certainly receive competing advice.

Some aides will argue that Japan, South Korea, and Australia want the United States to intervene because all three see the US–Taiwan relationship as an indicator of Washington's commitment to their own security. If the United States abandons Taiwan, the thinking goes, then America's Pacific allies will pursue independent military capabilities (up to and including nuclear weapons). Worse yet, they could acquiesce to Chinese hegemony.

But the American president will also hear the opposite case: that US allies in the region care more about risk than they do reputation, and that Taiwan is too hard to defend. After all, Washington could drag Canberra, Seoul, and Tokyo into the fight. And Beijing might retaliate against all three anyway even if they try to remain on the sidelines or provide support from afar. Worst of all from the perspective of America's allies, a quick US victory is far from assured. A prolonged stalemate, a nuclear escalation, a Pyrrhic victory, or an outright defeat could all lead to an America too exhausted to help them for years—or decades—to come.

The question of whether Taiwan serves as a leading indicator—a proverbial canary in the coal mine—for US allies in Asia is therefore likely to be at the forefront of any US president's mind in the earliest stages of a cross-Strait war. Unfortunately, history, policy, or theory are not particularly informative in terms of how Australia, Japan, and South Korea might react to American action (or inaction). Historically, although the United States has served as Taiwan's chief patron and protector for more than seventy years, Washington abrogated its formal defense treaty, the Sino-American Mutual Defense Treaty, with Taipei in 1979 and has maintained a carefully calibrated posture of ambiguity toward the island ever since.

As a matter of policy, this so-called strategic ambiguity means that if China attacks Taiwan, the president occupying the Oval Office when the crisis unfolds will have tremendous latitude in deciding whether to respond and how. Yet, predicting how a given president might react is tantamount to guesswork. The first Trump administration was a good friend to Taiwan, but in private President Donald Trump appeared reluctant to rescue it from attack.[3] Meanwhile, the Biden administration was more circumspect in its policies toward Taipei, yet President Joe Biden repeatedly and publicly made known his intent to defend Taiwan —only to have his statements "walked back" by his own staff.[4]

International relations theory is likewise indeterminate. The only reasonably confident assertion it offers is that the presence or absence of a formal treaty between Washington and Taipei is immaterial, given the anarchic nature of the international system. The absence of an international court or supranational military force with the power (and legitimacy) to enforce contracts and punish aggression creates a permissive environment in which Taiwan must fear for its safety, while rendering any promise to come to its aid inherently suspect. When it comes to how US allies might respond to American action—or inaction— some scholars offer compelling arguments that the United States will defend Taiwan to preserve its reputation as a reliable ally. Others contend, however, that America's formal treaty partners in the region may be just as concerned about being drawn into an unwanted war with China as they are about being left vulnerable should Washington abandon Taipei.

Even the degree to which Japan, South Korea, and Australia are willing to risk their own security to protect Taiwan is not an especially useful guide. As vibrant liberal democracies, all three would clearly be appalled to see a fellow democracy violently annexed by an authoritarian regime, and all three have taken steps to improve the readiness of their respective military forces.[5] All three governments have likewise stated their desire for peace and stability in the region,[6]—an understandable position given that their trade-based economies rely heavily on access to the Chinese market and the free, predictable movement of goods through the Taiwan Strait. Taken together, however, these positions do not necessarily imply that Japan, South Korea, or Australia wants the United States to defend

Taiwan if doing so risks the loss of their shared security guarantor or the collapse of East Asian commerce. Each has rational incentives to overstate its commitment to the status quo, yet none has publicly or explicitly endorsed US military intervention on Taiwan's behalf, let alone pledged to take an active role in its defense.

Unfortunately, arguments on both sides of this critical debate often rest more on assumptions about how Japan, South Korea, and Australia might respond to American intervention or abandonment than on rigorous assessments of what those allies are actually saying. Moreover, policy discussions in Washington seldom consider the full range of plausible outcomes in a cross-Strait conflict. Implicit in many arguments is the assumption that the United States would prevail if it chose to intervene. Yet a rational strategy requires accounting for the possibility of failure as well as success. Absent such nuance, it becomes too easy to assert that the United States must either defend or abandon Taiwan—on the grounds that the credibility of its alliance network and extended deterrence posture in the Indo-Pacific hangs in the balance.

This book aims to help policymakers understand how America's most militarily capable treaty allies in East Asia—Japan, South Korea, and Australia—might reassess their perceptions of US credibility based on how Washington responds to an attack on Taiwan. It draws on more than 100 interviews conducted over a three-year period with Japanese, South Korean, Australian, Taiwanese, and American policymakers, military officers (both active and retired), scholars, and analysts. As such, it offers one of the most rigorous open-source assessments currently available of allied expectations toward the United States in a cross-Strait conflict scenario.

Key Finding

At Least When it Comes to Defending Taiwan, Reputation Matters, but Reliability Matters More

This study finds that existing reputational arguments for defending Taiwan are incomplete. While it is undoubtedly true that Japan, South Korea, and Australia prefer deterrence to prevail in the Taiwan Strait in order to maintain the status quo, it does not necessarily follow that they expect—or desire—American intervention at all costs.

Should Beijing opt for war, all three would likely be surprised if the United States remained on the sidelines, and any perceived abandonment would almost certainly damage America's reputation in the eyes of both their leaders and publics. Yet even so, it does not necessarily follow that Canberra, Seoul, and Tokyo want Washington to defend Taipei at all costs. The interviews conducted for this study suggest that while reputation matters to these core allies, reliability—understood as the extent to which each believes Washington is both willing and able to protect their core national interests[7]—matters more. As much as Japan, South Korea, and Australia value America's reputation for honoring its commitments, it is not a reputation they expect the United States to uphold at the expense of its own survival. They understand that a dead patron is a useless one. Increasingly, they also recognize that both defeat and pyrrhic victory are plausible outcomes in a cross-Strait conflict.

Such findings resonate with the theoretical distinction between reputation and reliability first advanced by the Australian international relations scholar Iain Henry.[8] Henry suggests that US allies want more from Washington than "indiscriminate loyalty" toward the other members of its vast alliance network. Instead, what each ally really wants is for Washington's interests to overlap with its own, and for Washington to maintain the wherewithal to protect those interests.[9]

This conceptual distinction between reputation and reliability is significant because the two can at times be in tension. To be sure, if there were no doubt about America's capacity to defeat China in a war over Taiwan while preserving the military means to defend Japan, South Korea, and Australia against other potential threats, then reputation and reliability would effectively converge. The same would be true if Washington, Tokyo, Seoul, and Canberra shared identical security priorities. In such cases, bolstering a reputation for resolve would also enhance perceptions of reliability as an ally.

Unfortunately, it appears more likely than not that the United States will confront a tradeoff between reputation and reliability in a conflict over Taiwan's status. Efforts by Washington to fulfill its existing commitments—perceived, implied, or otherwise—to Taipei could come at the expense of its ability to subsequently defend Canberra, Seoul, or Tokyo. Interviews conducted for this study with subject matter experts in and on Japan, South Korea, and Australia indicate that although these allies place significant value on America's reputation for honoring its commitments, and although they express concern over the prospect of Taiwan falling under Chinese control, such concerns are tempered by increasing doubts about whether the United States could prevail at an acceptable cost. Compounding these anxieties is the belief shared across all three capitals that Washington—or Beijing—might entangle them in a war they would prefer to avoid.

Furthermore, Tokyo, Seoul, and Canberra do not share identical national security priorities. For Seoul, the foremost concern remains North Korea, which continues to pose an existential threat. South Korean experts expressed apprehension that a Taiwan contingency might either draw the country into an unwanted conflict or undermine its position vis-à-vis Pyongyang. These concerns often outweighed anxieties about the implications of US abandonment of Taipei for South Korea's own security. In contrast, experts in Japan and Australia were generally more alarmed by the reputational costs of Washington failing to defend Taiwan. Even so, they too voiced serious concern about the risks of a major, protracted conflict that could lead to American military defeat or lasting diminishment. Ultimately, both Japanese and Australian experts emphasized that, provided the United States does not fully withdraw from the Western Pacific in the face of Chinese expansionism, their governments would have little choice but to continue relying on the alliance, regardless of the outcome of a Taiwan conflict.

To be sure, this conclusion was neither anticipated nor preferred at the outset of this project, which aimed to assess how Australia, Japan, and South Korea view America's reputational stakes in a war over Taiwan. The initial hypothesis—and, candidly, the assumption and the hope we the authors held—was that US credibility would suffer significantly if Washington failed to defend Taipei. Such a conclusion would have simplified the logic of deterrence: the higher the reputational stakes, the easier it would be for the United States to persuade others that its commitments must be upheld, and that intervention in defense of Taiwan is essential to maintaining broader credibility.

Instead, the findings suggest that America's most militarily capable allies in East Asia hold a far more nuanced understanding of the relationship between reputation and credibility. If this analysis is correct, it has profound implications for US credibility and extended deterrence in the region: namely, that credibility does not rest solely—or even primarily —on whether Washington defends Taiwan. Rather, the sine qua non for sustaining US extended deterrence commitments is military capability.

Given the acknowledged risk that a US military intervention could result in defeat or a pyrrhic victory, leaders in Japan, South Korea, and Australia recognize that protecting American reputation might ultimately undermine American reliability. And in the final calculus, these treaty allies are more concerned with Washington's ability to defend them than with its willingness to defend others.

All of this said, the study has one important limitation worth highlighting at the outset. All but one of the interviews on which this book is based were conducted between early 2021 and early 2024, and therefore prior to the US presidential election in November 2025. The interview questions were therefore premised on the assumption that a war over Taiwan's status would unfold in a world in which the United States remains broadly committed to its existing global network of formal alliances. In other words, interviewees were asked how Australia, Japan, and South Korea might reassess their perceptions of US credibility based on the way Washington responds to an attack on Taiwan. But they were not asked to consider how such reassessments might play out if China attacks Taiwan *after* Washington had previously abrogated its commitments to a number of longstanding allies (e.g., the North Atlantic Treaty Organization). A generally less predictable US approach to alliances could well have implications for how Canberra, Seoul, and Tokyo think about the tradeoffs between American reputation and reliability. This question is not merely hypothetical, as the second Trump Administration has suggested that it might be willing to walk away from long-established alliances. However, addressing this is a task for future research.

Why Focus on Reputation and Reliability?

Allied perceptions of American reputation and reliability represent just one piece of a larger puzzle. There are, in fact, multiple rationales for defending Taiwan. While different justifications resonate with different audiences, it is important to recognize that no single argument—when considered in isolation—is likely to persuade the average, war-weary American voter that the sacrifice of American lives and resources is warranted for Taiwan's defense. Rather, the strongest case for defending Taiwan emerges only when these rationales are considered collectively. Five such arguments currently dominate the policy discourse in Washington.

The first rationale holds that the United States should defend Taiwan to protect global norms and rules.[10] Permitting China to annex Taiwan by force—particularly in the aftermath of Russia's 2022 re-invasion of Ukraine—would further undermine the so-called rules-based liberal international order that emerged after the Second World War and expanded in the post–Cold War era. Such an outcome could trigger a domino effect, encouraging other authoritarian regimes to pursue aggressive actions of their own, emboldened by Beijing's success and the perception of international passivity. Norms against nuclear proliferation might also begin to erode, as countries like Japan and South Korea reconsider their longstanding commitments to nuclear restraint and reevaluate their first-principles reliance on the American nuclear umbrella. Collectively, these normative shifts could signal the end of Pax Americana in East Asia and usher in a new era characterized by instability, Chinese regional hegemony, and a return to Hobbesian power politics.

The second argument centers on the preservation of Taiwanese democracy.[11] In the years following the collapse of the Soviet Union, liberal democracy appeared to have emerged as the uncontested ideal of modern governance. Under Xi Jinping, however, China has advanced a competing narrative—one that promotes Communism and technocratic authoritarianism as a superior alternative. As the world's most powerful liberal democracy, the United States bears a unique responsibility to support vulnerable democratic partners. Taiwan's proximity to China puts it at risk. The rapid erosion of Hong Kong's autonomy underscores this danger, leaving Taiwan as the only democracy in Greater China and offering a sobering preview of what Taiwanese society might face under Chinese control. Beijing's harsh repression of dissent in Hong Kong leaves little doubt about the fate awaiting those in Taiwan who resist Chinese Communist Party (CCP) rule. Beyond its strategic significance, Taiwan's democracy holds symbolic value: it offers reformers in China a beacon of hope and demonstrates to global skeptics that a robust democratic system can flourish in a majority-Han society shaped by Confucian traditions and a recent legacy of brutal authoritarian rule.[12]

The third justification is that the United States must defend Taiwan to safeguard both the American economy and those of its allies and partners.[13] Taiwan is deeply integrated into the global economy and consistently ranks among Washington's top ten trading partners—exceeding the United States' trade volume with countries such as India,

France, or Italy.[14] More significantly, Taiwan punches above its weight in the global technology ecosystem due to its dominance in advanced semiconductor manufacturing.[15] Taiwanese firms produce more than 90% of the world's most advanced microchips, account for nearly two-thirds of global contract chipmaking, and [16] 30% of the global market in chip testing and packaging. Any conflict that impedes Taiwanese chipmaking —whether a war, blockade, quarantine, or other major disruption—could cost the American technology sector at least a half-trillion dollars annually and [17] more than ten trillion dollars in overall economic activity. The snarled supply chains experienced during the COVID-19 pandemic offer only a limited preview of the far more severe consequences that would arise should Taiwan's semiconductor industry be compromised or destroyed.[18]

The fourth rationale is that the United States should defend Taiwan to deny China a decisive strategic or military advantage in the Asia Pacific.[19] If Beijing were to take control of Taiwan, it would acquire an "unsinkable aircraft carrier" in the First Island Chain—enabling Chinese air and naval forces to project power into the Western Pacific with far fewer constraints.[20] A Chinese military presence in Taiwan would also place Chinese forces dangerously close to Japan's outlying islands, likely prompting Tokyo to consider drastic countermeasures to mitigate the risk of further Chinese expansion. Such concerns would not be misplaced. Although Beijing would undoubtedly insist that its ambitions are limited to unification with Taiwan, it would hardly be the first great power to find its appetite whetted by victory. Indeed, annexation would mean that China either defeated the United States militarily or deterred it from intervening—both outcomes that could embolden hawkish Chinese nationalists within the Communist Party to press for further strategic gains. Even those among China's elite who might otherwise be content with resolving the Taiwan issue could come to view the postwar landscape as fraught with perils—such as Japanese "revisionism" or a vengeful United States—that warranted establishing a strategic buffer around Taiwan.

The fifth justification brings us to the focus of this book: the role of reputation in alliance maintenance. According to the reputational argument, the United States must defend Taiwan to preserve its credibility in the eyes of key allies like Japan, South Korea, and Australia.[21] Nor would the consequences of abandonment necessarily be confined to East Asia. As Ross Babbage forcefully argues, failure to protect Taiwan risks undermining American credibility across the entirety of an interconnected network of alliances, "as many of America's closest allies would be brought to question the deterrence and defensive value of their strategic relationships with the United States."[22]

The idea that Washington would go to war with Beijing over Taipei simply to reassure Tokyo, Seoul, and Canberra of its reliability may appear paradoxical, if not self-defeating. Yet, the underlying logic is a well-established—if also intensely debated—component of deterrence theory, as discussed next. Indeed, no less an authority on deterrence than Thomas Schelling famously argued that reputation is "one of the few things worth fighting over."[23] As a practical matter, the United States has spent the past eighty years constructing a complex, overlapping network of bilateral and multilateral alliances across the globe. Because every alliance ultimately rests on a measure of faith—specifically, that the other party will risk everything when the chips are down—it follows that US allies in Asia and beyond are watching closely to see how Washington responds to an attack on Taiwan.

The Scholarship on Reputation

This fifth and final rationale is the focus of this book because it lies at the heart of how the US foreign policy community conceptualizes what is at stake in the Taiwan Strait: namely, that the United States must defend Taiwan or risk eroding allied confidence in the credibility of American commitments across Asia and beyond. The academic literature largely supports this view. Scholars have long argued that a country's ability to deter adversaries from attacking its partners—what the literature terms *extended deterrence*—depends significantly on its reputation for honoring past commitments and standing by allies in their times of need. In essence, while retaliating in defense of the homeland is inherently credible, promising to strike back when someone else is attacked is not. In Thomas Schelling's famous formulation, "no one doubts that US troops will defend California. I have, however, heard Frenchmen doubt whether US troops can be counted on to defend France."[24]

Adversaries and allies alike have rational grounds to question any commitment to defend a third party. Making good on such a promise involves real risks and costs. It is unsurprising that in the heat of a crisis, both policymakers and the public may recoil at sacrificing blood and treasure to protect others. The anarchic and competitive nature of the international system exacerbates this challenge. In the absence of a supranational authority to enforce agreements or punish betrayal, states that are abandoned by their allies have little recourse. Moreover, anarchy obscures intentions, encourages bluffing and strategic ambiguity, and increases the likelihood of misjudgment. While distrust among adversaries is to be expected, the same conditions often breed suspicion even among long-standing partners and treaty allies.

Extended deterrence commitments lose credibility when both allies and adversaries begin to question whether the state offering security guarantees is willing or able to uphold them. Because credibility cannot be definitively established in advance, it is only logical for others to assess a patron's reputation—its record of honoring similar commitments in the past—as a proxy for its likely behavior in the future. This challenge is especially acute for the United States, given the scope of its global alliance network and the vast distances American forces must traverse to fulfill many of those defense obligations.

Scholars have long sought to understand the relationship between extended deterrence, credibility, and reputation.[25] Early debates centered on whether reputation can be objectively assessed, or whether it is inherently subjective—shaped largely by one state's interpretation of another's willingness to act.[26] More recent scholarship suggests that reputation is both measurable and causally significant. By leveraging new methodological tools and larger datasets, this body of work identifies three primary ways in which reputation and credibility influence the effectiveness of extended deterrence: personality and psychology, impacts of power projection, and alliance maintenance.

Psychological and personality-driven research on credibility finds that states "invest more heavily in reputation building if they believe a game will be repeated many times" and tend to do so when they assess a high likelihood of future conflict.[27] These findings further suggest that reputational concerns are closely tied to perceived future threats to the status quo posed by specific countries. Moreover, the personalities of individual leaders shape how states assess the likelihood of future conflict. For example, Keren Yarhi-Milo argues that hawkish states with leaders who are concerned with others' perception of their status will be most concerned with maintaining their reputations.[28] Self-monitors, in her description, are individuals who are particularly sensitive to cues about appropriateness of behavior and are willing to modify that behavior during crises. Furthermore, self-monitors also view reputation for resolve as a dilemma of "social standing," and thus will be more likely to demonstrate this reputation in most crises. Relatedly, recent research finds that leader-specific signals and domestic political environments shape how conflict is perceived—and, consequently, how potential protégé states interpret a major power's behavior.[29] Consequently, an individual leader's personality can influence both their perception of their own reputation and the way other states interpret their behavior.[30]

Finally, the literature indicates that a reputation for failing to uphold alliance commitments does indeed undermine a security guarantor's future credibility. For example, LeVeck and Narang find that states are generally less inclined to enter new alliances with those that have previously violated their commitments.[31] However, they also find that states who violate alliance commitments during "harder times" are more likely to form new alliances than those that did so in "easier times."

Scholars have further observed that the formality of an alliance also influences reputational consequences.[32] Reneging on informal commitments is unlikely to diminish a state's reputation to the same degree as failing to uphold a formal obligation. In fact, Kim, Byun, and Ko found that the United States' "abandonment" of its two-decade-long war in Afghanistan actually increased confidence among South Korean and Chinese observers in the credibility of US commitments to East Asia.[33]

Of course, the literature also makes clear that reputation is not the only factor allies and partners consider when assessing the credibility of their patron's extended deterrence commitments. Military power —particularly the capacity to project it—also plays a critical role. For example, Horowitz et al. find that both potential allies and adversaries interpret a security guarantor's level of military spending as a signal of its willingness to uphold its threats and assurances.[34] Hunzeker and Lanoszka argue that allies view the forward deployment of ground troops as an especially salient signal of credibility.[35] Similarly, Daehee Bak finds that advancements in military technology, such as rapid transportation and offshore basing, have diminished the extent to which geographic distance undermines the credibility of commitments made from afar. Bak argues that "the presence of active troops from allies and the existence of allies' military bases in a protégé country are likely to be one of the most substantial determinants of successful extended deterrence."[36] He further argues that "a challenger is expected to be less likely to initiate a conflict against a target when ally troops and military bases are operating in the target's territory." Todd Lehmann builds on these insights by showing that, between 1985 to 2018, states with greater force projection capacity tended to deploy fewer troops abroad.[37] However, he also finds that these states spread the troops that they do deploy across more countries. Thus, the greater a state's power projection capacity, the more broadly it seeks to exercise extended deterrence.

Roadmap

The remainder of the book is organized as follows: The rest of this chapter addresses several conceptual, methodological, and historical issues, including a brief overview of the US–Taiwan relationship from the Cold War to the present. Chapter 1 explores plausible conflict scenarios. Although the interviews conducted for this study deliberately elided the complex and messy details surrounding the sources and outcomes of a cross-Strait war in order to focus on the longer-term implications of US intervention or non-intervention, we acknowledge that potential crisis and conflict dynamics cannot be ignored entirely. Different types of crises and conflicts may carry distinct implications for American credibility. The chapter concludes by outlining three broad "worlds" in which the United States could plausibly find itself following a Chinese attack on Taiwan.

Chapters 2, 3, and 4 form the empirical core of the book, presenting the findings from the interviews. These chapters are organized geographically. Chapter 2 begins with Japan, both because it is closest to the Taiwan Strait and because it will play the most important role in any US-led coalition response. Chapter 3 turns to South Korea, which—though farther from Taiwan—may face even tighter constraints on how it can respond. Chapter 4 focuses on Australia. Despite being the most geographically removed, Canberra will still confront a difficult set of choices.

The final chapter revisits the main argument and outlining key policy recommendations that follow from it.

BACKGROUND AND METHODOLOGY

This book examines the extent to which a US decision to defend or abandon Taiwan should hinge on reputational considerations. We adopt this focus because one of the most frequently cited justifications for why Taiwan "matters" to the United States is rooted in reputation: namely, if Washington is prepared to turn its back on the Taiwanese people after nearly seventy years of serving as their patron and protector, why should policymakers in Japan, South Korea, or Australia place continued faith in the credibility of American security commitments?

This is a contentious policy question, reflected in a long-running scholarly debate over the extent to which states should be willing to fight in order to uphold their reputation for resolve. In the case of Taiwan, one camp argues that abandoning the island would fundamentally undermine American credibility across the region. According to this view, Tokyo, Seoul, Canberra, and others—concerned that Washington might similarly leave them in the lurch—would begin to pursue independent military capabilities, including nuclear weapons, or seek closer alignment with Beijing. The opposing perspective contends that fighting for Taipei solely to reassure other allies is misguided. Proponents of this view argue that reputational concerns are overstated; that Taiwan's geopolitical situation is sui generis and thus offers limited insight into the credibility of US commitments elsewhere; or that an American military exhausted by a war over Taiwan would be less capable of defending other regional allies in the future.

Based on three years of interviews with practitioners, scholars, and analysts in the region, this study finds that Japan, South Korea, and Australia ultimately place greater value on American reliability—defined here as the extent to which they believe Washington retains the military capacity to protect their core national interests—than on American reputation.

A Brief History of US–Taiwan Relations

Of course, America's reputation is at stake in the Taiwan Strait largely because, in one form or another, the United States has served as Taiwan's principal security guarantor since the early days of the Cold War. However, Washington's decision to abrogate its mutual defense treaty with Taipei in 1979, coupled with its longstanding posture of strategic ambiguity, has created a situation in which no one—by design—can say with certainty how the United States would respond to an attack on its former ally. To understand why such uncertainty surrounds a security relationship nearly seventy years in the making, a brief review of the history and evolution of US–Taiwan relations is instructive.

While Taiwan's history spans thousands of years, US interest in the island's security can be traced to the aftermath of the Chinese Civil War. When Mao Zedong's Communist Party prevailed and established the People's Republic of China (PRC) in 1949, Chiang Kai-shek and his Kuomintang (KMT) forces retreated to Taiwan, where they proclaimed the Republic of China (ROC) to be the sole legitimate government of all China.[38] For decades, both the PRC and the ROC claimed to represent the Chinese people in their entirety.

Prior to the Korean War, little consensus existed within the Truman administration over how to structure US–ROC relations.[39] President Harry S. Truman, his Secretary of State Dean Acheson, and the Joint Chiefs of Staff—then chaired by General Omar N. Bradley—believed that, unlike the protection of Japan and the Philippines, the defense of Taiwan did not constitute a vital US interest.[40] Nor did Truman or his advisers consider Chiang much more than a nuisance. The Korean War, however, changed the perceived stakes by convincing Truman that a KMT-controlled Taiwan could serve as a bulwark against Communist China.[41] Within a week of North Korea's surprise invasion, President Truman committed troops to the Korean Peninsula and ordered the US Seventh Fleet to deter a similar attack on Taiwan, stating, "the determination of the future status of Formosa must await the restoration of security in the Pacific, a peace settlement with Japan, or consideration by the United Nations."[42] When China intervened directly in the Korean War in late 1950, the United States retaliated by resuming direct military assistance to Chiang in early 1951.

Despite taking these steps to deter a Chinese attack on Taiwan, President Truman refrained from offering Chiang Kai-shek explicit security guarantees, fearing such assurances might embolden him and entangle the United States in another crisis. Instead, Truman stated that the purpose of dispatching the Seventh Fleet was "to prevent attacks by Communists on Formosa as well as forays by Chiang Kai-shek against the mainland, this last to avoid reprisal actions by the Reds that might enlarge the area of conflict."[43] In essence, the United States and the Republic of China were aligned by circumstance rather than shared strategic objectives. As Steven Goldstein described: "Very simply, while one ally sought to use the alliance primarily as an offensive tool, the other saw it primarily as a defensive mechanism. Chiang had not gone to Taiwan to create a government-in-exile or to be an American strategic asset. The island was a place to regroup his forces and to prepare to take the battle back to the mainland."[44]

In contrast to his predecessor, President Dwight D. Eisenhower took a more affirmative view of Taiwan's role in exerting pressure on Communist China. In 1953 he withdrew the Seventh Fleet, enabling the KMT to fortify Taiwan's outlying islands.[45] Following the end of the Korean War and the First Taiwan Strait Crisis, Eisenhower pursued a formal treaty with the Republic of China.[46] National Security Council memorandum 146/2 outlines US interests in Taiwan at the time, which included incorporating the island into the US defense posture in East Asia and relying on Republic of China forces to strike the People's Republic of China in the event of PRC intervention in Vietnam or Korea.[47]

The Sino-American Mutual Defense Treaty, signed in December 1954 and ratified in February 1955, formally obligated the United States to come to Taiwan's defense if China attacked it or the outlying Pescadores.[48] But the relationship proved short-lived. Although the Eisenhower administration remained fully committed to Chiang—going so far as to base ground, air, and naval assets in Taiwan[49]—President John F. Kennedy took a more skeptical view of the KMT. His administration went so far as to signal to Beijing that Washington would not support Chiang if he attacked China. Kennedy also declared that American support was limited to diplomatic backing, economic development, and vaguely specified defensive commitments.[50]

The Vietnam War could have provided an opportunity to deepen the relationship between Taiwan and the United States, particularly given China's support for North Vietnam. Yet by this point in the Cold War, Washington had little appetite for a direct confrontation with Beijing. Instead, the war in Vietnam ultimately contributed to the unraveling of America's formal commitment to the island. President Richard Nixon sought Beijing's help pressuring North Vietnam to return to the bargaining table.[51] He also believed the unfolding Sino-Soviet split presented strategic opportunities that the United States could exploit by pursuing rapprochement with Beijing. For its part, the People's Republic of China (PRC) insisted that the future of US–PRC relations depended on the United States withdrawing all military forces from Taiwan, severing diplomatic relations with Taipei, and revoking the Sino-American Mutual Defense Treaty.[52] The deterioration in US–Soviet relations in the late 1970s gave President Jimmy Carter added incentive to pursue full normalization of diplomatic ties with the People's Republic of China. Carter argued that Taiwan was naturally defensible and that continued arms sales would be sufficient to keep the island from falling. However, as Shelley Rigger notes, he also appears to have acknowledged that the Republic of China was likely to collapse soon after the US shifted recognition.[53] In any case, the United States formally withdrew from the Sino-American Mutual Defense Treaty and pulled all military forces out of Taiwan in 1979.

Complicating the situation for President Carter, Taiwan enjoyed broad bipartisan support in Congress, which was less sanguine about being complicit in Taiwan's demise. Congress quickly passed the Taiwan Relations Act (TRA) as a stopgap following Carter's unilateral abrogation of the Sino-American Mutual Defense Treaty.[54] Much of the TRA focuses on the operational, administrative, and legal requirements for maintaining relations with Taiwan in the absence of formal state-to-state recognition. From a strategic standpoint, however, the key provisions appear in the law's second and third sections, which establish the expectation that Taiwan's status will be decided peacefully, commit Washington

to furnishing Taiwan with sufficient arms to maintain its own defense
(as determined by the president and Congress), and obligate the United
States to maintain the capacity to resist "any resort to force or other
forms of coercion."[55]

Taken in conjunction with the so-called Three Communiqués—and later
the Six Assurances—the TRA has defined the US–Taiwan relationship
since 1979. To be sure, the TRA represented a "second-best" option for
what Taiwan lost in terms of formal security guarantees.[56] The TRA does
create a binding legal obligation with the power to constrain unilateral
executive action in certain respects (e.g., to maintain the capacity to resist
any resort to force). Nevertheless, the TRA does not mandate that the
United States defend Taiwan in the event of an armed conflict with China.
The result is a US policy designed to dissuade the PRC from attacking
while simultaneously providing Taiwan with a degree of assurance of US
support—but not so strong a guarantee that it might embolden the island
to take unilateral steps to alter the status quo. This attempt to thread the
policy needle has come to be known as strategic ambiguity.

In the more than four decades since the passage of the TRA, the United
States has consistently emphasized that neither China nor Taiwan should
attempt to unilaterally change the cross-Strait status quo, and that any
resolution should be achieved peacefully and reflect the principle of
self-determination. At the same time, the United States has deliberately
refrained from specifying the circumstances under which it would come
to Taiwan's aid in the event of a Chinese attack.

Subsequent US presidents have largely adhered to this framework. In
1996, President Bill Clinton deployed two aircraft carrier battle groups
to the waters off Taiwan in response to Chinese missile tests. However,
the following year, during his summit with Chinese President Jiang
Zemin, the joint statement they issued reiterated that the United States
adhered to its "one China" policy and the principles set forth in the Three
Communiqués, with no mention of the TRA.[57]

Five years later, President George W. Bush characterized the US commitment to Taiwan as an obligation to use "whatever it took to help Taiwan defend herself." Yet less than two years after that, US Deputy Assistant Secretary of Defense Richard Lawless told Taiwan's Deputy Minister of National Defense Chen Chao-min that Taiwan "should not view America's resolute commitment to peace and stability in the Taiwan Strait as a substitute for investing the necessary resources in its own defense." In November 2003, Deputy Secretary of State Richard Armitage reaffirmed that the Taiwan Relations Act is not a defense treaty. And in April 2004, Assistant Secretary of State James Kelly, testifying before Congress, responded to Chen Shui-bian's recent reelection by warning Taiwan of "limitations" to US support for constitutional changes in Taiwan. In the same hearings, however, Assistant Secretary of Defense for International Security Affairs Peter Rodman also warned Beijing that attempts to use force would "inevitably" involve the United States.

President Barack Obama's term of office coincided with the administration of Taiwanese president Ma Ying-jeou, a period marked by rapprochement between China and Taiwan. As a result, the Obama administration was largely spared from having to make significant changes or clarifications regarding US commitments to Taiwan. Obama's successor in the Oval Office was less fortunate, taking office just as Ma was succeeded by the more independence-minded Tsai Ing-wen.

In keeping with his mercurial style, Donald Trump's approach to Taiwan suggested an inconsistent commitment to the island. On December 2, 2016, then President-elect Trump spoke by phone with ROC President Tsai, becoming the first incoming or incumbent US president since the cessation of formal diplomatic relations known to have spoken with a Taiwanese president. In a Fox News interview on December 11, 2016, President-elect Trump brought into question America's commitment to the "One-China" policy, but after taking office he then recommitted to the policy on a phone call with Xi Jinping on February 9, 2017. Subsequently, the Trump administration opened a new US$250 million de facto embassy in Taipei; approved the sale of over US$13 billion in American weapons; and passed two major pieces of legislation to expand the scope of US–Taiwan relations. Nonetheless, he also expressed doubts throughout his presidency that Taiwan could be defended or was worth the effort. In his memoir, former National Security Advisor John Bolton recounts President Trump comparing Taiwan to the tip of a Sharpie marker, while likening China to the Oval Office Resolute Desk.[58]

President Biden went further than his predecessors in expressing his intent to protect Taiwan from China. On four separate occasions within just over a year, he stated clearly that the United States would intervene militarily if China attacked the island.[59] These remarks constituted some of the most forward-leaning statements of US intentions to defend Taiwan in the modern era. However, in each instance, officials from the Biden administration subsequently walked back his comments to preserve a degree of strategic ambiguity.

In addition, during the Biden administration, Speaker of the US House of Representatives Nancy Pelosi led a congressional delegation to Taipei in August 2022. Her meeting with President Tsai Ing-wen marked the highest-level visit by a sitting US government official in twenty-five years. This trip was followed in April 2023 by a meeting in California between Tsai and House Speaker Kevin McCarthy. In response, China expressed its dissatisfaction with these meetings by fundamentally changing the military status quo in the Taiwan Strait. In the aftermath of Pelosi's visit, Beijing effectively ended its tacit, seventy-year commitment not to send naval vessels across the median line of the Strait and increased its military operational tempo, including near-daily aircraft incursions into Taiwan's air defense identification zone (ADIZ).[60]

Complicating matters further is the growing consensus among foreign policy elites—reflected in both the Trump and Biden administrations' respective National Security Strategies—that the United States and China are locked in a great power rivalry, with Taiwan seen as a crucial partner in that competition.

Ultimately, whether the United States would deploy combat forces to defend Taiwan remains uncertain. It is against this backdrop of historical and ongoing ambiguity that this study examines how a decision to intervene in—or abstain from—a cross-Strait conflict might affect Washington's reputation in Asia and beyond.

Methodological Approach

To gain a better understanding of how Japan, South Korea, and Australia think about American credibility and reputation as it relates to a cross-Strait contingency, we spent three years conducting more than 100 virtual and in-person interviews with subject matter experts in and on Australia, Japan, South Korea, Taiwan, and the United States. As we discussed earlier, the "null hypothesis" guiding this effort—one that also reflected the authors' personal preference—was that US allies in Asia would place significant weight on America's reputation for resolve, as demonstrated by a willingness to defend Taiwan even in the absence of a formal security commitment. That said, the purpose of this study is not to test existing international relations theories, nor to propose a new one. The goal was more modest: to examine existing theoretical understandings of how allies use reputation and reliability to assess the credibility of their patron's extended deterrence commitments, and to determine which of these theories best align with how three critical allies actually think about a potential war over Taiwan.

This approach carries a number of caveats. We fully acknowledge that this project does not constitute a rigorous test of the underlying theories. China has not invaded Taiwan—and, we hope, never will—so the insights drawn from these interviews are necessarily speculative since no one can predict the future. Moreover, Taiwan is in many ways an outlier in the international system—a sui generis case that may not fully reflect how reputation and reliability function elsewhere or in different issue areas. That said, precisely because Taiwan represents such a high-stakes and strategically significant case, understanding how key US allies perceive the credibility of American security commitments in this context is important for US security in East Asia, as well as offering valuable insight into the dynamics of alliance politics more broadly.

We used a two-pronged process to select potential interviewees. First, we systematically reviewed recent policy literature on cross-Strait relations to identify elite policymakers (current and former), high ranking military officers (serving and retired), academic scholars, and think tank analysts with substantive expertise on Taiwan-related issues. Second, we used a "snowballing" approach—a well-established social science method —by asking each interviewee to recommend other subject matter experts we should consider.[61] We conducted semi-structured interviews, posing a core set of standardized questions to all participants while allowing for individualized follow-up based on their specific responses. Each interview lasted approximately one hour. In the standardized portion, we asked interviewees to assess how they might reevaluate American credibility in the context of three plausible "worlds," each representing a basic outcome likely to follow from a Chinese-initiated attack on Taiwan:

- China fails to annex Taiwan because of a successful US-led military intervention
- China successfully annexes Taiwan despite a US-led military intervention
- China successfully annexes Taiwan because the United States does not intervene

The next chapter discusses these three notional outcomes in greater detail. We deliberately chose not to focus our interviews on a fourth logical—but ultimately implausible—scenario: a cross-Strait war in which the United States remains on the sidelines but China nevertheless still fails to annex Taiwan. The geographic proximity of China, the military imbalance between China and Taiwan, and the relative ease with which Taiwan could be isolated render such an outcome highly unlikely and ultimately unrealistic.[62]

Our decision to conduct primarily virtual interviews over a three-year period was a necessary adaptation to the unique geopolitical and epidemiological conditions at the time. We launched this project in January 2021, which happened to coincide with the height of the COVID-19 pandemic, when travel restrictions in the region forced us to resort to virtual interviews. Although we were initially skeptical about the effectiveness of virtual interviews, we soon discovered several advantages. First, virtual interviews made it easier to schedule meetings with high-ranking officials by allowing us to accommodate their demanding schedules more flexibly than would have been possible with budget- and time-limited in-country visits. Second, the virtual format afforded us greater opportunity to reflect on and process information between interviews.

Overseas research is also prohibitively expensive, particularly in the aftermath of the COVID-19 pandemic. As a result, such trips typically require compressing numerous back-to-back meetings into a short period, leaving little time to reflect on interviewee responses or to adjust questions in light of unexpected findings. In contrast, conducting virtual interviews over the course of several years allowed us to refine our lines of inquiry and incorporate emerging events as they unfolded (as discussed in the next section). Finally, because virtual interviews are relatively inexpensive, we were able to conduct follow-up meetings with select subject matter experts to clarify or deepen our understanding of key insights.

To be sure, we recognize the potential limitations with a virtual-only approach. One initial concern was that interviewees might be more hesitant to discuss sensitive issues over the internet. To address this, we conducted a final round of in-person interviews in Tokyo and Taipei during the summer of 2023. Ultimately, we found that most subject matter experts were just as forthcoming in virtual settings as they were in face-to-face meetings. Moreover, we observed no meaningful differences in the substance or candor of responses across the two formats.

We should also note that our original goal was to complete all interviews within a year. However, a series of major foreign policy developments convinced us to adopt a longer-term approach. These included the Biden administration's withdrawal from Afghanistan; the announcement of the AUKUS agreement linking Australia, the United Kingdom, and the United States; alarming revelations about China's rapidly expanding nuclear arsenal; the Tsai administration's decision to significantly increase defense spending and reintroduce extended conscription; South Korea's presidential election; Russia's re-invasion of Ukraine; and the outbreak of the Israel-Hamas conflict. Each of these developments prompted additional rounds of interviews. These subsequent interviews ultimately reinforced our central findings, and the study benefited considerably from the additional time taken to confirm the robustness of our conclusions.

Potential Drawbacks and Limitations

Before proceeding, it is important to acknowledge several other plausible limitations and potential sources of bias in our approach. First, readers will note that this book does not cite or otherwise attribute specific comments, insights, or opinions to individual subject matter experts. This omission reflects a deliberate methodological decision made early in the study. We also agreed to grant complete anonymity to any interviewee who requested it. As a result, no specific names are referenced in the case study chapters, and attentive readers will therefore notice that the list of interviewees acknowledged at the beginning of this book does not correspond to the full number of experts interviewed.

We recognize that granting blanket anonymity opens us to the critique that we "heard what we wanted to hear" from the interviewees. Particularly skeptical readers might even suspect that our findings were manufactured out of whole cloth. While we were aware of these risks, we concluded that anonymity was both justified and, in many cases, necessary. The topics we explored—especially questions regarding the possibility of a US defeat—are highly sensitive, and in some circles, even taboo. Granting anonymity allowed many of the interviewees—several of whom remain in influential positions—to speak candidly and offer their unvarnished assessments. To mitigate concerns about interpretive bias, we have made a consistent effort to indicate the degree of consensus (or lack thereof) among the interviewees, using terms such as "unanimous," "majority," and "plurality." We also highlight dissenting or minority perspectives when we judged them to be especially insightful or likely to carry influence, even if they were not broadly representative.

Second, this project relies heavily on elite-level interviews. It is well understood that foreign policy experts often hold views that differ markedly from those of the general public and the politicians who represent them. Foreign policy elites are also frequently criticized for operating within an echo chamber that reinforces the disconnect between their worldviews and broader societal preferences. A related concern is that all of the interviewees were fluent in English, raising the possibility that we disproportionately heard from a rarified, self-selected subgroup in each country. To mitigate this potential bias, we sought to interview elites across the political spectrum in Australia, Japan, South Korea, the United States, and Taiwan, and we contextualize our findings with publicly available polling data wherever possible.

This limitation notwithstanding, we believe the nature of the Taiwan question renders a focus on elite practitioners methodologically defensible. Despite the attention Taiwan receives among US foreign policy specialists, a recurring theme in the interviews was the relative scarcity of Taiwan-specific expertise among US allies in the Asia-Pacific region. This may stem from the imperative to concentrate on China itself, from the comparatively smaller national security and foreign policy communities in these countries, or from other structural factors. Whatever the cause, the consequence is a shared perception that, when critical decisions regarding Taiwan must be made, a relatively small number of expert voices in Japan, South Korea, and Australia are likely to wield disproportionate influence.

Third, our semi-structured approach meant that not every expert was asked the exact same set of questions. Ideally, a standardized set of questions would have allowed for a more direct comparison across the three case studies. In practice, however, aside from a core set of pre-formatted questions used to frame each discussion, individual interviews followed distinct paths. This divergence reflected both the natural flow of conversation and the influence of real-world developments during the course of the project. More importantly, it stemmed from the fact that the three countries we studied view their strategic challenges and interests in fundamentally different ways. Capturing both the commonalities and the distinctions among them—as we do in the chapters that follow—required flexibility beyond a rigid script.

Finally, as with any interview-based study—whether focused on elites or the general public—there is always the possibility of unintentional bias. Although we made a concerted effort to speak with experts across the political spectrum in each country, we may have inadvertently overlooked certain perspectives. Some interviewees might have felt compelled to say what they thought we wanted to hear, though we suspect that seasoned experts and elites are generally less susceptible to such pressures. Others may have responded strategically, offering views intended to influence our conclusions rather than reflect their true beliefs. A further limitation is that even subject matter experts cannot know with certainty how they or their governments would respond in the event of war in the Taiwan Strait. Nearly all of the interviewees acknowledged that the manner in which a conflict unfolds—whether as a slow-burning crisis or a rapid escalation, whether Taiwan resists or capitulates, whether China limits its operations to the island or strikes US bases in the region—would significantly shape national responses. Because the intentionally simplified hypothetical outcomes we outlined cannot capture the full range of plausible contingencies, it remains possible that we have overlooked important caveats to our main findings.

We acknowledge these risks and made a good faith effort to remain mindful of them throughout the research process. It is also important to reiterate that the conclusions we reached were not the ones we expected —or initially hoped—to find. Both authors have spent significant time living and traveling in Taiwan, and both would personally prefer to see the United States defend the island in the event of an attack. We also share the broadly held scholarly view that reputation matters. If anything, our prior assumptions and preferences might have predisposed us against the conclusion we ultimately reached. That we arrived at this conclusion despite those inclinations underscores its significance. In the end, even if our approach is imperfect, we believe in the inherent value in attempting to listen carefully to what our allies are actually saying.

Definitions

During the course of the interviews, it became clear that policymakers, military officers, and scholars frequently used the same terminology to mean different things. To avoid confusion and ensure conceptual clarity, it is therefore important to define several key terms at the outset.

We begin by defining *deterrence* as the effort to persuade another actor —specifically, China—to refrain from altering the status quo when it would otherwise prefer to do so. While deceptively simple in concept, deterrence has generated a vast body of academic literature seeking to unpack its many dimensions and complexities.[63] We do not have the time or space to examine that literature in any detail, but it suffices to note that the scholarship identifies three basic factors on which successful deterrence depends.

First, the deterring state must convince its target that it is credible. Credibility, in turn, depends on the target's belief that the deterring state is both capable of making good on its threats should deterrence fail (in other words, that it *can* do what it says it is going to do), and resolved enough to do so given that it is usually costly and risky to make good on a threat (in other words, that it *will* do what it says it is going to do).

Second, the deterring state must send clear signals to ensure that the target understands how the status quo is defined and what actions would constitute a transgression or challenge to it. These signals must, of course, include a credible threat of the costs the target will incur if it violates the status quo. Less obviously—but no less importantly—the deterring state must also provide assurances that the target will not be punished if it refrains from such violations. Without such assurances, the target may conclude that it is doomed regardless and thus might as well "go down swinging."

Third, the deterring state must have a clear understanding of how much the target values the underlying issue, as well as the target's tolerance for risk and pain. Deterrence is unlikely to succeed if the issue is of marginal importance to the deterring state but of existential significance to the target. Moreover, the threat must involve costs that the target finds genuinely unacceptable. If the promised punishment is one the target is willing to endure to alter the status quo, deterrence is almost certain to fail. At the same time, threatening a level of pain that exceeds what the deterring state is itself willing to bear is equally unwise. Yet, history suggests that deterring states often assume, incorrectly, that their adversaries share similar thresholds for risk and suffering—an assumption that can lead to miscalculation.

Although not the focus of this study, it is worth noting that we define compellence as the inverse of deterrence: an effort to persuade another actor to change the status quo when that actor would prefer to maintain it. In this sense, deterrence and compellence constitute the two primary forms of what Thomas Schelling refers to as coercive diplomacy.

Returning to deterrence, this study adopts Glenn Snyder's distinction between its two basic forms: *deterrence by denial*, which seeks to raise the costs of altering the status quo until doing so becomes untenable; and *deterrence by punishment*, which relies on the threat of intolerable retaliation in response to any violation of the status quo.[64] Scholars and analysts generally associate deterrence by denial with the deployment of strong conventional military defenses, while credible deterrence by punishment is typically understood to require the possession of nuclear weapons.

Of course, the focus here is not on how Washington can deter Beijing from attacking the United States. Rather, the goal is to understand what Washington should do in a cross-Strait war to convince Tokyo, Seoul, and Canberra that its efforts to deter Beijing from attacking them remain credible. This requires engaging with the concept of *extended deterrence*. While deterrence refers to efforts to prevent an adversary from altering the status quo by attacking oneself, extended deterrence involves convincing a potential aggressor not to attack an ally. The former is inherently more credible; the latter is not. As Schelling famously put it, "no one doubts that US troops will defend California. I have, however, heard Frenchmen doubt whether US troops can be counted on to defend France."[65] As with deterrence, effectively practicing extended deterrence requires credibility, clear signaling, and a deep understanding of the adversary's values and pain thresholds. However, extended deterrence introduces another requirement: *reassurance*. Whereas deterrence involves signaling threats and assurances to the target, extended deterrence demands convincing the ally that the protecting state will indeed honor its commitments should a conflict arise.

Reassurance is, of course, easier said than done, because allies and adversaries alike understand that fulfilling a threat made on behalf of another often carries the risk of war. Scholars have identified a range of techniques and mechanisms to enhance the credibility of such inherently suspect promises. One method is to use what James Fearon calls a *costly signal*, or a signal for which the act of sending incurs or creates a cost that "the sender would be disinclined to incur or create if he or she were in fact not willing" to follow through on the commitment.[66] Building on the works of Schelling and others, Fearon outlines two principal methods for sending costly signals. The first involves "hands tying," which may include deploying so-called tripwire forces (such as NATO's enhanced Forward Presence battlegroups in Europe), making public declarations that politically constrain future backtracking, or sharing nuclear launch authority with the ally. The second involves imposing sunk costs, such as constructing large overseas bases on allied territory that serve no strategic purpose unless the ally is attacked.

A third way of reassuring an ally is to establish and maintain a reputation for having followed through on such commitments in the past. This is what scholars refer to as a reputation for resolve, which is the central focus of this book. This study formally defines reputation for resolve as "the belief others hold about an actor's willingness to stand firm and face costs, based on that actor's past behavior."[67] We contrast reputation with reliability, which—borrowing from Iain Henry's important work introduced earlier—we define as the degree to which a given ally considers Washington to be both willing and able to protect *that ally's* core national interests.[68]

To conclude, and in the interest of precision and concision, we offer definitions of a few additional terms that appear throughout this book. We adopt a narrow definition of *ally* and *alliance*, drawing on Bruce Russett's standard: "a formal agreement among a limited number of countries concerning the conditions under which they will or will not employ military force."[69] In theory, individual alliances can assume a wide variety of forms. However, in practice, states tend to converge on what Raymond Kuo refers to as a dominant alliance form, although what this dominant archetype looks like can and does vary over time.[70] As a practical matter, we consider Washington and Taipei to have been allies for the duration of the Sino-American Mutual Defense Treaty (1954–1979). In contrast, we use the term "partnership" to describe the relationship after 1979. To capture two important risks associated with joining an alliance—or what Glenn Snyder refers to as the "alliance security dilemma"[71]—this study defines abandonment, entanglement, and entrapment as follows: *Abandonment* refers to a situation in which one ostensible ally fails to fulfill its commitment to support or defend the other ally. Entanglement arises when one ally feels compelled to participate in an expensive and/or unnecessary conflict solely to uphold prior explicit commitments. Entrapment is a specific form of entanglement in which one ally deliberately provokes a conflict in order to draw the other, unwillingly, into it.[72]

Asymmetry and symmetry have become frequent buzzwords in discussions of cross-Strait policy. In this study, we use these terms to refer specifically to relative force employment—that is, how one side conducts military operations in relation to how the other side fights.[73] We use the term *symmetric force employment* to describe situations in which one side chooses to fight in the same manner as its opponent. In contrast, *asymmetric force employment* refers to cases in which one side deliberately adopts an opposing style of warfare. We distinguish symmetry and asymmetry from the use of conventional and unconventional forces. Conventional forces are organized, equipped, and trained to attack, occupy, and hold or control ground, airspace, or maritime territory. Unconventional forces, by contrast, are organized, equipped, and trained to harass, disrupt, and deny control to the adversary.

Finally, the term *gray zone* appears throughout the book. Although widely used, the term *gray zone* is often applied inconsistently. Here, we use *gray zone* to refer specifically to the deliberate, coordinated, and incremental use of provocations, intrusions, and other "salami-slicing" (incremental encroachment) tactics—employing conventional and/or unconventional military forces—to test existing red lines, undermine resolve, and establish new "facts on the ground," without *generating a decisive military reaction from the target or its allies.*[74]

NOTES

1. We recognize that the choice will not be entirely binary. As demonstrated by US support for Ukraine following Russia's 2022 re-invasion, intervention can take many forms. In the event of a Chinese attack on Taiwan, the US president will almost certainly demand—and the national security team will almost certainly attempt to present—a spectrum of options between full-scale military defense and outright abandonment. Several such alternatives are discussed in subsequent chapters. Nevertheless, for a range of reasons—including Taiwan's proximity to China and distance from the United States, the cross-Strait military imbalance, the limited capacity of US allies and partners in the Indo-Pacific (including Taiwan) to mount an effective defense without direct US combat support, and the geographic difficulty of sustaining an island nation under attack—it is reasonably accurate to suggest that, in practical terms, a future American president would face a stark choice: war or abandonment.

2. See, for example, Heath, Lilly, and Han, *Can Taiwan Resist a Large-Scale Military Attack by China?* 1; Metz and Sand, "Defending Taiwan."

3. Rogin, *Chaos Under Heaven*, 44.

4. Quinn, "Biden Says, for Fourth Time."

5. Examples include Tokyo's decision to reposition military assets closer to Taiwan, participation in (apparent) contingency planning with Washington, and informal "2+2" dialogues involving high-ranking members of Japan's Liberal Democratic Party and Taiwan's ruling Democratic Progressive Party. Analysts similarly point to Australia's participation the both the so-called "AUKUS" trilateral security pact with Washington and London and the so-called "Quad" with Washington, Tokyo, New Delhi, and Canberra. Seoul's newfound willingness to discuss longstanding historical disputes with Tokyo also serves as concrete evidence that American allies are willing to set aside differences and prioritize defense because of a shared interest in maintaining peace and stability in the Taiwan Strait. See Liff, "No, Japan is Not Planning"; Chung, "Japan to Build Munitions"; Chen, "Taiwan, Japan Ruling Parties"; Reuters, "US and Japan Draw Up."

6. White House, U.S.-Japan Joint Leaders' Statement, "U.S.-Japan Global Partnership for a New Era", (2021); The White House, U.S.-ROK Lead-

ers' Joint Statement, (2021); The White House, Readout of President Joe Biden's Meeting with Prime Minister Anthony Albanese of Australia, (2022).

7. Henry, "What Allies Want," 53.
8. This study was not designed to rigorously test any particular academic theory or paradigm. Nonetheless, it would be remiss not to note the striking alignment between our findings and the predictions of Henry's Alliance Audience Effect theory. We also acknowledge that Henry was among the Australian experts interviewed for this project. His interview—along with his article "What Allies Want" and his subsequent book *Reliability and Alliance Interdependence*—was influential in shaping our understanding and framing of the insights gathered through this research.
9. Henry, *Reliability and Alliance Interdependence.*
10. See, for example, Statement by Ely S. Ratner, Assistant Secretary of Defense for Indo-Pacific Security Affairs, Office of the Secretary of Defense, Before the House Armed Services Committee, 118th Congress, (September 19, 2023); Statement by Ely S. Ratner, Assistant Secretary of Defense for Indo-Pacific Security Affairs, Office of the Secretary of Defense, Before the 117th Congress, Committee on Foreign Relations, United States Senate, (December 8, 2021); Gordon, Mullen, and Sacks, *U.S.-Taiwan Relations in a New Era*, 9; Alperovitch, "Taiwan Is the New Berlin"; Menendez, "This is How the US Will Stand."
11. See, for example, Gordon, Mullen, and Sacks, *U.S.-Taiwan Relations in a New Era*, 10; Cunningham, *The American Case for Taiwan*, 2–3; Bellocchi, "The Strategic Importance of Taiwan," 70–72; Statement by Ely S. Ratner, Assistant Secretary of Defense for Indo-Pacific Security Affairs, Office of the Secretary of Defense, Before the 117th Congress, Committee on Foreign Relations, United States Senate, Short; Rachman, "Why Taiwan Matters,"; Kanapathy, "Countering China's Gray-Zone Activities"; Alperovitch, "Taiwan Is the New Berlin."
12. Kanapathy, "Countering China's Gray-Zone Activities," 28.
13. See, for example, Rittenhouse Green and Talmadge, "Then What?"; Kanapathy, "Countering China's Gray-Zone Activities."; Menendez, "This is How the US Will Stand"; Yu, "Five Reasons"; Rachman, "Why Taiwan Matters "; Bellocchi, "The Strategic Importance of Taiwan," 67–70; Statement by Ely S. Ratner, Assistant Secretary of Defense for Indo-Pacific Security Affairs, Office of the Secretary of Defense, Before the House Armed Services Committee, 118th Congress, Short; Statement by

Ely S. Ratner, Assistant Secretary of Defense for Indo-Pacific Security Affairs, Office of the Secretary of Defense, Before the 117th Congress, Committee on Foreign Relations, United States Senate, Short; Gordon, Mullen, and Sacks, *U.S.-Taiwan Relations in a New Era.*

14. Sacks and Hillman, "The Time Is Now."
15. Kanapathy, "Countering China's Use of Force," 31–33.
16. Li and Cheng, "How Taiwan Became the Indispensable Economy"; Central News Agency, "Xi Prefers 'Peaceful' Unification of Taiwan.".
17. Li and Cheng, "How Taiwan Became the Indispensable Economy"; Welch et al., "Xi, Biden and the $10 Trillion."
18. Li and Cheng, "How Taiwan Became the Indispensable Economy."
19. See, for example, Babbage, *The Next Major War*, 133; Bolton, *The Room Where It Happened*, xxvi; Yu, "Five Reasons"; Cunningham, *The American Case for Taiwan*; Statement by Ely S. Ratner, Assistant Secretary of Defense for Indo-Pacific Security Affairs, Office of the Secretary of Defense, Before the 117th Congress, Committee on Foreign Relations, United States Senate, Short; Colby, "Why Protecting Taiwan Really Matters"; Bellocchi, "The Strategic Importance of Taiwan," 62–67; Gordon, Mullen, and Sacks, *U.S.-Taiwan Relations in a New Era*; Kanapathy, "Countering China's Gray-Zone Activities," 28–31; Alperovitch, "Taiwan Is the New Berlin"; Bosco, "Taiwan and Strategic Security"; Mearsheimer, "Say Goodbye to Taiwan"; Colby and Mitre, "Why the Pentagon Should Focus on Taiwan."
20. A more tempered version of this argument holds that China could gain an operational advantage by putting surveillance and target acquisition sensors on Taiwan, thereby modestly extending the range of its long-range maritime precision strike sensors and weapons. See, for example, Sweeney, *How Militarily Useful Would Taiwan Be*, 5–6; Biddle and Oelrich, "Future Warfare in the Western Pacific"; Steinberg and O'Hanlon, *Strategic Reassurance and Resolve*, 242–243. For a skeptical take on the military advantages that might accrue to China if it seizes Taiwan, see Porter and Mazarr, *Countering China's Adventurism*, 9–11; Caverley, "The Taiwan Fallacy."
21. See, for example, Sullivan, *A Test of Will*, 14–15; Bolton, *The Room Where It Happened*, xxv; Friedberg, "Will We Abandon Taiwan?"; Glaser, "U.S.-China Grand Bargain?"; Santoro and Cossa, *The World After Taiwan's Fall*; Cunningham, *The American Case for Taiwan*, 7–9; Bellocchi, "The Strategic Importance of Taiwan," 72–76; Gordon, Mullen, and Sacks, *U.S.-Taiwan Relations in a New Era*, 9–10; Haas and Sacks, "To Keep the

Peace"; Colby and Mitre, "Why the Pentagon Should Focus on Taiwan"; Lohman and Jannuzi, "Preserve America's Strategic Autonomy"; Tucker and Glaser, "Should the United States Abandon Taiwan?" 32.

22. Babbage, *The Next Major War*, 133.
23. Schelling, *Arms and Influence*, 124.
24. Schelling, *Arms and Influence*, 35.
25. For a recent review of the reputation literature, see Jervis, Yarhi-Milo, and Casler, "Redefining the Debate."
26. For work on the relationship between reputation and signaling, see Copeland, "Do Reputations Matter?"; Morrow, "Capabilities, Uncertainty, and Resolve"; Fearon, "Signaling Foreign Policy Interests." For a critical take on this link, see Mercer, *Reputation and International Politics*; Press, *Calculating Credibility*; Tang, "Reputation, Cult of Reputation."
27. Tingley and Walter, "The Effect of Repeated Play"; Sechser, "Reputations and Signaling."
28. Yarhi-Milo, *Who Fights for Reputation*.
29. McManus and Yarhi-Milo, "The Logic of 'Offstage' Signaling"; McManus and Nieman, "Identifying the Level."
30. Lupton, *Reputation for Resolve*.
31. LeVeck and Narang, "How International Reputation Matters."
32. Morrow, "Capabilities, Uncertainty, and Resolve"; Leeds and Anac, "Alliance Institutionalization"; Johnson, Leeds, and Wu, "Capability, Credibility"; Leeds, Long, and Mitchell, "Reevaluating Alliance Reliability"; Leeds, Mattes, and Vogel, "Interests, Institutions"; Leeds and Savun, "Terminating Alliances"; Crescenzi et al., "Reliability, Reputation, and Alliance Formation"; Mattes, "Reputation, Symmetry, and Alliance Design."
33. Kim, Byun, and Ko, "Remember Kabul?"
34. Horowitz, Poast, and Stam, "Domestic Signaling."
35. Hunzeker and Lanoszka, "Landpower and American Credibility."
36. Bak, "Alliance Proximity."
37. Lehmann, "Projecting Credibility."
38. For an especially incisive critique of the way Washington handled its post–World War II relationship with Taipei, see Kerr, *Formosa Betrayed*.
39. Goldstein, *The United States and the Republic of China*, 6.
40. Khan, *The Struggle for Taiwan*, 56–58.
41. Yarhi-Milo, Lanoszka, and Cooper, "To Arm or to Ally?", 104.
42. Truman, "Statement by the President, Truman on Korea."
43. Truman, *Memoirs by Harry S. Truman*, vol. II, 337.

44. Goldstein, *Suspicious Allies*, 6.
45. Yarhi-Milo, Lanoszka, and Cooper, "To Arm or to Ally?", 6.
46. Goldstein, *Suspicious Allies*, 7.
47. Goldstein, *Suspicious Allies*, 9–10.
48. See Articles VI and VII, "Mutual Defense Treaty Between the United States and the Republic of China," (1954). https://avalon.law.yale.edu/20th_century/chin001.asp.
49. Yarhi-Milo, Lanoszka, and Cooper, "To Arm or to Ally?", 105–107.
50. Goldstein, *Suspicious Allies*, 8.
51. Goldstein, *Suspicious Allies*, 8.
52. Goldstein, *Suspicious Allies*, 21.
53. Rigger, "The Taiwan Relations Act," 11.
54. American Institute in Taiwan, Taiwan Relations Act, (1979).
55. Taiwan, Short Taiwan Relations Act, Section 2(b)(6).
56. DeLisle, "The Taiwan Relations Act at 40," 35–36.
57. William J. Clinton and Zemin Jiang, China-US Joint Statement.
58. Bolton, *The Room Where It Happened*, 311.
59. *President Joe Biden: The 2022 60 Minutes Interview*; The White House, "Remarks by President Biden and Prime Minister Kishida Fumio"; The White House, "Remarks by President Biden After Marine One Arrival"; ABC News, "Full transcript of ABC News' George Stephanopoulos' Interview with President Joe Biden."
60. Shattuck and Lewis, *Breaking the Barrier*.
61. For an overview of both this approach and potential drawbacks, see Geddes, Parker, and Scott, "When the snowball fails."
62. For example, according to the U.S. Department of Defense, the People's Liberation Army Eastern and Southern Commands alone have nearly five times more ground troops, six times more destroyers, 17 times more submarines, and four time more war planes than the entire Taiwanese military. Beijing also spends at least 20 times more on defense than Taiwan. Office of the Secretary of Defense, *Military and Security Developments Involving the People's Republic of China, 2022*.
63. For a representative sample of this sprawling literature and its evolution since the mid-twentieth century, see Brodie, *Strategy in the Missile Age*; Snyder, *Deterrence and Defense*; Schelling, *The Strategy of Conflict*; Schelling, *Arms and Influence*; Blechman and Kaplan, *Force without War*; Mearsheimer, *Conventional Deterrence*; Freedman, *Deterrence*; Narang, *Nuclear Strategy in the Modern Era*; Sechser and Fuhrmann,

Nuclear Weapons and Coercive Diplomacy; Gartzke and Lindsay, *Elements of Deterrence.*

64. Snyder, "Deterrence and Power," 163.
65. Schelling, *Arms and Influence*, 35.
66. Fearon, "Signaling Foreign Policy Interests," 69.
67. Lupton, *Reputation for Resolve*, 3.
68. Henry, "What Allies Want," 53.
69. Russett, "An Empirical Typology," 262–263. This definition is similar to the one used by the Alliance Treaty Obligations and Provisions dataset, which holds that alliances are "written agreements, signed by official representatives of at least two independent states, that include promises to aid a partner in the event of military conflict, to remain neutral in the event of conflict, to refrain from military conflict with one another, or to consult/cooperate in the event of international crises that create a potential for military conflict." Leeds, "Alliance Treaty Obligations," 7.
70. Kuo, *Following the Leader.*
71. Snyder, "The Security Dilemma."
72. We take these definitions from Lanoszka, *Military Alliances in the Twenty-First Century*, 52 & 77. For a deeper discussion of these and related alliance pathologies, see Snyder, "The Security Dilemma"; Christensen and Snyder, "Chain Gangs"; Morrow, "Arms versus Allies"; Kim, "Why Alliances Entangle"; Beckley, "The Myth of Entangling Alliances."
73. Hunzeker and Lanoszka, *A Question of Time*, 26.
74. Lanoszka, "Russian Hybrid Warfare," 178; Kuo, *Contests of Initiative*, 2.

CHAPTER 1

CONFLICT SCENARIOS

This book explores how a war over Taiwan's status might reshape East Asian assessments of American power, interests, and credibility. Whereas most existing studies focus on the causes and conduct of such a conflict, the primary objective of this study is to assess its broader implications for the United States' alliance relationships in the region and Washington's long-term ability to deter and compel. By setting aside the complex and contingent details surrounding the origins and outcomes of a cross-Strait conflict, we aim to evaluate whether—and to what extent—concerns about credibility and reliability should factor into a US decision to intervene militarily.

That said, the nature of potential crisis and conflict scenarios cannot be entirely set aside. There are plausible reasons to believe that different types of crises and conflicts may carry distinct implications for American credibility. To take an extreme example, it is difficult to imagine that US allies in East Asia would question Washington's resolve if it chose not to respond to a Taipei-initiated first strike against Beijing. By contrast, US inaction in the face of an unprovoked, all-out Chinese attack on Taiwan is far more likely to trigger fear, uncertainty, and strategic reassessment among America's regional allies.

It is therefore useful to outline a basic typology of coercive options Beijing might realistically consider. A review of the existing work suggests that there are six such scenarios worth considering in detail:[1]

- A sustained campaign of subversive manipulation and provocation in the so-called gray zone
- A blockade of Taiwan's main island
- A surprise attack on one or more of Taiwan's offshore islands
- A coercive strike campaign
- A full-scale invasion and occupation of Taiwan
- Nuclear options

Each scenario reflects a distinct pathway through which Beijing might attempt to achieve the same fundamental objective: asserting political control over the Taiwanese people. While it is useful to examine them individually, this study proceeds from the assumption that these options could also be employed in combination[2]—either sequentially or concurrently—as part of a broader campaign leading up to full-scale occupation.

Gray-Zone Subversion

Experts use the term "gray-zone warfare" to describe Beijing's ongoing attempts to coerce Taiwan at the lowest end of the kinetic spectrum. Unfortunately, the term "gray zone" has become something of a catch-all phrase to refer to a range of different types of diplomatic, economic, and military coercion. As stated in the previous chapter, this study adopts a more precise definition: the term refers to the deliberate, coordinated, and incremental use of provocations, intrusions, and other gradualist tactics—employed by both conventional and unconventional military units—to challenge existing red lines, undermine resolve, and establish new "facts on the ground" without *generating a decisive military reaction from the target or its allies.*[3]

This study treats Chinese behavior as a gray-zone provocation only when it involves conventional and/or unconventional military units—in other words, when it includes the use or threatened use of violence. As a result, we exclude purely diplomatic, propagandistic, and economic actions from this category. For example, we do not consider Beijing's efforts to persuade Taiwan's diplomatic allies to shift recognition from Taipei to the People's Republic of China as gray-zone subversion. The same applies to economic coercion, including threats, punishments, and inducements, as well as state-sponsored mis- and disinformation campaigns. While these measures are undeniably part of the broader landscape of China–Taiwan relations, they fall outside the scope of gray-zone provocations as defined in this study.

Similarly, because gray-zone subversion—according to our definition—constitutes an attempt to challenge the status quo without triggering military escalation, we distinguish it from overt and unambiguous forms of state-directed military violence (or threats thereof), including the seizure of one of Taiwan's outlying islands, a blockade of Taiwan itself, long-range air and missile strikes against military or civilian targets, and, of course, an all-out invasion.[4]

Unlike the more overt uses of force discussed next—which, thankfully, remain hypothetical—Chinese gray-zone incursions are real and persistent. Beijing routinely mounts gray-zone provocations against Taiwan and has done so for some time. Taiwanese government offices and civilian corporations are under constant cyberattack.[5] The People's Liberation Army (PLA) conducts military exercises that simulate blockades, amphibious landings, and strikes against high-value Taiwanese targets.[6] Chinese aircraft also intrude into Taiwan's ADIZ on a near-daily basis.[7]

Regardless of the specific form they take, China's gray-zone operations share a common goal: to gradually intimidate and coerce Taiwan into acquiescing to Beijing's demands.

Air and Sea Blockades

If Chinese leaders decide to move beyond gray-zone tactics, they may still choose to stop short of a full-scale invasion. One alternative option is the launch of a multi-domain blockade of Taiwan's main island. Indeed, Western analysts increasingly worry that a blockade is the most likely way that Beijing will try to use force against Taiwan.[8] The PLA appeared to rehearse such blockade operations during a four-day, large-scale military exercise surrounding Taiwan following Speaker of the House Nancy Pelosi's trip to Taipei in August 2022—and again following the Taiwanese presidential election in early 2024 and Taiwan's National Day celebrations that October.[9]

The reasons Beijing might consider a blockade of Taiwan are straightforward. As a densely populated island, Taiwan is especially vulnerable to being cut off from the outside world.[10] Taiwan's 23 million citizens depend on maritime imports for 97 percent of their energy needs,[11] and the combination of domestic food production and available stockpiles could sustain the population for only about six months.[12]

China's geographic proximity to Taiwan, combined with the scale of its military forces, provides Beijing with multiple options to attempt to isolate the island from the international community. The most immediate risks are economic. Taiwan is a vital node in global supply chains, and its economy relies heavily on consistent access to international suppliers and markets. Disruptions to these connections would result in severe and immediate economic consequences. In 2024, the Bloomberg Economic Institute estimated that a blockade of Taiwan could impose a global economic cost of US$10 trillion, with Taiwan's economy contracting by more than 12 percent in the first year alone. Even businesses and consumers not directly involved in foreign trade would feel the effects, as unemployment and inflation would likely surge.

The long-term effects of a blockade could prove even more corrosive. The longer such a campaign drags on, the more enduring and possibly irreversible the economic damage is likely to be. Multinational corporations that have long depended on Taiwan as a key link in global supply chains may begin to relocate operations or seek to decouple from the island altogether. Even if the blockade is only partial or porous, soaring insurance premiums could render commercial engagement with Taiwan financially untenable. At the same time, a brain drain is likely, as educated and affluent Taiwanese seek to leave the island—an outcome that Beijing may view as beneficial and actively encourage through continued pressure. The consequences for Taiwan's semiconductor sector—the crown jewel of its economy—could be particularly devastating.

Offshore Island Grab

In discussions of cross-Strait tensions, analysts and commentators frequently assert that Taiwan lies just 90 miles from China. This characterization, however, is inaccurate. Taipei exercises jurisdiction over several hundred outlying islands, many of which are considerably closer to the Chinese mainland than the main island of Taiwan (Formosa).[13] These islands—often small in size (the largest measures less than 150 square kilometers), sparsely populated (some are uninhabited, while the most populous has approximately 120,000 residents), and lightly defended —present tempting targets. The Dongsha (Pratas), Kinmen, Matsu, and Penghu island groups are especially vulnerable. Kinmen's main island lays less than 10 kilometers away from the Chinese city of Xiamen;[14] the Matsu islands are within 20 kilometers of the Chinese coastline; and the nearly one hundred Penghu islands lie in the Taiwan Strait between Taiwan and China.

These island chains are located astride likely invasion routes, making it likely that Chinese military forces would seek to neutralize or occupy them as part of any full-scale assault on Taiwan's main island.[15] However, some analysts argue that a limited attack on one or more of Taiwan's outlying islands could serve Beijing's political objectives while avoiding the high costs and risks associated with a full-scale invasion. Seizing Taiwan proper would require the PLA to mobilize hundreds of ships and aircraft, along with several hundred thousand troops—an undertaking that would be virtually impossible to conceal. Such a buildup would likely trigger Taiwanese defensive preparations and allow the United States time to surge forces into the region. In contrast, a much smaller force could capture an outlying island with little warning, potentially catching both Taipei and Washington off guard. Moreover, US military intervention would be less certain:[16] as a matter of law and policy, most of these islands are not covered under the Taiwan Relations Act; and as a matter of operational feasibility, the rapid pace of a limited seizure would likely outstrip the US military's ability to respond in time to prevent it.

At least in theory, presenting Taiwan and the United States with a surprise fait accompli could have a profound impact on Taiwanese and American resolve, entirely disproportionate to the lost territory's military utility or strategic value. By demonstrating resolve and military capability, Beijing might hope to convince Taiwanese leaders and citizens of the futility of resisting, while also signaling to Washington, Tokyo, Seoul, and Canberra that Taiwan's situation is untenable. At a minimum, the seizure of an outlying island could prompt greater hesitation and debate among leaders in all four capitals than an unambiguous full-scale invasion might. Western leaders already question whether their publics would be willing to go to war with China to defend Taiwan. Expecting them to risk war to retake a small, isolated, and militarily insignificant island may prove a bridge too far.

Coercive Strike Campaign

Beijing has at least one other kinetic alternative short of mounting a full-scale invasion: it could conduct standoff strikes against Taiwan, with or without a corresponding air and naval blockade.[17] The PLA might fire missiles near, over, and into Taiwan; conduct bombing runs using both manned and unmanned aircraft; employ People's Liberation Army Navy (PLAN) vessels to strike targets at sea, in port, or near the coastline; and orchestrate cyberattacks against critical government, military, and civilian installations and infrastructure. A standoff strike campaign could also involve covert operatives and sleeper cells tasked with assassinating key leaders, sabotaging critical infrastructure, and inciting public unrest.

If Beijing were to initiate a standoff strike campaign, its objective would likely be to destroy, degrade, or neutralize Taiwan's military capabilities in order to undermine both its capacity and will to resist. Potential targets include radar installations; long-range strike platforms and their associated infrastructure; air and missile defense systems; command, control, communications, computers, intelligence, surveillance, and reconnaissance (C4ISR) nodes; airfields; naval ports; ammunition and fuel depots; high-value military assets such as surface ships and Taiwan's domestically produced diesel-electric submarines; and potentially key government leaders. Chinese leaders would almost certainly hope that, once a significant portion of Taiwan's offensive and defensive military capability is neutralized, public and political pressure would compel Taipei to seek terms for peace.

To further constrain Taiwan's military options, Beijing might also target key infrastructure, including the island's power grid, transportation chokepoints near military installations—particularly those housing armor and mechanized units—fuel reserves, and the landing sites of undersea cables that connect Taiwan to the global internet.

The more the PLA strikes these types of targets, the higher the likelihood of civilian casualties. Whether Beijing views such "collateral damage" as a bug or a feature of its campaign remains uncertain. It is difficult to assess whether Chinese leaders believe they can erode Taiwanese will to resist through precision strikes limited to military infrastructure alone, or if they anticipate that targeting civilian populations will also be necessary in a protracted strike campaign. On the one hand, a substantial body of social science research suggests that harming civilians tends to strengthen popular resistance rather than diminish it.[18] On the other hand, political leaders and military planners throughout history have often assumed—mistakenly—that inflicting terror and unacceptable levels of pain on civilian populations will lead those populations to turn against their own governments.

Full-Scale Invasion

Beijing's most complex option is a full-scale invasion. Such an undertaking would constitute one of the largest military operations in history. While the invasion could unfold in a variety of ways—and western analysts should expect China's military to surprise them with its operational and tactical flexibility and creativity—ultimate success will hinge on whether the PLA can accomplish three core tasks in advance of launching an attack.

Isolate

Severing Taiwan's access to the outside world will be a top priority for the PLA, as continued inflows of weapons, ammunition, spare parts, fuel, medicine, and food would strengthen both Taiwan's resolve and its capacity to resist. To prevent this, any Chinese plan to isolate the island would almost certainly include measures aimed at deterring external support—and provisions to interdict such support should deterrence fail.

Blind

Whether Beijing would strike US bases in Japan or South Korea during the opening stages of a full-scale invasion remains speculative. That it would do so against Taiwan, however, is virtually certain. To maximize the chances of success, the PLA would need to blind, disrupt, or otherwise degrade Taiwan's ability to detect, target, and intercept incoming forces —particularly strike aircraft—and weaken Taiwan's ability to coordinate defensive operations and conduct counterstrikes against targets inside China. A large-scale and destructive strike campaign would therefore almost certainly precede—or more likely, coincide with—the onset of a blockade.

Degrade

Once Taiwan's ability to detect incoming missiles, aircraft, and surface ships—and to coordinate its military defenses—has been sufficiently degraded, the PLA would likely intensify its strikes to hammer away at Taiwan's remaining capabilities and its national resolve. These operations would set the stage for the most challenging and decisive phase of the campaign: putting Chinese boots on Taiwanese ground.

Landing operations are likely to commence when PLA leaders assess that the main invasion force can come ashore without incurring unacceptably high losses from remaining Taiwanese defenders. It is reasonable to expect the PLA to begin by deploying special operations forces, airborne units, and air assault troops. These initial "shock troops" may arrive even before the joint strike campaign by the PLA Rocket Force (PLARF), PLA Air Force (PLAAF), and PLA Navy (PLAN) has fully concluded —an approach that would significantly increase the risk of fratricide. Meanwhile, Chinese forces will move to take control of the Kinmen, Matsu, and Penghu islands, assuming they have not already done so.

The large-scale introduction of ground combat troops will follow. If the PLA Air Force (PLAAF) has secured air superiority and the joint strike campaign has sufficiently degraded Taiwan's air defenses, the PLA will likely seek to insert as many conventional ground units by air as possible —hence the imperative to seize and hold airfields. Nevertheless, Beijing will ultimately need to deploy hundreds of thousands of ground troops to overcome Taiwanese defenses and secure key population centers. The Greater Taipei Area alone is home to approximately seven million people and spans nearly 900 square miles. No military in the world possesses sufficient transport aircraft to airlift the number of troops—let alone the accompanying vehicles, weapons, ammunition, food, and fuel—required to take and hold such a target. The bulk of the invasion force will need to arrive by sea.[19]

Deterring Outside "Interference"

As Chinese military operations and strikes unfold in and around Taiwan, China will simultaneously seek to limit external intervention by various means. Beijing will do everything in its power to deter the United States from deploying military forces to aid Taiwan in the event of an invasion— and, to a lesser extent, to dissuade Tokyo, Seoul, and Canberra from offering meaningful support for such an effort. At a minimum, the Chinese government can be expected to exert diplomatic and economic pressure, accompanied by explicit or implicit threats, as it begins massing combat power. Beijing will also attempt to constrain or deny American access to regional airspace, ports, airfields, and military bases through whatever means of pressure it can leverage.

If these non-kinetic efforts fail to dissuade Washington and its allies from directly intervening, Beijing will likely rely on its conventional anti-access, area denial (A2/AD) capabilities. By threatening to use long-range strike weapons against US bases, aircraft, and ships, Beijing might hope to convince Washington that the costs of moving forces into theater will be unacceptably high. Alternatively, if Beijing concludes that American intervention is inevitable, it might authorize preemptive strikes against US forces stationed in Japan. Such action, however, would be unmistakably escalatory and would almost certainly ensure direct American and Japanese involvement in the conflict.

Nuclear Options

A more ominous possibility also exists: rather than relying solely on conventional weapons to deter or defeat Washington, Chinese leaders might contemplate issuing nuclear threats, or even initiating a nuclear first strike.[20] Nor, it must be said, is it beyond the realm of possibility that the United States might feel compelled to use nuclear weapons to defend Taiwan.[21]

To be sure, the specter of a nuclear detonation may seem farfetched given Beijing's professed commitment to a "No First Use" policy. Yet there are several reasons not to dismiss the risk outright. First, China's pledge makes an exception for scenarios involving threats to its homeland—and Beijing unequivocally regards Taiwan as an integral part of its territory. Second, Chinese leaders may (correctly, in our view) conclude that relying solely on conventional anti-access capabilities places them on the horns of a dilemma. On one hand, launching preemptive conventional strikes against US and Japanese bases and assets in the region could inflame political and public sentiment in Washington and Tokyo without decisively degrading allied military capabilities. On the other hand, waiting for US or Japanese forces to fire the first shot could leave the PLA at a tactical disadvantage, particularly if American and Japanese forces have time to mass before engaging. To avoid this dilemma, Beijing may consider issuing nuclear threats. Moreover, Chinese leaders might assess that the best way to avoid a protracted and costly conflict is to seize Taiwan quickly—before the United States and its allies can mount an effective response. If Beijing doubts Washington's willingness to "trade Los Angeles for Taipei," it could calculate that a limited nuclear threat or demonstration might deter US intervention and, in doing so, shatter Taiwan's will to resist.

At a minimum, Washington should expect Beijing to rattle the nuclear saber early in any invasion scenario. Much as Vladimir Putin made thinly veiled nuclear threats and issued largely symbolic orders to his nuclear forces during Russia's re-invasion of Ukraine,[22] Chinese leaders are likely to employ similar tactics to stoke Western fears of nuclear escalation. Public statements, implicit warnings, and conspicuous nuclear posturing should all be expected—and interpreted as part of a deliberate strategy to deter external intervention.

Washington should be cautious not to brush aside such threats as mere bluster or cheap talk. As several interviewees emphasized, Beijing may be more willing to cross the nuclear threshold than many American analysts assume. A full-scale invasion of Taiwan represents not only an existential threat to Taiwan but also to the Chinese Communist Party—

and to Xi Jinping personally. To the extent that China's leaders question the value of a post-conflict world that doesn't include them, they may be prepared to consider nuclear options, including tests, demonstrations (such as a high-altitude detonation), or even a preemptive strike against Taiwan. That Beijing might annihilate the very place it seeks to reclaim may seem irrational—if one assumes that the People's Republic of China is motivated primarily by material interests such as profit or prestige. If, however, Beijing views Taiwan primarily through the lens of historical humiliation and national identity, then the idea of "destroying the island to save the nation" has a coldly utilitarian logic. After all, if Taiwan can be reduced to smoldering rubble at the push of a button, what remains to fight over? In a major 2021 policy address, Xi Jinping underscored this point by quoting Chairman Mao: "Do not hesitate to ruin the country internally in order to build it anew."[23] In this context, the threat of nuclear escalation by Xi, and China's willingness to kill the patient in order to save it, cannot be dismissed out of hand.

Research Focus

We have outlined China's potential courses of action because these represent the scenarios regional security experts considered when discussing how different outcomes might affect the United States' alliance relationships. Having done so, however, a natural question arises: why devote attention to analyzing a future in which Beijing opts to launch an all-out war on Taiwan—particularly given our premise that a full-scale invasion represents both the worst-case scenario and, arguably, the least likely?

Our reasoning is straightforward. We do not believe Beijing can compel Taiwan without either launching—or credibly threatening to launch— a full-scale invasion. We also suspect that Chinese leaders understand this dilemma. Blockades, seizures of outlying islands, and coercive strike campaigns all suffer from the same core limitation: unless they quickly break the will of Taiwan's government and population, they provide Washington and its allies time to respond. The only way for Beijing to mitigate that risk is to mobilize an invasion force alongside any blockade, island grab, or strike campaign. Even if Beijing prefers to avoid the costs and risks of occupying Taiwan's main island, the most effective way to make these "lesser" forms of aggression credible—whether in the eyes of Taipei or Washington—is to convince them that an all-out invasion could follow.

As such, any meaningful discussion of how allies might react to scenarios in which Taiwan falls to China must include the prospect of invasion. Gray-zone provocations, blockades, and even stand-off strikes leave the United States with enough strategic flexibility that allies may shrug off their implications. But when it comes to how Japan, South Korea, and Australia perceive Washington's Taiwan choices as reflective of their own circumstances—the "there but for the grace of God" question— an American decision whether or not to respond to an invasion is the true litmus test.

When the Dust Settles

Having thus concluded that the aftermath of an invasion offers the most analytically relevant context for examining questions of US credibility and reliability, we turn to a description of the scenarios presented to the interviewees. In doing so, we prioritized parsimony over complexity, framing potential outcomes along two key binary dimensions: whether the United States intervened in the conflict, and whether Taiwan retained its independence. The intersection of these binaries yields four distinct scenarios, which we present in the following matrix:

Table 1. Matrix of Possibilities.

	Taiwan remains independent	China controls Taiwan
United States does not intervene	1	2
United states intervenes	3	4

The US Does Not Intervene, but Taiwan Remains Independent

Given the relative disparity between China and Taiwan in terms of population, military capabilities, and economic resources, this outcome is so implausible as to be considered functionally impossible. Accordingly, we did not explore it in depth during the interviews, though it warrants brief mention here for the sake of completeness. Should the United States choose not to intervene in response to an unambiguous Chinese attack and Taiwan nonetheless manage to preserve its independence, Taiwan, the United States, and their allies would be in a comparatively stronger position. That said, the implications for the broader US alliance network would remain difficult to predict.

From China's perspective, this outcome would constitute not only a tactical and operational defeat but also a strategic catastrophe. In recent decades, China has oriented its military modernization efforts around the objective of prevailing in a Taiwan contingency. Its emphasis on anti-access/area denial (A2/AD) capabilities is intended to erode US military advantages in the Western Pacific and reduce the likelihood of effective intervention by Washington. If Taiwan were able to defend itself without US assistance, it would signal that China's efforts had been in vain and that it had focused its preparations on the wrong adversary. The PRC would likely emerge from such a conflict bloody and demoralized.

Meanwhile, the reunification of Taiwan has been a core strategic objective for China since the founding of the PRC and has only increased in importance under Xi Jinping. In a speech marking the centenary of the CCP, Xi reaffirmed that "resolving the Taiwan question and realizing China's complete reunification is a historic mission and an unshakable commitment of the Communist Party of China,"[24] and has asserted on multiple occasions that the Taiwan question cannot be passed down from generation to generation.[25] Through these repeated statements, Xi has tied his own legacy to bringing Taiwan under Beijing's control. Were Taiwan to retain independence in the face of a Chinese effort to bring the island to heel by force, the CCP could suffer a crippling blow to its legitimacy, with potentially disastrous knock-on effects. With this in mind, it is difficult to envision what a Chinese defeat would actually look like as long as Xi remains in power. Unless he—or the CCP itself —lost control of the country, a failed invasion would likely be viewed as a temporary setback, followed by a period of rearmament with the intent to try again.

For the United States alliance system, this outcome is more ambiguous. A Taiwanese victory and the preservation of Taiwanese democracy would undoubtedly align more closely with US strategic interests than the alternative. However, the rationale for maintaining a forward-deployed US military presence in East Asia as a deterrent to war rests on a shared consensus that Washington will intervene in the event of aggression and that US allies depend on it to do so. If Taiwan were forced to confront China alone—and nonetheless prevailed—US allies in Japan, South Korea, Australia, and the Philippines, as well as strategic partners such as Singapore, would likely undertake a bottom-up reassessment of their relationships with Washington and their own security postures. The United States would have shown itself to be unreliable, and China would be revealed as a paper tiger. Defense experts and policymakers would likely approach this reassessment through one lens, and ordinary citizens through another. In democratic societies, partisan politics would likely shape the discourse, with attitudes toward future relations with the United States becoming a salient political issue.

The ultimate consequences would vary by country, but the overarching point remains: the blow to US credibility as an ally would be significant, and the perceived need for American protection could diminish. Nevertheless, we considered this scenario sufficiently implausible that we did not explore it in depth with regional experts. Instead, the implications for the alliance system in the event of American nonintervention following a full-scale Chinese invasion are examined more thoroughly in the analysis of scenario two.

The US Does Not Intervene, and China Takes Taiwan

The second scenario depicts an unambiguous victory for China and a voluntary abstention from intervention on the part of the United States. In this state of the world, Beijing has achieved much of what it claims to seek. Most notably, it has succeeded in asserting political control over Taiwan. Taiwan's de facto independence is extinguished, China's territorial integrity is secured, and the ambiguous 1949 conclusion to the Chinese Civil War is laid to rest. In addition to gaining control over Taiwan's territory and resources—discussed further below—the PRC also secures a significant narrative victory. The annexation of Taiwan represents the culmination of a core national ambition. It enables Beijing to claim that it faced down the forces of American hegemony and emerged victorious. With the United States having chosen not to intervene, Beijing can credibly assert that its military ascent and economic influence made its victory over Taiwan a fait accompli.

In addition to securing a narrative victory, China would gain control over Taiwan's territory and resources. These include not only natural resources—both on land and in surrounding maritime areas—but also, potentially, the crown jewel of Taiwan's industrial base: the world's most advanced and productive semiconductor fabrication capabilities. As the COVID-19–related supply chain disruptions made clear, access to leading-edge semiconductors has become a critical chokepoint for countless global industries. Control of advanced chip production could give China the edge in the emerging battle for AI dominance, with lasting consequences for decades to come.

Beyond access to natural and productive resources, Chinese control over Taiwan could also confer a major strategic advantage by granting Beijing unfettered access to the Pacific.[26] Such an outcome could significantly advance Beijing's ambitions to exert unchecked regional hegemony over East Asia. The PRC would immediately control a significant portion of the First Island Chain, with its forces positioned less than 100 nautical miles from the southernmost island of the Japanese archipelago.

From a military planning and resourcing perspective, the PLA would no longer need to structure its force posture around the objective of seizing Taiwan. This would free resources for the development of enhanced force projection capabilities, including a more robust blue-water navy capable of operating far beyond Taiwan's immediate vicinity.

For the United States, the losses would be inversely commensurate with China's victories. Most notably at the operational level, Washington would lose access to the island General Douglas MacArthur famously described as an "unsinkable aircraft carrier." With the loss of Taiwan, Washington's ability to project power and operate with relative freedom in the Western Pacific would be significantly diminished. Both naval and air operations would be affected, as the US military would be forced to adapt to a new strategic environment in which the PRC exercises control over the airspace and maritime approaches that it previously contested with Taiwan.

Stepping back from the military implications, a US decision not to intervene in a conflict that ends in Beijing's favor could deliver a significant blow to American credibility as an ally. In such a scenario, Washington's continued ability to maintain its regional position and uphold its alliance network would depend on persuading allies that its commitment to Taiwan was categorically different from its formal treaty obligations to Japan, South Korea, Australia, and the Philippines. The absence of a formal defense treaty with Taiwan may facilitate that argument. However, as detailed in the chapters that follow, interviews with regional experts indicate that many would nonetheless be shocked if the United States failed to come to Taiwan's aid when the stakes were highest.

Helpful to the US cause of alliance maintenance would be that, in this scenario, China emerges as an even more powerful—and potentially more menacing—actor. This development could have the effect of reinforcing Washington's alliance network despite the misgivings of its regional partners. Even if the United States were seen to have abandoned Taiwan in a time of need, it would remain the only credible counterbalancing force to an even stronger PRC. If regional actors such as Japan, South Korea, and Australia wish to retain some independence from Beijing's orbit, they would likely be compelled to draw even closer to the United States, despite their misgivings—and perhaps closer to one another as well. This could involve doubling down on domestic military modernization, an effort long encouraged by many in the US defense community in both bilateral and multilateral settings. It would also almost certainly entail increased defense cooperation with—or purchases from —the United States. Improved domestic capabilities among these US allies could enhance deterrence against potential PRC aggression, foster more equitable burden sharing, and reduce free-riding on US security guarantees.

Following a PRC victory of this type, East Asia could move into a less stable, more dangerous configuration, in which an emboldened Beijing advances more openly revanchist territorial ambitions. However, it is also conceivable that removing the persistent irritant of Taiwan's unresolved status could yield a less militaristic PRC—one that perceives its core national interests as secure and thus feels less need for further adventures afield. For Washington, while this outcome would force a deeply uncomfortable reckoning, the end of its security commitments to Taiwan might also free up resources to pursue other strategic objectives. Moreover, in the context of the bilateral relationship between China and the United States, the resolution of Taiwan's status could eliminate the most volatile flashpoint that has bedeviled relations for decades. Absent the risk of confrontation over Taiwan—and assuming the lingering animus of direct conflict could be mitigated—one can envision a scenario in which the United States and the PRC find greater scope to collaborate on shared global challenges, including climate change, nuclear nonproliferation, international narcotics trafficking, and stability on the Korean Peninsula.

Before turning to other possible outcomes, it is important to note that much in this scenario hinges on what Taiwan looks like after the cessation of major combat operations. Taking the island is one thing; holding it is another. If the people of Taiwan conclude that their defeat is total and irreversible—and that life under Chinese Communist Party (CCP) rule promises greater stability or prosperity than the alternative—Beijing may achieve not only a military victory but also a relatively smooth imposition of political and administrative control. However, if Taiwan refuses to accept defeat, and a protracted, well-resourced insurgency takes shape, the situation could become far more complex. The likelihood of such an outcome increases significantly if the Taiwanese government and military have taken prior steps to train and equip local partisans in preparation for a potential campaign of guerilla warfare[27]—China may find that holding Taiwan becomes even more difficult than taking it in the first place.

Historical and recent examples from both colonial occupations and modern conflicts illustrate how post-conflict stabilization efforts can become protracted, resource-draining quagmires rather than strategic or operational successes. The United States' two-decade failure in Afghanistan and Israel's ongoing challenges in Gaza and the West Bank offer readily apparent parallels. Taiwan's relatively large population, combined with the natural advantages afforded to guerrilla fighters by dense urban environments and mountainous jungle terrain, would make a sustained insurgency difficult to suppress. Even if only a small fraction of the population chose to resist and were adequately armed, these freedom fighters could present a formidable and enduring challenge to Chinese control. Should Taiwanese forces and civilians dig in and actively oppose Beijing's authority, the prospects for improved relations between China and the United States would likely diminish. In such a scenario, Washington may feel compelled to support Taiwanese partisans—motivated by both solidarity with a struggle for democratic self-determination and the strategic incentive to tie up the Chinese resources needed to quell a domestic insurgency.

The US Intervenes, and Taiwan Remains Independent

Of the four plausible outcomes considered in this study, this is the scenario that nearly all of the experts interviewed regarded as the most likely. Decades of sustained US presence in the region—including repeated assurances from Washington to allies, partners, and adversaries alike that the United States is a steadfast and reliable partner—have cultivated a widespread confidence among regional observers that the United States would almost certainly intervene in defense of Taiwan in response to unambiguous Chinese aggression. Furthermore, based on an assessment of relative capabilities at the time of this analysis, the experts consulted broadly agreed that, with US support (and likely assistance from regional allies), Taiwan would probably prevail. Even so, despite this scenario remaining the prevailing assumption, it warrants further elaboration and analysis—particularly because the costs of a US victory may be far greater than is commonly presumed.

First, by way of definition, in a scenario in which the United States responds to an attack or near-attack by clearly and decisively coming to Taiwan's aid, a victory for the United States would be characterized by the preservation of the status quo ante—that is, the retention of Taiwan's de facto independence. While this outcome could potentially lead to a further step toward de jure independence, such a development is not inevitable. Distinctions between de facto and de jure independence were not explored in detail in the interviews conducted for this study.

For China, this scenario would represent both an operational defeat and a strategic setback. As previously noted, the CCP under Xi Jinping derives a significant portion of its legitimacy from its asserted ability to undo the "century of humiliation" China faced at the hands of foreign powers. Central to this narrative is the CCP's pursuit of maximalist territorial claims, particularly its insistence on sovereignty over Taiwan. Should Beijing fail to bring Taiwan under its control in the face of military resistance, it is reasonable to expect that segments of the Chinese population would begin to question the CCP's continued legitimacy and its claim to a national mandate.

Nonetheless, even in the context of what appears to be a clear-cut Chinese defeat and an American—and Taiwanese—victory, both timing and subsequent developments remain critically important. If Chinese forces are repelled swiftly and without incurring significant losses in personnel or critical capabilities, such as air and sea lift, it is plausible that Beijing would seek to regroup and prepare for another attempt. Taiwan looms so large in China's strategic thinking that a failed assault—absent a decisive degradation of China's military capacity—may simply prompt a period of recalibration and rearmament. Indeed, Beijing is likely to employ strategic patience in a conflict over Taiwan, deliberately choosing the timing and character of its operations to maximize the advantages conferred by geographic proximity and a more enduring national will.[28] In this context, defeat would not constitute a permanent condition but rather a temporary setback and delay in the pursuit of strategic objectives.

In contrast, a protracted conflict may suggest a more decisive outcome, in the sense that if a drawn-out war still ends in a Chinese defeat, it is likely that Beijing will have incurred substantial losses in personnel and equipment. However, a prolonged conflict would also deplete US resources. Should China employ its capabilities effectively, even a brief war could inflict serious damage on the United States, including the loss of American lives and significant military assets—potentially extending to high-value platforms such as aircraft carriers. In such a scenario, Washington could face the prospect of a Pyrrhic victory: preserving Taiwan's independence but at great cost.[29]

Existing scholarship offers limited direct guidance for this scenario, in part because of the United States' position as a global hegemon and the inherent complexity of modeling the dynamics of the American political process. Elected leaders in both Congress and the White House would inevitably need to respond to public opinion, yet it remains uncertain whether—and to what extent—the broader US public, particularly voters in politically consequential states and districts, would continue to support Taiwan in the face of mounting casualties. It is therefore conceivable that the United States could intervene, achieve battlefield success, and deliver a significant blow to China's regional military ambitions, yet still emerge from the conflict substantially weakened—both in terms of its capacity to project power in the Western Pacific and its domestic political will to sustain such commitments.

In this scenario, Taiwan retains its independence and China emerges chastened, but the United States may nonetheless adopt a more restrained or even isolationist posture. If the Taiwan issue were resolved definitively—particularly in the form of a shift from de facto to de jure independence—Beijing's threats to the island might no longer resonate as urgent with US voters. In such a case, North Korea would remain the only clear regional security rationale for maintaining a substantial American military presence in East Asia. Domestic political pressure could therefore build for a "peace dividend," in the form of a drawdown of US commitments in the region. Paradoxically, China might then find itself in a world in which it has lost a war, failed to subjugate Taiwan, and yet nonetheless succeeded in one of its core long-term objectives: accelerating the erosion of US military presence and influence in East Asia.

For America's allies in the region, the prospect of a US pullback following a victory in Taiwan poses a significant challenge. Unlike the United States, South Korea, Japan, the Philippines, and to a lesser extent, Australia, will continue to contend with China as a neighbor. Regardless of the outcome in Taiwan, the reality that China has been East Asia's regional hegemon for most of recorded history remains unchanged, and China will retain its substantial advantages in size, population, and productive capacity. Additionally, South Korea will continue to face an existential threat from North Korea, a challenge entirely separate from the Taiwan issue. As explored in greater detail in subsequent chapters, if a victory in Taiwan leads to Washington's disengagement from the region, America's allies may find the associated costs of such a shift to be more than they are willing to bear.

The US Intervenes, but China Takes Taiwan

From the perspective of the United States and its allies, this is the worst possible post-conflict outcome of the four scenarios considered. It was also the scenario that interviewees were least comfortable discussing, even when reassured that their responses would remain anonymous. The prospect of the United States fighting for Taiwan and losing is so dire that even experts who focus on these issues find it difficult and unsettling to consider, even as a hypothetical.

If the United States comes to Taiwan's aid and ultimately loses, the likely result would be an epochal change—a regional and global reordering of power, reminiscent of the reconfiguration that followed Japan's victory in the Russo-Japanese War at the outset of the twentieth century.

Modern US wars have not always resulted in clear victories. Indeed, the outcomes in Korea, Vietnam, the second Iraq conflict, and Afghanistan fall somewhere between ambiguous victories and outright defeats. However, none of these conflicts involved a direct, force-on-force war against a peer competitor. In a confrontation over Taiwan's status, the United States would face China over an issue that ranks among Beijing's top strategic priorities. As the world's sole superpower, though an aging one, the United States inherently has more to lose and less to gain than its adversary in such a conflict. China would enter the fray with a recently modernized, untested force that has not engaged in sustained conflict since the Vietnam War, while the US would confront it with a battle-hardened (though war-weary) military that has been actively engaged in combat—albeit in a different type of warfare—for the past twenty years. A Chinese victory would represent a shocking tactical, operational, and strategic defeat for the United States. To understand the magnitude of such a defeat, it is necessary to further explore the follow-on consequences.

China would emerge in a significantly improved strategic position. As described earlier in scenario 2, with control over Taiwan, the PLA Navy would have unfettered access to the Western Pacific and the waters beyond. It would be within easy operable range of the southernmost islands in the Japanese island chain and could use Taiwan as a base of operations for aircraft and missile forces. Beyond the geographic advantage, definitively resolving the Taiwan question in Beijing's favor would eliminate one of the most significant planning constraints on Chinese military operations. Without the need to prepare for an amphibious invasion and subsequent occupation of Taiwan, Chinese military planners would gain the flexibility to shift focus to other scenarios, expanding their strategic vision to include more ambitious options for power projection.

There are no guarantees regarding how these new options would manifest. Beijing has repeatedly asserted that it has no irredentist ambitions and that once Taiwan is under its control, it will not seek further military expansion. However, with the constraints of Taiwan contingency planning removed, Beijing would at least be able to explore other options and consider developing its forces to project power in a manner commensurate with its expanding global economic interests.

Of course, as previously described, China's ability to shift its focus to other areas would depend to some extent on the degree of functional control it can exercise over Taiwan and the state of the Chinese military once the dust has settled. In this scenario, the Taiwanese government and people will have a say. If Taiwan accepts defeat and submits to its new status, the PRC military may face few constraints. However, if Taiwan launches a protracted guerrilla-style campaign—something that would only be feasible if Taiwan's government has prepared politically, logistically, and militarily for popular resistance—China may be forced to deal with at least a low-level conflict for an extended period after nominally bringing the island under its control. In such a case, Taiwan could become a drain on resources and an albatross for China.

For Washington, once it has licked its wounds, a clear and unambiguous defeat could present an opportunity to fully reassess its posture in East Asia. While some possible outcomes of this reassessment, including a complete retreat from the region, may seem unthinkable now, a decisive US defeat would almost certainly shift the so-called Overton window in unpredictable ways. Suffice it to say, such a defeat would likely mark the beginning of an entirely new paradigm in world affairs.

With the Taiwan issue settled, the only remaining unsettled conflict in East Asia of strategic concern to the United States would be the North Korean nuclear program. However, as extensively discussed in the interviews conducted for this study, if China becomes significantly stronger, one likely outcome is that South Korea increasingly moves into Beijing's orbit. This would suggest that the challenges of a divided Korean peninsula could shift from being Washington's concern to becoming more of Beijing's problem.

In such a scenario, it might become sensible—albeit painful—for the United States to accept China as a regional hegemon in Asia, similar to the role the United States held in the Western Hemisphere at the dawn of the twentieth century.

This is an unfamiliar and uncomfortable scenario for US strategists to contemplate. It would necessitate a rethinking of US military posture and strategy, particularly as it could undermine the justification for a continued US troop presence in Japan and South Korea. Some in these countries already question the utility of large US bases. After witnessing a significant defeat, pro-US alliance voices in Tokyo and Seoul will likely find it difficult to counter critics in their countries who argue that the cost of hosting US forces now outweighs the benefits. At the very least, US skeptics across the region will gain the upper hand and likely use their newfound leverage to advocate for sharply curtailing or even ending the US military presence altogether.

A clear-cut military defeat would also compel a reevaluation of Americans' national self-conception, a painful and uncertain process that could lead to the country lashing out rather than introspecting. In this scenario, Japan and Australia would find themselves in a precarious position. Without the protective umbrella of US support, they would be forced to forge a new understanding with Beijing regarding their place in a PRC-dominated Asia-Pacific, which would have significant implications for their domestic political landscapes. Indeed, the rise of an unrivaled, hegemonic China could have unpredictable electoral consequences, possibly even threatening their status as democracies if their citizens turn to strongman-style leadership for reassurance.

The world described in this scenario would mark the most profound departure from Asia's recent past and present. It would be a tragedy for the citizens of Taiwan who seek to determine their own destiny. For the United States, it would signal a new era with different possibilities, and perhaps even improved outcomes, albeit within a completely different strategic context.

Where Does That Leave Us?

It bears repeating that it is neither a given nor an inevitability that Beijing will resort to military force against Taiwan. While Chinese leaders may choose to "roll the iron dice," they will have a range of military options for addressing the Taiwan issue. Although an all-out invasion seems the most likely course of action for China to resolve its "Taiwan problem" through force, it is important to acknowledge that no one outside of Xi Jinping's inner circle—perhaps not even Xi himself—can predict the exact methods that will be considered. Regardless of how a military campaign for Taiwan unfolds, we have outlined four basic ways in which all potential scenarios might play out. Having briefly described China's military options and the four most plausible political-military outcomes, the focus now turns to assessing how the United States' most steadfast military allies in the region are likely to respond to these possible aftermaths.

Notes

1. See, for example, Pottinger, *The Boiling Moat*; Blackwill and Zelikow, *The United States, China, and Taiwan*; Pettyjohn, "War with China"; Cancian, Cancian, and Heginbotham, *The First Battle*; Kuo et al., *Simulating Chinese Gray Zone*; Blumenthal et al., *From Coercion to Capitulation*.
2. For example, a full-scale invasion would almost certainly include gray zone operations to mask the military build-up, the seizure of outlying islands to increase freedom of maneuver, a blockade of the island to achieve air and naval superiority, standoff strikes to prepare landing zones and neutralizes Taiwanese defenses, and nuclear saber rattling to discourage a US response. But Beijing could also combine these options even if it decides against undertaking a risky, full-scale invasion. One could easily imagine Beijing initiating a blockade, only to threaten the subsequent annexation of Kinmen and Matsu, followed by standoff strikes if Taipei refuses to comply.
3. Lanoszka, "Russian Hybrid Warfare," 178–179. See also Kanapathy, "Countering China's Gray-Zone Activities."; Mazarr, *Mastering the Gray Zone*; Kuo et al., *Simulating Chinese Gray Zone*.
4. Cyber-attacks present a definitional challenge under this rubric. For the purposes of this analysis, we consider cyber-attacks to constitute gray zone activity only when they do not disable critical infrastructure and are not being conducted in support of a larger, traditional military operation.
5. The U.S. Department of Commerce business guidance for Taiwan notes the island's disproportionally high incident of cyber-attacks, citing 2022 figures of 30 million attacks per month. See U.S. Department of Commerce, *Taiwan – Cybersecurity*.
6. Reuters, "China Trying to 'Normalise' Military Drills." .
7. Taiwan's Ministry of Defense releases daily reports on Chinese incursions into its air defense identification zone; see Republic of China (Taiwan), Ministry of National Defense, *Guofang Xiaoxi* 國防消息 [Defense News],"Real Time Military Updates."
8. Jestrab, *A Maritime Blockade of Taiwan*.
9. Kwan, "China Begins Live-Fire Military Drills"; Mai, Wang, and Wu, "Mainland China Kicks Off PLA Blockade"; Mahadzir, "China Targets Taiwan."

10. With 649 residents per square kilometer, Taiwan has the world's 17th highest population density. See World Population Review, "Taiwan Population 2024."
11. Webster, "Does Taiwan's Massive Reliance…?"
12. Ferreira and Critelli, "Taiwan's Food Resiliency."
13. Taiwan also lays claim to islands in the Senkaku, Spratley, and Pratas island chains.
14. In fact, Beijing has suggested that it will build a bridge between Kinmen and the Chinese city of Xiamen. See Wu, "Bridge Dilemma."
15. Easton, *The Chinese Invasion Threat*, 114–115.
16. Kanapathy, "Countering China's Gray-Zone Activities."
17. Kanapathy, "Countering China's Use of Force," 88–89.
18. Pape, *Bombing to Win*; Horowitz and Reiter, "When Does Aerial Bombing Work?"; Allen and Machain, "Understanding the Impact of Air Power"; Chamberlin, *Cheap Threats*; Allen, "Time Bombs"; Post, "Flying to Fail."
19. By way of historical comparison, Operation Husky, the allied invasion of Sicily during World War II, is an appropriate analogy in terms of the size of the island to be taken and the force defending it. The Allied landing force numbered more than 160,000 men and required some 2,950 ships to transport it. For a more thorough comparative analysis between the Battle of Sicily and a potential invasion of Taiwan see Mike Pietrucha, "Amateur Hour Part I."
20. For a deeper exploration of potential nuclear scenarios and associated risks, see Stokes, *Atomic Strait*; Sweeney, *Why a Taiwan Conflict Could Go Nuclear*; Talmadge, "Would China Go Nuclear?"; Cunningham and Fravel, "Assuring Assured Retaliation." For an excellent analysis of Chinese perceptions of strategic stability, see Logan, "Chinese Views of Strategic Stability."
21. As Sweeney points out, "some of the main advocates for more openly planning to defend Taiwan have also expressed interest in enhancing U.S. tactical nuclear options for Chinese and Russian conflict scenarios"; Sweeney, *Why a Taiwan Conflict Could Go Nuclear*, 6. See, for example, Colby, "Against the Great Powers"; Giarra, "Time to Recalibrate."
22. Freedman, "Going Nuclear."
23. Xi, "Yishiweijian."
24. Xinhuanet, "Full Text: Speech by Xi Jinping."
25. Reuters, "China's Xi Says Political Solution for Taiwan Can't Wait Forever"; Xinhuanet, "Xinhua Headlines: Xi Says."

26. For a dissenting view, see Porter and Mazarr, *Countering China's Adventurism*; Caverley, "The Taiwan Fallacy."
27. At present, we are skeptical that Taiwan is taking the necessary steps to make a protracted and well-resourced insurgency a viable possibility. See Hunzeker, Wu, and Marom, "A New Military Culture for Taiwan"; Lee and Hunzeker, "The View of Ukraine from Taiwan"; Hunzeker and Lanoszka, *A Question of Time*, 99–102.
28. Culver, "The Unfinished Chinese Civil War."
29. For a deeper assessment of the implications of a protracted conflict between the United States and China, see Rehman, *Planning for Protraction*; Montgomery and Ouellet, "American Defense Planning."

Chapter 2

Japan

Japan is the starting point for this study because it is both Washington's closest ally to Taiwan geographically and will inevitably serve as the linchpin in any potential US-led alliance responding to Taiwan's defense.[1] First among equals in terms of its population, economy, and military capability, Tokyo stands as Washington's most steadfast partner in opposing Beijing. Japan is also more concerned than Washington's other allies in the region about the implications of Chinese aggression against Taiwan for its own security, making it the most willing to bear significant costs in support of cross-Strait deterrence. Crucially, Japan's response to a Chinese attack on Taiwan would shape how Canberra and Seoul would act. Australian and South Korean interlocutors in this study emphasized that Japan's role in a US-led effort to assist Taiwan would directly influence their own willingness to support US requests for assistance.

Without downplaying the importance of Japan's very real historical and economic ties with Taiwan, Japan's interest in maintaining peace and stability in the Taiwan Strait stems first and foremost from Taiwan's geographic proximity and the presence of US forces in Japan. Japanese strategists therefore conclude that Tokyo will inevitably find itself in the line of fire, even if it would prefer to remain uninvolved. Given that

Japan will suffer regardless of the outcome of a cross-Strait war, Japanese interviewees were in unanimous agreement that the best course of action by far is to avoid or deter conflict. Achieving this goal, they emphasized, requires both a capable Japan Self-Defense Forces (JSDF) and a robust US military presence in the Western Pacific.[2]

However, if deterrence fails despite Washington and Tokyo's best efforts, does it follow that Washington can automatically count on Tokyo to help defend Taiwan?[3] Or must Washington intervene to uphold its reputation for resolve in the eyes of Japanese leaders and voters? The interviews suggest that the answer to both questions is no.

When it comes to Japan's role in a cross-Strait war, the interviewed Japanese experts were clear: there is no guarantee that Japanese military forces will rush to Taiwan's defense. Instead, a range of factors will shape Tokyo's calculus, the most important being what Washington does. If the United States fails to lead or becomes directly involved, it is almost certain that Japan will abstain from the conflict. None of the Japanese experts interviewed believes that Japan will fight for Taiwan if the United States stays on the sidelines, attempts to "lead from behind," or opts for a non-military response (though some experts noted that recent changes to Japan's national security decision-making apparatus have given Tokyo the option to respond, even without US involvement). Other critical variables will include whether China preemptively strikes US bases in Japan, whether Taiwanese military forces hold out long enough to buy time for outside intervention, and whether Beijing's actions are crafted with enough "implausible deniability" to spark a domestic and constitutional debate among Japanese elites and voters.

In terms of America's reputation, both Japanese elites and voters would undoubtedly be shocked if Washington left Taipei to its fate. However, while Japanese elites might expect the United States to defend Taiwan, they are even more concerned with ensuring that the US military retains its ability to protect Japan. Moreover, interviewees were clear that the abandonment of Taiwan would not automatically trigger the collapse of the US–Japan alliance. As long as Washington maintains a robust military presence in Japan and the Western Pacific, and as long as pro-US elites in Japan effectively manage public opinion, the alliance is expected to endure.

In any of the negative scenarios—abandonment, defeat, or Pyrrhic victory—the Japanese public will likely demand an explanation as to why they should continue to put up with a major US military presence. This issue, already a sensitive subject, would become even more challenging for Japanese politicians, especially those representing areas with large military bases, such as Okinawa. Elite opinion would play an important role in shaping the public response to these situations. A useful parallel can be drawn with the US withdrawal from Afghanistan. Several interviewees noted that the Japanese public's initial reaction to the withdrawal was marked by concerns about US reliability. However, expert opinion eventually prevailed, framing the narrative that, despite the chaotic nature of the withdrawal, it ultimately allowed the United States to reallocate resources toward its defense and deterrence missions in the Pacific. Public opinion polling results corroborated these views, showing that the Japanese public did not emerge from the Afghanistan withdrawal with increased skepticism of the US military or the alliance.[4]

This chapter summarizes the findings related to specific aspects of the security challenges posed by Chinese aggression toward Taiwan, with a particular focus on the implications for Japan and its alliance relationship with the United States. It begins by outlining Japanese views on the Taiwan issue, followed by an examination of Japanese perspectives on the US–Japan alliance. The chapter further explores how the alliance could be affected by various US actions in the event of a Taiwan contingency.

How Japan Views the Stakes of a Cross-Strait War

Japanese Elites and Voters Support Taiwan

The Japanese experts interviewed clearly regard Taiwan as a critical security issue for Japan. The most frequently cited characterization was that Taiwan serves as the southern anchor of the first island chain. Chinese control over Taiwan's main island would fundamentally jeopardize Japan's security, especially given that it would place Chinese military forces less than 100 miles from Japanese territory. Additionally, a Chinese naval presence on Taiwan's main island would grant the PRC the ability to interdict both military and civilian shipping in and around the Taiwan Strait, the Miyako Strait, and the Bashi Channel, which surround Taiwan to the west, north, and south, respectively.

The view that Taiwan matters to Japan extends beyond the country's foreign policy elite; the Japanese public also holds Taiwan in high regard. Interviewees expressed near-unanimous consensus that pro-Taiwan sentiments are broadly shared among Japanese voters, a perspective supported by public opinion polling.[5] Several experts pointed to the historical ties between Japan and Taiwan as an important reason for this affinity.[6] Others highlighted the Japanese public's enduring sense of gratitude for Taiwan's extensive aid to Japan following the March 2011 earthquake. Furthermore, the interviewees asserted that the average Japanese voter would be sympathetic toward Taiwan, particularly in the case of an unprovoked, full-scale invasion in which Taiwan's leaders neither unilaterally declared independence nor took any similarly provocative actions. They also stated their belief that most Japanese voters support stability in the Taiwan Strait, desire the maintenance of the cross-Strait status quo, and understand the security risks to Japan posed by a Chinese takeover of Taiwan.

Elites and Voters Are More Divided about China, but Attitudes Are Trending Negative

When it comes to Japanese attitudes toward China, interviewees suggested that Japanese elites and voters generally fall into two broad groups. The first camp prioritizes the US–Japan alliance and tends to take a more hawkish stance toward China. The second camp seeks a more balanced approach, emphasizing the importance of maintaining stable ties with China while also valuing the US–Japan relationship. Although elite opinion largely mirrors public opinion regarding China, one interviewee noted that a given expert's views often align with their own regional focus: those specializing in the US alliance tend to be more hawkish, while those focusing on East Asian regional affairs are more inclined to advocate for a balanced approach to China.

Most of the interviewed experts suggested, or at least intimated, that the hawkish camp in Japan is growing larger, particularly within the Ministry of Foreign Affairs. One expert suggested that Japanese officials who have dealt with Beijing's increasingly bellicose actions are more likely to interpret these provocations as signs of Xi Jinping's long-term intentions for the region. Another interviewee noted that Chinese assertiveness and saber-rattling are pushing more Japanese experts to align with some of the more hawkish voices in the US government, particularly the US Department of Defense. Several interviewees brought up the warning by then head of US Indo-Pacific Command Admiral Philip Davidson that China might try to annex Taiwan by 2027,[7] although one expert did assert that the equivalent timeline among Japanese experts is more likely a few years longer, by 2030 or thereabouts.

One source spoke in detail about the perspective of Japanese experts on Xi Jinping's current position and his likely goals. This expert believes that Xi holds a Sino-centric view of global affairs, with the ambition of surpassing both Deng Xiaoping and Mao Zedong in his leadership legacy. The expert argued that the only way Xi can achieve this lofty goal and justify his extended rule is by accomplishing what his predecessors could not. Bringing Hong Kong to heel was one such achievement. According to this interviewee, Taiwan is now Xi's next logical objective. Since China still faces a capability gap compared to the United States and its allies, the source anticipates continued expansionism and militarization in the South China Sea, possibly culminating in an island grab over Taiwan. Additionally, the expert mentioned that many Japanese analysts expect China to continue opportunistically expanding its sphere of influence anywhere it can find an exploitable vacancy. The interviewee shared their perspective on China's credibility: "Sometimes as individuals we say, 'I promise.' But to the Chinese, a treaty or a promise is a one-way street. 'You have to honor this treaty, but I don't have to.' And most of the time Beijing does not maintain its side of the equation. It depends on its feeling. That is the Chinese way."

Finally, sources highlighted that Japanese experts see Xi's position as structurally precarious. The longer Xi remains China's undisputed leader, the more he frustrates and alienates the cohort of ambitious Party officials below him who are being denied opportunities for advancement. One interviewee asserted that many of Xi's staff believe he should step down at the end of his third term, but that Xi's decision not to name a potential successor at the 2022 Party Congress suggests that he may be positioning himself to seek a fourth term in 2027. If Xi pursues this route, the source believes that the risk of an attack on Taiwan will increase, as Xi may seek a justification for extending his rule in the face of potential opposition from within the CCP.

National Defense—Including Taiwan—Is a Priority, yet Obstacles Remain

In December 2022, the Kishida government made headlines when it released three new strategic documents. Taken together, the National Security Strategy, National Defense Strategy, and Defense Buildup Program underscored Tokyo's focus on the risk of a direct attack on Japan, while signaling an intent to make substantial improvements to Japan's independent defensive capabilities.[8] Whether these documents represented a tectonic shift in Japanese security policy or the logical next step along an already-established trajectory is a matter of debate.[9] Regardless, Tokyo's stated goal of increasing all national security spending from 1% to 2% of gross domestic product (GDP) is a significant departure from Japan's historically stagnant defense budgets.[10] It also represents a victory for critics who have long argued that Tokyo must take a more active role in protecting itself from attack and contribute more actively to the US alliance. These budgetary increases will ostensibly allow the Ministry of Defense and the JSDF to pursue much-needed defense capabilities, especially those related to missile defense and long-range counterstrike.

These documents were also noteworthy for reaffirming Tokyo's commitment to maintaining peace and stability in Taiwan. The National Security Strategy, in particular, references Taiwan seven times and goes so far as to categorize Taipei as "an extremely important partner and precious friend of Japan, with whom Japan shares fundamental values including democracy, and has close economic and personal ties."[11] In doing so, the 2022 National Security Strategy mirrored an overarching willingness among senior Japanese officials to talk more openly about Taiwan.[12] The new defense spending targets should also make it easier for the JSDF to plan for Taiwan contingencies. As one former JSDF officer described, "The Ministry of Finance has used the '1% constraint' as a way to tamp down on efforts to lean into the Taiwan problem. So, if the Ministry of Defense came and said, 'We need X, Y and Z to deal with this problem set,' Finance would use the 1% as a sort of 'one in one out policy' to get the services to figure out what they would need to give up to get things." The interviewees indicated their belief that increased Japanese defense spending is both a response to and an enabling factor for greater focus on Taiwan security contingencies.

When assessing the degree to which Taiwan "matters" to Tokyo, one Japanese expert made an important comparison between Taiwan and the Senkaku Islands. When asked how Japan might react to a Chinese attack on or seizure of the Senkakus (which Japan considers sovereign territory and which Washington has indicated are covered under the US–Japan Mutual Defense Treaty), the expert responded that:

> The Senkakus are very small islands, and so we could understand if [the US] Congress said no [to getting involved]. But Taiwan is very different from the Senkakus. Taiwan is far more important strategically, geographically, politically, economically, because if China occupies Taiwan, then the South China Sea belongs to China. And if the South China Sea belongs to China, then Japan's supply lines to the Middle East and other parts of the world become very tricky. And if China takes Taiwan, it makes it even easier for the PLAN to go to Guam or Hawaii. So, if something happens in the Taiwan Strait, the US must come to help Taiwan.

Another interviewee, meanwhile, reversed this logic, suggesting that Japanese voters would view US support for Taiwan as a proxy for American willingness to defend the Senkaku Islands. As this source explained, "[Japanese voters] will think, 'If the US won't help defend Taiwan, why would they help defend uninhabited islands like Senkaku?' They will doubt the US commitment to Japan and will view past presidents' assertions that Article 5 covers Senkaku as hollow statements... though they might also be glad to have avoided a war with China."

Of course, regardless of what Japan's security strategy says about Taiwan, or the extent to which Japanese elites view an attack on Taiwan as a threat to Japan, several practical impediments continue making it difficult for Tokyo to prepare for a cross-Strait conflict scenario.[13] One such obstacle is that cross-Strait relations have become so salient that the topic has turned into something of a third rail in Japanese politics. As one diplomatic official put it, "the Cross Strait issue is so important that it has become taboo to discuss openly in public, especially war scenarios, due to concerns vis-à-vis our big neighbor and our position regarding our understanding of the One China Policy." While experts in non-public forums, such as think tanks and Track II dialogues, can engage in more substantive conversations and exercises, a de facto freeze on public commentary complicates both internal planning and the inevitably necessary step of convincing the public why it might be in Japan's interest to defend Taiwan.

Another issue is the difficulty Japan and Taiwan face in coordinating politically and diplomatically. One interviewee noted the multiple creative pathways through which US and Taiwanese officials can interact, contrasting these with the administrative and operational constraints that preclude Japan from doing the same. Another expert noted that the United States' One China Policy is accompanied by the TRA and the American Institute in Taiwan. Together, these mechanisms have provided Washington with the flexibility to sell advanced weapons, maintain direct military-to-military ties, conduct joint exercises, and sustain a supportive policy across decades of different presidential administrations. Japan, in comparison, has no legal analogue to the TRA. As a result, Tokyo has been cautious about establishing direct communication and ties with Taiwan. However, Tokyo is finding creative ways to work around these obstacles. For example, the Ministry of Defense now sends a civilian official to serve as a liaison in Taiwan instead of solely relying on a retired JSDF officer.[14] Nonetheless, as a former JSDF officer put it, "We want to support Taiwan, but Japan's Ministry of Foreign Affairs says that under Japan's One China Policy, Japan cannot."[15]

Broad Public Support for Taiwan Will Not Necessarily Mean Support for Military Action

Beyond the question of whether the JSDF will have the funding and capabilities it needs to provide meaningful support in a cross-Strait conflict, there is also no guarantee that the Japanese public's affinity for Taiwan will translate into widespread support for using the Japanese military to defend Taiwan in a war. Interviewees identified several factors that could impact public support. Foremost is the degree to which Chinese military operations impinge on Japanese territory and security. Unanimously, the interviewees were unable to imagine a realistic invasion scenario that did not also affect Japan. As one former defense official succinctly put it, "There is no way for China to attack Taiwan without impacting Japan's security." Some interviewees pointed to the limited size of the theater of operations and the short distance between Taiwan and Yonaguni as evidence that Chinese military operations will inevitably intrude into Japanese air and sea space. Others highlighted the risk that Beijing might preemptively strike US bases in Japan and/or conduct cyberattacks against Japan's military, government, and civilian infrastructure. These interviewees therefore thought it more likely than not that a Chinese attack on Taiwan will lead Tokyo to deploy naval forces to protect its own territory and assets, and to invoke Article V of the Treaty of Mutual Cooperation and Security between Japan and the United States, thereby obligating Washington to respond.[16] These experts also agreed that treaty obligations could similarly require Tokyo to support a US military response to Chinese aggression against Taiwan even in the absence of a direct threat to Japan.[17]

That said, if China does manage to attack Taiwan without directly threatening Japanese security, the Japanese public might be prove even less willing to support involving the JSDF. Interviewees similarly suggested that contingencies short of a full-scale invasion, such as the seizure of an outlying Taiwanese island or a joint air and naval blockade, are likely to divide Japanese voters over the best way to respond.[18] Japan's business community also acts as a source of restraint in cross-Strait conflict. The majority of interviewees singled out Japanese business interests as the constituency most likely to oppose any hardline position on China, including over Taiwan. To be sure, interviewees repeatedly emphasized that, despite the Chinese market being far more important than Taiwan's to Japan's economy,[19] strategic concerns will likely trump economic interests. Nonetheless, there was agreement among Japanese, American, and Taiwanese subject matter experts that Japan's business community might demur from this consensus to some degree. Part of this dynamic stems from the relationship between the Japanese government and the private sector, which sources noted is different in Japan compared to the United States due to the close ties that large Japanese conglomerates maintain with the Japanese government. Politically, sources also pointed to an economic wing within the Liberal Democratic Party (LDP) that advocates for Sino-Japanese cooperation and generally believes that Japan's economic future depends on stable trade relations with China. Several interviewees identified this faction as the most likely political bloc in Japan to fear US entanglement more than US abandonment when considering possible Taiwan outcomes.

Interviewees listed some specific economic issues that they believe pose the most significant complications for Japanese support of Taiwan. Several noted the challenges involved in excising China from intricate supply chains, emphasizing the substantial shift in production from Japan to China within the last few decades.[20] Interviewees also pointed to Japan's dependence on China in key areas, such as access to rare earth minerals for production and China's consumer markets as a source of demand. They predicted that some within Japan's pro-balancing camp would hesitate to approve aggressive measures such as Magnitsky-type sanctions targeting Chinese officials responsible for human rights violations. Additionally, sources noted that Beijing is fully aware of these economic interdependencies and would likely exploit them to widen divisions within Japanese political factions, as well as between Washington and Tokyo, to the greatest degree possible.

Japanese Experts Do Not Expect South Korea to Play a Role in a Cross-Strait Conflict

Until now, the focus has been on how Japanese experts view China and Taiwan. However, it is also worth briefly examining how Japanese elites consider South Korea's potential role in a cross-Strait contingency, if indeed they think about it at all. Their views are best summarized as "dubious." The experts interviewed were overwhelmingly skeptical that Seoul would make a meaningful contribution to any US–Japan effort to counter a Chinese attack on Taiwan. As one interviewee bluntly put the matter, "We cannot keep them on our side anymore, but we can still work not to push them too close to China."

To be sure, those interviewed expressed understanding and sympathy for Seoul's predicament. South Korea's history and geography were central to their analysis. More than one interviewee described South Korea as a "half island" forming an inseparable part of the First Island Chain and sitting astride the Yellow Sea, a key sea-lane into the East China Sea. They also noted the country's history of depredation at the hands of larger and more powerful neighbors. As one Japanese interviewee put it:

> Imagine you were the Korean nation, surrounded by the Manchurians, Chinese, and Japanese in the past, and now surrounded by the Russians, Chinese, and Americans. This is a terrible place to live. What's the best way to survive? Keeping the balance among the monster neighbors. If you confront and fight, you will be destroyed. It's a small peninsula with a dead end on the southern side and on the north a huge gateway for invasion. Because they know they are vulnerable, they've tried for centuries to maintain balance among the neighbors. The best way is to identify the most powerful among those monsters and pay tribute. This means they will guarantee your existence, if not your independence. This has been the Korean foreign policy for centuries.

Thus, in the eyes of Japanese strategists, Seoul's strategic dilemma, coupled with its understandable focus on the far closer—and existential—threat from Pyongyang, relegates Taipei to an afterthought (at most) in Korean strategy and politics. Of course, the Japanese interlocutors also pointed out that just because Seoul might not be interested in a cross-Strait war does not mean that a cross-Strait war will not be interested in Seoul. They expect that any crisis over Taiwan's status will almost certainly impact South Korea. After all, the presence of US forces and assets in the country means that any escalation over Taiwan will inevitably raise questions about South Korea's role.

Several of the Japanese interviewees offered a word of caution for American planners on this point. They suggested that, beyond simply not focusing on Taiwan, South Korea is unlikely to want to play a role in any effort to repel a Chinese use of force. Such reluctance would almost certainly preclude the use of South Korean assets to support a US-led military campaign. In fact, it could extend to denying Washington permission to utilize its bases and ROK-based forces in support of the same. The interviewees implied that this reluctance is why Tokyo does not include South Korea (or Australia, for that matter) in its strategic decision-making regarding Taiwan.

Experts in Japan are fully aware that difficult Korea-Japan relations make cooperation on an issue like Taiwan even more challenging. Despite recent breakthroughs in Tokyo's relationship with Seoul,[21] the interviewees expressed pessimism about achieving anything resembling NATO-like readiness and interoperability in the region. Sources also highlighted the significance of domestic politics in South Korea. Several interviewees expressed versions of the sentiment that there is no hope for cooperation under a liberal administration in Seoul, but that when conservatives are in power in Seoul—as was the case at the time of publication—there is at least some room to maneuver, prepare, and collaborate.

How Japan Views the United States

Washington, the Indispensable Ally

There is no question that those interviewed view the United States as a vital security guarantor. Even Japanese experts who acknowledge China's relative ascendance and believe that Tokyo will need to cooperate with Beijing nevertheless made clear that they continue to see the United States as a more important and reliable partner now and for the foreseeable future. Indeed, most of the interviewees spoke at length about America's central role in both protecting Japan and maintaining regional stability. As one former national security official put it in a representative comment:

> We are convinced this US-led liberal order is a good thing. This Western system based on people's free will is the most important.

And it isn't just a Western system, it is a universal system. China is waking up, but they are moving in the opposite direction. They are embracing yesterday's totalitarian ideas—like the Meiji. They believe they can change the world overnight by the use of force. China is trying to revive communism. The only way we can stand against this is if we are united. But without the US we cannot be united and do this.

A JSDF official was more succinct: "We can't defend ourselves by ourselves. We need the US, especially militarily." The obvious implication is that Japanese foreign policy elites believe that the absence of US leadership will jeopardize Japanese peace and security.

They Also Trust That Washington Will Defend Tokyo... but Cracks in that Consensus Are Emerging

The question of whether the United States would actually deploy military forces to defend Japan from attack cuts to the heart of Japanese concerns about American credibility. These fears of abandonment are not unique to the US–Japan relationship. Indeed, such concerns are a natural—and rational—worry for any partner in any military alliance. War is costly and risky. Without a supranational authority in the international system capable of compelling states to honor their commitments, there is nothing to prevent an ally from getting cold feet when the true costs of fulfilling its defense promises become clear.

Given the supposed ubiquity of abandonment concerns, it was therefore surprising to find that most experts expressed unwavering confidence in the strength of the US–Japan alliance. They also conveyed a strong sense that Washington remains committed not only to Japan's defense but also to maintaining stability in the Indo-Pacific.

To be sure, this sentiment was tempered by a view expressed by some interviewees, though not all, that the United States is entering a period of relative retrenchment. Indeed, even those who expressed a desire for clear and consistent US leadership voiced concerns that US domestic politics could force Washington to pull back from the region in the coming years. The concern was framed around the fear that US domestic politics in general—and growing pro-isolationist sentiments in particular—could undermine Washington's commitment to Japan and the wider region. This worry was not seen as being characteristic of just one political party. For instance, one interviewee contrasted the Biden administration's emphasis on infrastructure and domestic spending to China's continued focus on military modernization. Another expert noted that, despite consistency in US declaratory policy, the increasingly vocal pro-isolationist voices in Congress and both parties create uncertainty, as they suggested, "when it comes to an actual crisis, we don't know how the United States will react." A third interviewee was especially blunt, stating: "A big concern for us are America First sentiments. They are neither Republicans nor Democrats, they are isolationists. This is the biggest fear for us. The weakened leadership of the US is a weakened global order. And Japan has no friends that can replace the United States."

When asked about the US actions most likely to reassure Japanese voters and elites that Washington remains committed to Japan and likely to make good on its security guarantees, interviewees highlighted US-led diplomatic dialogues, military exercises, and consistent messaging in declaratory policy.

Importantly, one Japanese officer remarked "We are always thinking about how to increase US credibility to Japan." Japanese experts view US credibility as crucial to Japan's security and perceive it as a dynamic element that Japan has a vested interest in strengthening. This perspective underscores that Japan, like any state dependent on a geographically distant partner for security, will seek tangible demonstrations of reassurance, regardless of its faith in the alliance. At the highest level, these statements suggest that behind Tokyo's expressed trust in Washington, there lies a set of rational concerns recognizing that US commitment cannot be taken for granted. Given how frequently interviewees expressed enthusiasm for any efforts to bolster the perceived credibility of US support, it is evident that any US initiatives to demonstrate or enhance its commitment to the region would be enthusiastically welcomed by most relevant Japanese security experts.

How Japan Thinks About US Options in a Cross-Strait Conflict

Tokyo is Not Particularly Worried that Washington Will Drag it into a War over Taiwan

If abandonment fears represent one side of the alliance coin, concerns about entrapment lie on the other.[22] Entrapment occurs when a state finds itself obligated to defend an ally that has triggered a conflict through aggressive or provocative actions. Given the prominence of entrapment concerns in some US foreign policy circles,[23] one might expect similar worries in Japan. However, the Japanese experts and elites interviewed were not particularly worried about the United States provoking a cross-Strait conflict. Some experts downplayed the likelihood that Washington might drag Tokyo into a cross-Strait war because they were confident that Japanese leaders could maneuver diplomatically, avoid direct involvement, or find loopholes if they were so inclined.[24] For example, one interviewee suggested that Japan has consistently been adept at finding workarounds. He cited several historical precedents, including the Korean War, when Japan sent minesweepers but did not become directly involved in combat, and the Vietnam War, when Japan allowed Japan-based American B-52s to conduct bombing runs only after first leaving Japanese airspace and heading away from Vietnam.

Other interviewees provided more sober assessments of entrapment risks. Most, in fact, approached the topic with realism, perhaps tinged with a sense of resignation, acknowledging that Tokyo's necessary reliance on Washington made entrapment nearly inevitable. As one former senior Ministry of Foreign Affairs official put it, "Neither the US nor Japan has any choice. If the US wants to compete with China, they need us. And we are being threatened by China, and we need the US. This is not a master-servant relationship. This is two strategic thinkers realizing that they need each other. No single country can compete with China. So, credibility is important, but there aren't many other choices."

One dissenting voice on the issue of entrapment came from a senior Ministry of Foreign Affairs official, who suggested that the average Japanese voter might not be as sanguine about entrapment risks as Japanese foreign policy experts. Specifically, he pointed out that some voters do worry that Washington could spark a cross-Strait crisis. As he explained, "The US likes war scenarios, but the world isn't 1945 anymore, and Asia isn't the Middle East. We trust Xi Jinping more than America not to start a war." However, this viewpoint was an outlier. The prevailing sentiment among those interviewed was that the US alliance remains Japan's best—or its least worst—option for preserving stability in the face of China's proximity and power.

The experts interviewed also acknowledged the operational realities involved in a US-led defense of Taiwan. They were in unanimous agreement that Washington would have no choice but to utilize its assets and bases in Japan if it were to intervene in a cross-Strait contingency. Similarly, all agreed that Beijing would likely consider preemptive strikes against US forces in Japan, and that the Japanese public would perceive such an attack as one on Japan itself.

The interviewees were divided on whether Beijing would risk a preemptive strike on Japanese soil. While none dismissed the risk out of hand, several experts suggested that Beijing would carefully weigh the operational benefits of striking US bases in Japan against the strategic costs of triggering Japan's involvement in the conflict. Other experts believed that Beijing had already made up its mind, concluding that Japan's involvement is inevitable. As one interviewee noted, "Based on the Chinese strategic literature, China tends not to give the Japanese the benefit of the doubt, which would suggest that taking out the bases—rolling the iron dice—is worth the risk."

Japanese Assessments of US Reputation

Having established the context, the study now turns to its primary focus: examining how Japan might reassess US reputation based on Washington's response to an attack on Taiwan. To address this issue, interviewees were asked to consider how Japan might react to each of the three plausible outcomes that collectively encompass the basic ways a cross-Strait war might conclude. To recap, these three basic outcomes are that the United States military remains on the sidelines as China attacks and takes Taiwan, the United States military intervenes but fails to prevent a Chinese takeover, or the United States military successfully thwarts a Chinese invasion. The analysis begins with Japan's likely response to non-intervention, followed by its reactions to a US defeat and a US victory.

Non-Intervention Would Damage US Reputation... but the Alliance Would Survive

It is worth noting that simply broaching the question of non-intervention elicited obvious discomfort among nearly all interviewees. The prospect of Washington abandoning Taipei was clearly not something that Japanese security experts were eager to contemplate. However, despite the apparent taboo surrounding the topic, interviewees provided insights which were both nuanced and, importantly, diverse in their responses to this unsettling question.

Almost all interviewees agreed that Japan's reaction to non-intervention would depend largely on the way the conflict unfolds and how Washington explains—or fails to explain—its inaction to Tokyo. For instance, it would be easier for Japanese elites and voters to accept non-intervention if they believed that both Tokyo and Washington were caught off guard by ambiguous indicators and events leading up to Beijing's full-scale attack. The same might hold true if Taiwanese defenses collapsed immediately or if Taipei capitulated before the United States had time to surge military assets into the theater. None of the interviewees believed Washington should wage a clearly hopeless fight for Taiwan solely to maintain the American reputation for resolve.

The manner in which Beijing attacks Taiwan, and the extent to which such actions threaten or impact Japanese territory, will also influence Tokyo's reaction to non-intervention. Several experts suggested that Japan would be less critical of a decision not to respond to the seizure of one of Taiwan's minor outlying islands compared to an attack on Taiwan's main island or a major population center, such as Penghu County in the Penghu Islands. Similarly, the closer PLA ships and aircraft come to Japan's outlying islands, the more strongly Tokyo will expect a decisive response from Washington.

The most important factor from the Japanese perspective is whether Beijing strikes the Japanese homeland to preempt US forces in Japan and/or Japanese counterstrike assets. The interviewees were adamant that any attempt to reassure Tokyo about Washington's commitment to Japan's defense would fall on deaf ears if the US military fails to react to a direct attack on Japan, even if Beijing's intent was clearly only to keep Washington and Tokyo on the sidelines.

Some Think Abandoning Taiwan Will Undermine US Reputation

Many—though not all— interviewees said that Japanese faith in the credibility of American commitments would be severely shaken if Washington abandoned Taipei. They argued that Japan's dependence on the US–Japan alliance, combined with the fundamental uncertainty surrounding Washington's willingness to defend Japan from attack, leads Tokyo to obsess over the signaling value of US actions. As one scholar put it, "The Japanese alliance is riddled with loopholes. This is why Japan is conditioned to be extra sensitive to what the US does or doesn't do, beyond what the treaty language says." For this reason, Japanese leaders and voters are highly attuned to even the slightest indicators of US intention. The scholar went on to say:

When the US Seventh Fleet pulled out its carrier in response to the Fukushima nuclear disaster, the Japanese public viewed this as a signal of a lack of US commitment to Japan's security. Even if it's understandable from a rational perspective why Washington couldn't commit its forces, it would be seen in Japan as a real breach of faith and would have consequences. It wouldn't unravel the alliance overnight, but it would gradually erode the alliance over time. I would go so far as to say, even if the conflict were Taiwan's 'fault,' lack of a US response would be read in Tokyo as the United States neglecting, or even abandoning, a major partner.

A small number of interviewees even suggested that Japanese voters would consider Washington's "failure" to defend Taiwan as tantamount to a declaration that the United States no longer intends to maintain its position as a Pacific power. In the words of one analyst, "If the US didn't react to whatever unlawful, illegal, unacceptable military operation against Taiwan, you would lose all the allies in Asia."

Few of the experts interviewed took the argument this far. However, it was consistently noted that abandoning Taipei would prompt Japanese voters to question the rationale for tolerating such a large US military presence in Japan. Many would wonder whether America's commitment to defend Japan is any deeper than what they perceived as its failure to protect Taiwan.

Yet Not Intervening Might Not Destroy Washington's Reputation... if Washington Gives Tokyo a Reason to Keep the Faith

Complicating the picture, interviewees did not universally believe that maintaining the credibility of Washington's commitment to Japan requires defending Taiwan. Several interviewees said the alliance could survive despite US nonintervention, provided that Washington clearly communicates its rationale for staying out of the conflict and helps Tokyo understand its position. Specifically, US policymakers would need to proactively offer a compelling explanation for why military intervention is not feasible—such as needing to "keep its powder dry" for the defense of Japan, or because Taiwanese defenses might collapse before US forces could arrive in sufficient numbers. Japanese leaders must understand and accept Washington's reasons, and, perhaps most importantly, the Japanese government and pro-US foreign policy elites must find a convincing way to explain American non-intervention to a potentially skeptical Japanese public.

Indeed, interviewees expressed the belief that even in the face of abandonment of Taiwan, Japanese security experts and foreign policy elites would still recognize that Japan has no realistic alternative but to rely on the United States for security. Across the conversations with security experts, there was unanimous agreement that the US alliance is the sine qua non of Japanese security, regardless of public opinion or reaction. Left with no viable alternative, even if the United States appeared to abandon Taiwan, these experts would still work to maintain the alliance for the sake of Japan's defense. They would likely also attempt to restore Washington's damaged credibility in the eyes of a skeptical Japanese public.

If Beijing were to achieve an "easy" victory over Taiwan—or at least do so without facing American military intervention—and thus emerge more emboldened than ever, the interviewees expect Japan's dependence on US support would only increase. One retired military officer framed Tokyo's lack of options in stark arithmetic terms: "If the US did nothing over Taiwan, the credibility of the US would be dead. Now, would this lead to the end of the Mutual Defense Treaty? I don't think so. It's basic math. Japan is 1. China is 3. The US is 4. 4+1 = 5. So, Japan would stick with the US."

In the wake of Taiwan's abandonment, left with the worst option except for all the others, most interviewees believe Japanese security experts and foreign policy elites would work overtime to maintain the US–Japan alliance. They would seek to justify or rationalize American inaction in the eyes of a skeptical Japanese public, while striving to restore or repair Washington's damaged credibility. Some interviewees suggested that this group might attempt to highlight the fundamental differences between US security guarantees to Taiwan and Japan by reminding Japanese voters that the Taiwan Relations Act is not a formal defense treaty and therefore less binding than Japan's treaty with the United States. Additionally, Japanese elites could argue that the loss of Taiwan would make Japan even more crucial to the United States both strategically and economically.

Nor will Washington be a helpless bystander in this situation. Several interviewees suggested that the United States will play a crucial role in shaping the narrative in Japan by helping Japanese elites counter public skepticism and ease fears. At a minimum, Washington must keep Tokyo informed throughout each step of the US decision-making process. While proactive communication will be essential in any scenario, the interviewees emphasized that it will become especially critical if Washington opts not to intervene. Surging military assets to help Tokyo defend its outlying islands; reinforcing US troop levels in Okinawa; and/ or making attempts to provide Taiwan with weapons, humanitarian relief, or civilian evacuation could all send a clear signal that Washington has no intention of abandoning Tokyo even if it is unable to save Taipei.

Some interviewees pointed out that strategic and operational realities might compel Washington to temporarily withdraw its forces to minimize casualties or to establish a better military posture. However, even these experts were careful to emphasize that if Washington wants to remain a credible Pacific power in Tokyo's eyes, it must find a way to quickly regain its position in the defense of Japan, strive to protect regional sea lanes, and maintain—if not reinforce—its posture in the broader Indo-Pacific.

Washington can also influence Japanese reactions to US non-intervention by taking steps to shape the broader context. For example, the US military could reinforce its position in the Pacific by deploying additional ships, aircraft, ground troops, missile defense systems, and critical enablers to Hawaii, Guam, Australia, and—where alliance politics allow—

South Korea, Thailand, and the Philippines. Conversely, a broader move toward retrenchment would likely have the opposite effect.

Several interviewees cited Afghanistan as an example. While they criticized the US pullout as ungainly and poorly handled, Japanese defense officials and foreign policy elites noted the formidable airlift assets that were still brought to bear and acknowledged that, in the end, it allowed Washington to redirect resources and focus to the Indo-Pacific.

Japan Will Not Defend Taiwan Without US Leadership

One additional point is worth noting regarding a US decision not to intervene. Interviewees expressed a strong consensus that Japan is highly unlikely to fight without the United States by its side. The prevailing view was that the JSDF's capacity to directly engage the PLA without US military support is—and will remain—quite limited.

At least one interviewee noted that, because the Japanese government has the legal authority to mobilize forces in response to an armed attack against a neighboring country that poses a clear risk to Japan's survival, a unilateral Japanese response is at least theoretically possible. Whether this hypothetical scenario could ever become a reality—and whether it would be sufficient to deter Beijing— are, of course, different questions entirely.

The issue prompted several experts to speculate about the types of military capabilities Japan might employ in a cross-Strait conflict without US involvement. Among the candidate capabilities were Japanese submarines, missile defense systems, and a range of non-kinetic assets, including satellites, cyber defenses, and electromagnetic monitoring and jamming. However, most interviewees believed that, in response to an attack on Taiwan and US non-intervention, the Japanese government would likely deploy naval, air, and ground units around Japan's outlying islands.

One expert pointed out that if Tokyo determines an attack on Taiwan constitutes a clear threat to Japanese security and initiates security operations in response, such a move would automatically trigger the US treaty obligation to assist Japan. In this instance, Japanese involvement could potentially compel a US response even if Washington remains ambivalent about supporting Taiwan. This observation illustrates that entanglement works both ways. It serves as a clear reminder that, regardless of Washington's response to an attack on Taiwan, demonstrating a firm commitment to Japan's defense will be essential to maintaining the US–Japan alliance.

A US Defeat is So Shocking That it is Barely Contemplated
After being asked how Japan might respond to a cross-Strait conflict in which Washington remains on the sidelines, interviewees were then asked to contemplate an even more unsettling question: how might Japan react to an attack on Taiwan in which the US military intervenes but suffers a decisive defeat?

The experts appeared to find discussing a US military defeat even more unsettling than the prospect of non-intervention. While interviewees typically responded quickly to most other questions, prompts concerning American defeat were often met with long pauses, nervous laughter, and remarks along the lines of "that's a good question." One possible inference is that regional allies have not contemplated a scenario in which the US military loses to the same extent as they have non-intervention or victory. If so, this suggests that the shock of a US military defeat could reverberate across the region in unexpected and hard-to-predict ways.

All interviewees agreed that a military defeat would be catastrophic. When asked to consider long-term implications for Japan and the US alliance, interviewees understandably tended to seek more context and detail. Typical follow-up questions included: Was this a massive, overwhelming defeat, or a close fight with a political resolution that allowed both sides to spin the outcome for their domestic audiences? Did China bloody the United States and Japan but lose the entire PLA Navy, most of its air force, and deplete its missile forces in the process? Did the scenario contemplate a temporary cessation of fighting in preparation for renewed conflict, possibly accompanied by horizontal or vertical escalation? Would a loss of Taiwan lead to an intensified Cold War and aggressive containment strategy to prevent further Chinese advances? While such questions might suggest that context would matter as much for a US defeat as it would for US non-intervention, the way in which interviewees requested clarification also indicated that such a scenario is not yet taken seriously or widely studied in Tokyo.

Indeed, it was notable that several experts, without prompting, referred to a series of highly publicized wargames in which the United States lost a Taiwan conflict.[25] They emphasized that these exercises were not truly predictive of how a cross-Strait conflict might unfold. Rather, they argued, the Pentagon was deliberately using these simulations to help identify capability gaps and doctrinal shortcomings. Some experts also brought up high-profile comments such as those by Admiral Davidson, suggesting that the United States is not prepared for a fight. Here too, such remarks were characterized as part of a bureaucratic strategy by which US Indo-Pacific Command was leveraging fears that the US military might lose, using them to secure increased funding from Congress. In other words, when confronted with a request to contemplate a hypothetical US loss, these experts seemed to revert habitually to the position that studying defeat was merely a tool for improving performance, rather than a plausible outcome or a basis for strategic and alliance planning.

Asking Experts to Rank their Preferred Bad Outcomes Yielded No Consensus

Having discussed both abandonment and defeat with the interviewees, the next question posed was which outcome they believed would be worse for Japan. The question was framed to elicit and explore Japanese perspectives on which would be more damaging to the alliance: challenging Japanese assumptions about America's reputation for resolve or shaking Japanese faith in US capability?

When weighing defeat against abandonment, interviewees' reactions and responses were decidedly mixed, with no clear consensus emerging. While all stressed that either scenario would be catastrophic, some suggested it would be worse for the alliance if the United States failed to intervene at all, while others indicated that a US defeat would be the worst possible outcome. A few interviewees insisted that the specifics of the situation would matter too much for them to opine without more details.

One expert expanded on why non-intervention would be the worst possible outcome, explaining that a military defeat could represent a temporary setback, whereas non-intervention would signify an outright abandonment, explaining:

> For US credibility, what matters most is your willingness to maintain the status quo. If the US fought seriously but was then overwhelmed by China, we should make Chinese control over Taiwan as temporary as possible. Defeat is not the end. Even if their military took over, what about the supply line? How can they endure and stay and remain on the island intact? The island will be isolated, and there might be an insurgency. There would be many options, many ways to continue fighting. Our goal is not to invade the continent, our goal is to maintain the status quo. If they occupy the island, we should pursue the status quo ante and get back to normalcy. The invasion and occupation by China is not the end of the game. If it's the end of the game, they win and we lose. But if we don't stop fighting, we will not win, but also won't lose. In a nutshell, it's a matter of the will of the US and Japan.

Other interviewees believed that the worst possible outcome would be for the United States to fight China and lose, although their responses tended to be more nuanced and focused on specific circumstances. Several suggested that in the face of this outcome, Japan would ultimately seek an accommodation or a separate peace with China. Others, however, believed Japan would still attempt to preserve the US alliance in some form, albeit with much greater reluctance and trepidation. The earlier discussions on "the long game" and the limited alternatives to US power were again cited: Japan has few strategic options, regardless of US decisions.

Nuclear Considerations

If US Capability and Reliability are in Question, Japan Will Consider Nuclear Weapons

Nuclear escalation emerged as a particularly frequent topic in discussions with interviewees, with some broaching the issue even before it was explicitly mentioned. Experts in and on Japan were notably consistent in their views of nuclear issues. Their main concern was that China would use nuclear rhetoric and saber rattling to exploit Japan's historical fears, aiming to deter the country from intervening in a cross-Strait conflict.

When discussing this issue, interviewees unanimously began with a reminder that nuclear risks are not hypothetical to the Japanese people. Having experienced the atomic bombings of Hiroshima and Nagasaki, as well as the 2011 Fukushima nuclear disaster, the Japanese public remains highly attuned to the specters of intentional and accidental nuclear catastrophe.

Interestingly, the issue of nuclear proliferation frequently arose when interviewees were asked to compare US non-intervention with US defeat. The interviewees acknowledged that both scenarios would likely ignite a nuclear debate in Japan. Most suggested that proponents of an independent Japanese nuclear capability would be more empowered than ever, with Tokyo likely signaling—both publicly and in private bilateral talks with Beijing—that it was seriously considering the pursuit of its own nuclear arsenal. One source proposed that Washington might attempt to dampen Japanese interest in nuclear weapons by stationing nuclear weapons in Japan and exploring a NATO-style launch-sharing arrangement.

Several interviewees, however, offered a counterpoint, arguing that possessing nuclear weapons remains an inviolable taboo in Japanese public life. They emphasized that reluctance to consider nuclear weapons is particularly strong among pro-Taiwan political leaders. As one expert explained, "Most of the LDP's attention is on getting the Japanese to commit to defend Taiwan. And as soon as you start talking about nukes, then it would become very difficult for Japanese to bear the thought of suffering yet another nuclear attack. So, I think the lack of discussion is largely strategic, at least at the public level. Although even in a private capacity I don't think these conversations are happening." According to this viewpoint, although a US defeat or the abandonment of Taiwan could spark debate about a Japanese nuclear deterrent, the anti-nuclear voices would likely remain strong.

Importantly, however, none of the interviewees believed that Tokyo would actually go through with developing nuclear weapons. One expert noted that Japan would need to withdraw from the Treaty on the Non-Proliferation of Nuclear Weapons (NPT) to do so, which would make it impossible for Japan to import the nuclear reactor fuel it needs for civilian power generation. Another interviewee pointed out that a nuclear Japan is unlikely to alter China's deterrence calculus in any case, given that Beijing is expanding its own arsenal and Washington maintains a significant overmatch.

Japan Worries More about Beijing's Nuclear Threats and US Readiness than about Nuclear Use

Taboos notwithstanding, most Japanese interviewees were remarkably frank and willing to discuss the possibility of nuclear escalation in a Taiwan conflict. Three themes emerged from their responses. First, Japanese foreign policy elites expressed confidence that Beijing will not actually use nuclear weapons—at least against the United States—in a war over Taiwan, even if the PLA began to lose. As one source put it, unless "Xi gets crazy," the prevailing sentiment among the interviewees was that "restraint would prevail among Chinese leadership." Another expert similarly noted, "If China lost in the initial fight, I think they would be more likely to protract the conflict, wear out US and Japanese ability to sustain it, and then try to come back for a second round, rather than escalate to nuclear."

At the same time, interviewees expressed concern that Beijing might resort to using nuclear saber-rattling and coercion against US allies and partners. One interviewee stated:

> I think China might consider using nuclear threats against Japan at the start of the crisis to convince the Japanese people to stay on the sidelines and not to intervene. Recall the 'Five Minute' video, in which China threatened to use nuclear weapons against the Japanese people and said China's nuclear no-first-use policy does not apply to Japan because Japan's history of invading China.[26] I'm not saying China wants to use nukes against anyone. But because of the legacy of Japan-China relations it could be justified or rationalized.

The fear in this case is that China would use nuclear threats to coerce Japan and other countries into staying out of the conflict. This expert recommended that Japan and the United States study Chinese nuclear strategy in order to prepare their publics—and potentially South Korea as well—to cope with this type of coercion.

To be sure, some nuclear coercion scholars argue that a nuclear threat is only credible when the target believes the initiator has both the capability and the resolve to follow through on its threat.[27] Thus, the view that Beijing will not use nuclear weapons and the fear that it might engage in nuclear saber-rattling are logically at odds. That said, the primary aim here is to document the perceptions and fears of US allies, rather than to label these perceptions as founded or unfounded. Moreover, fear is an inherently subjective emotion—one that Beijing might try to exploit, even if there is an "objective" sense that the risk of nuclear use remains low. In this context, even if security experts overwhelmingly conclude that the actual nuclear risk is low, the public may not share this conclusion and may still be susceptible to an intimidation campaign that exerts political pressure and constrains the options available to Japan's elected leaders.

Finally, many of those interviewed expressed hope that Washington would renew its focus on nuclear deterrence in relation to China. One expert raised concerns that the United States is out of practice on the basic fundamental requirements of extended deterrence. To paraphrase these concerns, there is a sense that it has been some time since the US last had to actively reassure a treaty ally facing imminent nuclear threats—and that the muscle memory developed during the Cold War is atrophying.

Another source implored US strategists to recognize that existing US nuclear strategy, doctrine, and posture were developed within a heavily Eurocentric context, focused on interactions between just two adversaries. According to this expert, the existing models are ill suited to fully capture the complexities of nuclear escalation in the Indo-Pacific. As this expert put it, "the European theater was relatively simple: one team, NATO, against one enemy, Warsaw Pact." In contrast, the Indo-Pacific is far more complex, involving multiple nuclear-armed states (China, Russia, North Korea, India, and Pakistan), multiple potential adversaries, and divergent threat perceptions among the US allies. In this source's opinion, the increased complexity, coupled with differing traditions of political philosophy compared to the European theater, demands greater attention from US nuclear planners.

Victory's Drawbacks

When discussing the "best case" scenario—a US-led victory—many interviewees pointed out that Japan has likely spent insufficient time considering the consequences of a Chinese defeat in Taiwan. Interviewees who have studied this issue unanimously believe that a Chinese loss would mean the end of Xi Jinping's leadership, if not the Chinese Communist Party's grip on power altogether. As one source put it, "The CCP's legitimacy comes from economic growth and prosperity, and the historical reunification of Taiwan. And if they lose one of those legitimacies, then the Chinese people will not follow the leadership of the CCP anymore."

The interviewees predicted that the loss of CCP legitimacy would plunge the region into deep uncertainty at best—if not outright chaos. They expected that Taiwan would declare formal independence, likely with Japan's support, and that Japan's policies and priorities would remain largely unchanged: continuing to rely on the US alliance while maintaining sufficient military strength to defend itself, without moving toward revanchism or expansionism. However, the interviewees also noted that the entire configuration of the regional order would need to be reworked, depending on how developments unfold in China.

Interviewees also discussed how Beijing might react as it began to realize it was losing the fight for Taiwan. Some experts suggested that—despite Xi's consolidation of control—such a scenario could lead to fissures between the CCP and PLA leadership. A particularly volatile scenario could emerge if the Party insisted that the fight continue but the military concluded it could no longer endure punishing losses. One security analyst also cautioned against underestimating Beijing's willingness to regroup and launch a second offensive, warning that retaliatory moves following a defeat were a serious possibility.

One source diverged from the others, predicting that, in the aftermath of a Chinese loss, Japan would likely respond by trying to "play the good cop"—that is, by focusing on diplomacy to buy time for China to put itself back together. This source described a perception that both Japan and Taiwan understand Chinese domestic politics better than the United States does, due to their proximity to the region and—especially in Taiwan's case—their greater ease in gathering and processing information in Chinese.

How Japan Thinks about Gray-Zone Scenarios and Escalation Risks

Finally, the matter of gray-zone competition was discussed, with Japanese experts—along with their Australian and South Korean counterparts—

overwhelmingly viewing it as Beijing's preferred approach to dealing with Taiwan.

The Risk of Inadvertent Escalation in the Gray Zone is Low... though Not Zero

Those interviewed were not particularly concerned that gray-zone competition might escalate into outright war. The experts generally believed that Taiwanese, Japanese, and American security forces are sufficiently professional, and that Xi Jinping has consolidated and centralized his power to such an extent that even a heated exchange would likely to remain under control. As one source explained, "I'm of the view that any severe escalations would be deliberate. And if there were an accident or a miscalculation, Xi would have the power and ability to pull back."

To be sure, some experts expressed concern that the risk of inadvertent escalation—due to an accidental or negligent collision or unauthorized use of force—is not zero. Several interviewees highlighted the limited, or nonexistent, crisis communication channels between Beijing, Washington, Tokyo, and Taipei. Additionally, some expressed an expectation that China's updated Coast Guard Law would lead Beijing to test US, Taiwanese, and Japanese red lines with increased intensity and frequency.[28] To mitigate the risk of an accidental or inadvertent conflict, several interviewees proposed measures aimed at further reducing tensions.

Suggestions along these lines included more advance planning for crisis de-escalation among the United States, Japan, and Taiwan, as well as efforts to engage China in establishing or re-establishing communication channels, such as hotlines. It is important to note that Beijing has thus far resisted the sort of strategic hotlines created between Washington and Moscow during the Cold War.[29] At the time of this publication, China had also refused to restore the cross-Strait communication mechanisms it cut after the Democratic Progressive Party (DPP) returned to power in 2016.[30]

Regional experts repeatedly pointed out the overall lack of effective military-to-military communications, which hinders efforts to deconflict in-theater operations and reduce the risk of accidental air or naval collisions, or other contingencies. While all parties are interested in controlling escalation and avoiding unintended retaliation, redlines remain insufficiently defined, and existing communication channels are inadequate for diffusing misunderstandings. One source suggested that, although clearly articulating redlines may increase tensions in the short term, the potential benefits in clarifying the operational picture and preventing misinterpretations outweigh this cost. Several sources recommended that Japan and the United States collaborate with China and Taiwan to establish an agreed-upon framework for managing accidental escalation and preventing events from spiraling out of control.

The Chance that Beijing Might Defeat Taipei in the Gray Zone is Even Lower

The interviewees were unanimously and deeply skeptical that Beijing might somehow find a way to annex or otherwise prevail over Taiwan via gray-zone provocations alone. As one expert framed the matter:

> Even in scenarios where we're talking about stronger uses of force —for example a naval blockade, or an air or missile bombardment— I have trouble seeing Taiwan folding. That gives me an even higher confidence that Taiwan wouldn't fold under cyber-attacks, or an attack disguised as humanitarian relief. I think China would still have to show its hand in a way that creates the possibility of third-party involvement. We think the PLA would like to win without fighting, but there aren't really shortcuts to this. And the idea of winning without fighting is un-PLA. It's certainly not the way Mao thought. 'There are no shortcuts to war.' And if we believe the PLA is a product of Maoist thought, the PLA recognizes that it will have to do a lot more to collapse Taiwan's will than just play in the gray zone.

The interviewees were generally in agreement that Taiwan is capable of handling Chinese cyber-attacks and disinformation. The Taiwanese government and public are well aware of these challenges and are actively addressing them. However, the interviewees view Taipei as more likely to struggle with Chinese campaigns of diplomatic isolation and economic coercion. In both cases, China's power is so much greater than Taiwan's that Taiwan cannot maintain its trade relationships or its already-limited presence in the international community—such as in global public health and trade bodies—without direct assistance and support from partners like Japan and the United States.

Even So, the Gray Zone Remains an Important Arena for Competition

Paradoxically, several Japanese experts suggested that because China is so unlikely to launch a conventional invasion due to the associated costs and risks, it therefore considers its gray-zone activities as relatively more important. According to this line of reasoning, Xi Jinping has so effectively consolidated power that any decision to go to war over Taiwan would be an entirely political one (i.e., the Chinese military has no autonomy or say in the matter), and Xi will not start a war because he is still too likely to lose.[31]

Even the experts who were reluctant to predict whether Xi might decide to attack one day still believed that the gray zone remains critical to Beijing's overarching strategy. As one retired senior military officer put it:

> From Xi's perspective, he is probably carefully calculating the risks, costs, and benefits. I think he sees Taiwan as being a part of his dream. He is not giving up or compromising on what he says. But his mind and his intentions are impossible to know. Even Xi himself may not know what he will want in a few years or a few months. So, I think he is trying to create favorable circumstances so that he will have options to exploit if and when he decides to make a conventional, full-scale effort. Meanwhile, through these gray zone activities and/or coercive diplomatic efforts, maybe

he gets lucky and things turn out such that Taiwan gives up, in which case, why not?

China's continuous provocations in Taiwan's ADIZ represent a unique challenge. Since China's air incursions do not technically violate territorial airspace, Japan itself will not respond directly. However, the constant incursions are placing strain on Taiwan's defenses, particularly by contributing to the wear and tear on its small fighter fleet due to the significant cumulative flight hours. Japanese experts noted that they face a similar challenge in the ongoing confrontation over the Senkakus, which have been managed through the Japanese Coast Guard. However, the interviewees refrained from offering recommendations to Taiwan. They expressed confidence that Taiwan can and will develop the appropriate response to these air and naval intrusions.

Given Japan's territorial sensitivities regarding Yonaguni Island and the Senkakus, it was perhaps unsurprising that the interviewees emphasized gray-zone scenarios involving incursions by Chinese vessels—fishing fleets were mentioned most often—and/or the seizure by China of outlying Taiwanese islands. Although by our definition, the seizure of an island (even an uninhabited one) crosses the line from a gray-zone activity into an act of war, it is still noteworthy that many of the Japanese interviewees specifically mentioned island grabs when responding to open-ended questions about gray-zone scenarios.

Multiple interviewees described essentially the same hypothetical sequence of events. China would begin by equipping ordinary fishing boats with communications equipment, and potentially armed crews. These fishing fleets begin probing by sailing close to and around Taiwan's islands in the South China Sea, and/or one of the outlying islands in the Taiwan Strait. Facing no direct armed opposition, the "fishermen" would land on an island and remain there, potentially claiming the territory as theirs by ancestral right. Interviewees suggested that such a scenario might be murky enough to prevent the US government or the Japanese Diet from responding decisively. They also suggested it could create the precursor for a Chinese *casus belli*, particularly if the Taiwanese Coast Guard responded with force. According to multiple interviewees, this scenario is the most concerning for Japan because it is seen as highly plausible and is also expected to fall below the threshold that would spark enough outrage among the Japanese and American publics to justify a fulsome response.

Deterrence Über Alles

Regardless of their specific views on outcomes, all interviewees repeatedly emphasized the importance of maintaining an effective US deterrence posture in the region. They reiterated that even an intervention by a capable US force that emerged victorious would still result in a horrible, bloody outcome for Japan. Given Japan's geography, strategists believe that the country would find itself in the line of fire in any conflict, and thus any victory would come at great cost. As one interviewee stated, "America will find a way to win. And probably without resorting to nukes. Yet from Japan's perspective, Okinawa will be in ruins and so will Tokyo. That would be very bad. So, our goal is to not start a war. To that end, we have to be willing to accept risk." A capable military is crucial for maintaining the alliance, but avoiding conflict altogether remains by far the best option.

NOTES

1. For an overview of the origins of the US-Japan alliance, see Swenson-Wright, *Unequal Allies?*; Cha, *Powerplay*; Izumikawa, "Network Connections."
2. For an assessment of how Tokyo can better prepare its military for a Taiwan contingency, and what Washington can do to help, see Koda, "The Sun Also Rises"; Newsham, "Japan as the "'Swing Vote'"; Cooper and Johnston, "Getting U.S.-Japanese Command"; Ross, "What's Missing."
3. For examples of this line of reasoning, see Nakada, "Aso"; Ashley, "Japan's Revolution"; Bercaw, "Yes, Taiwan Will Defend Taiwan."
4. Yusaku Horiuchi (Dartmouth College), Takako Hikotani (Gakushuin University), and Atsushi Tago (Waseda Univesity) fielded surveys in August 2020 examining whether the United States lost credibility in the eyes of the Japanese public due to the withdrawal from Afghanistan. See Welsh, "How Did the Japanese Public React."
5. A 2023 Pew Research Center survey found that 82% of those surveyed in Japan view Taiwan favorably. Huang and Clancy, "Taiwan Seen More Favorably." See also Nemoto and Iawata, "74% in Japan."
6. Taiwan was a colony of Japan from 1895, when the Qing government ceded control to Japan in the Treaty of Shimonoseki, until 1945 when control was nominally returned to the Republic of China following World War II. Taiwan was Japan's first colony, and Tokyo attempted to administer the island as a "model colony," investing heavily in economic modernization and the development of cultural ties.
7. Shelbourne, "Davidson: China Could Try."
8. National Security Strategy of Japan (Provisional English Translation) (2022); National Defense Strategy (Provisional Translation as of December 28, 2022), (2022); Defense Buildup Program (Provisional Translation as of January 17, 2023).
9. Tsuneo, "What's New in Japan's."
10. Adam Liff usefully points out that the oft-cited claim that Tokyo intends to double its defense budget is a misleading misinterpretation of the Kishida government's real target, which is 2% of GDP for *all* 'national security-related spending.' [Emphasis in the original]. According to Liff, the real goal is to increase defense spending by 35%--which, although

far less than a 100% increase, is still significant. See Liff, "No, Japan is Not Planning."

11. National Security Strategy of Japan (Provisional English Translation), Short, 14.

12. See, for example, Park, "Japan official, calling Taiwan"; U.S. Department of State, "U.S.-Japan Joint Press Statement"; White House, Short U.S.-Japan Joint Leaders' Statement, "U.S.-Japan Global Partnership for a New Era"; Bloomberg, "Japan Sees China-Taiwan Friction."

13. See Hornung and Johnstone, "Japan's Strategic Shift"; Tsuneo, "What's New in Japan's."

14. Kaneko et al., "Exclusive: Japan Elevates Taiwan Security."

15. Kaneko et al., "Exclusive: Japan Elevates Taiwan Security."

16. Japan, Ministry of Foreign Affairs of Japan, *Treaty of Mutual Cooperation*.

17. It is worth pointing out that the scholarly literature on alliance politics suggests that Tokyo and Washington can find ways to fulfill their treaty obligations without necessarily intervening in a cross-Strait war or even engaging with Chinese forces. Allies are remarkably effective at foot dragging, finding loopholes, sidestepping obligations, and meeting the letter of the law while ignoring its spirit when they do not think it is in their interest to fight. Beckley, "The Myth of Entangling Alliances"; Lanoszka, *Military Alliances in the Twenty-First Century*, 70–74.

18. One interviewee did suggest that the number of Japanese citizens living in Taiwan might push an otherwise reluctant Japanese public to support military action. Approximately 20,000 Japanese citizens were living in Taiwan as of 2022. "Number of Residents from Japan Living in Taiwan from 2013–2022," in *Statista* (2024). https://www.statista.com/statistics/1080654/japan-number-japanese-residents-taiwan/.

19. China is Japan's largest trade partner. Total trade between the two countries reached $335 billion USD in 2022, up more than 14% from the preceding year. See Japan, Ministry of Foreign Affairs, "Japan-China Economic Relationship."

20. Japanese direct investment in China reached nearly 10 billion in 2022, with China representing the 3rd biggest destination for Japanese FDI (after the United States and Australia). As of 2022, Japanese companies were operating at over 30,000 sites in China. Japan, "Japan-China Economic Relationship and China's Economy."

21. Examples include the March 2023 meeting between South Korean President Yoon Suk Yeol and Japanese Prime Minister Fumio Kishida, the Japan-ROK-US trilateral summit at Camp David in August 2023,

and recent increased military cooperation over missile defense and technological development. See White House, "The Spirit of Camp David"; Mirna Galic and Frank Aum, "What's Behind Japan and South Korea's Latest Attempt to Mend Ties?," *Analysis, United States Institute of Peace,* Mach 21, 2023, https://www.usip.org/publications/2023/03/whats-behind-japan-and-south-koreas-latest-attempt-mend-ties; Aamer Madhani, "US, Japan, South Korea to Announce Deeper Defense Cooperation at Camp David Summit," *Associated Press,* August 14, 2023, https://apnews.com/article/biden-yoon-kishida-camp-david-missile-defense-f3ce58da383f22 55ee479624645db542.

22. See the definitions of these terms in the introductory chapter.
23. See Posen, "Pull Back"; Posen, *Restraint;* Chong and Hall, "The Lessons of 1914"; Edelstein and Shifrinson, "It's a Trap!"
24. Such sentiments echo Adam Liff's observation that Tokyo has long sought to maintain a high degree of flexibility and maneuverability in its Taiwan policy. Liff, "The U.S.-Japan Alliance and Taiwan."
25. Copp, "'It Failed Miserably'"; Pettyjohn, Wasser, and Dougherty, *Dangerous Straits;* Cancian, Cancian, and Heginbotham, *The First Battle of the Next War.*
26. Feng, "China Officials Share Viral Video."
27. Sechser and Fuhrmann, *Nuclear Weapons and Coercive Diplomacy.*
28. Trung, "How China's Coast Guard Law."
29. Kine, "'Spiral Into Crisis'"; Kelly, "Xi Rejects US Offer."
30. Hernandez, "China Suspends Diplomatic Contact."
31. While our own view is that Xi's true personal calculus on the matter remains fundamentally unknowable, we acknowledge that we spoke with multiple individuals among the Japanese security community who feel strong conviction on this point.

CHAPTER 3

SOUTH KOREA

The discussion now turns to South Korea which—despite being farther away from any potential conflict over Taiwan than Japan—will nevertheless confront a difficult set of decisions. This claim might seem puzzling to some readers. After all, few allies are as deeply intertwined as South Korea and the United States. Their bond was forged on the battlefields of the Korean and Vietnam conflicts, formalized by a more than 70-year-old mutual defense treaty, and continuously reinforced by the exceptional degree of interoperability between US and South Korean forces.[1] However, these enduring ties should not be taken to mean that Seoul and Washington see eye to eye on the stakes and risks involved in the Taiwan Strait. While South Korea has a unique and close twentieth century relationship with the United States, it also has several millennia of historical ties with China, a deep reliance on exports to the Chinese market, and an unfinished war with an implacable foe whose closest ally is Beijing.

Over the course of this three-year study, interviews revealed that South Korean elites are both less concerned about the likelihood that China might attack Taiwan and more reluctant to become involved in a cross-Strait conflict than either their Japanese or Australian counterparts. In fact, if China were to attempt a forcible annexation of Taiwan, the interviews suggest that South Korea is the US ally most likely to breathe a (secret) sigh of relief if Washington decides to remain on the sidelines.

None of these points should be taken to suggest that South Korean leaders are callous or indifferent to Taiwan's plight. Instead, they shed light on what a cross-Strait war would mean for Seoul, particularly if Washington comes to Taipei's defense. Namely, a US-led military intervention would raise the specter of three equally distasteful scenarios: marginalization, abandonment, or entanglement.[2] Such concerns are eminently understandable. As the evocative saying goes, South Korea has long viewed itself as a shrimp among whales.[3] Throughout the entirety of the country's (and before that, the kingdom's) history, Korean leaders have found it necessary to seek allies to protect themselves from the predation of their stronger neighbors—whether those neighbors were Qing dynasty Manchus, Imperial Japan, or the potentially revanchist ambitions of Xi Jinping's China.

An unfortunate side effect of this dependence is that South Korea has inevitably also found itself at the mercy of its own alliance relationships. The need to maintain a good working relationship with its benefactor can compel Seoul to take sides when it would prefer to remain neutral. At its worst, this means Korea can be drawn into conflicts that it would much rather avoid.

Nor has Washington necessarily proven itself to be the most reliable of security guarantors. The Truman administration's indifference toward South Korea helped set the stage for the Korean War. Even after fighting side by side with the South Korean military for three years, Washington still resisted committing itself to Seoul's defense. It was not until the Eisenhower administration perceived a need to restrain South Korea— a view that South Korean president Syngman Rhee was all too eager to encourage—that Washington agreed to a formal alliance with Seoul. US concerns about South Korean adventurism even influenced the form that the alliance ultimately took.[4] More than seventy years on, fears of abandonment, entanglement, and junior status continue to shape how

South Korea thinks about its relationship with the United States. Further complicating these enduring qualms, Seoul must prioritize North Korea over all other potential security threats and contingencies, while also maintaining a stable relationship with its most powerful neighbor, China.

Such factors help explain why most of the South Korean scholars and subject matter experts interviewed appear to privilege reliability over reputation. For South Korea's safety and survival, North Korea matters far more than Taiwan. Moreover, whereas a Chinese attack on Taiwan would not directly endanger South Korea, Beijing's reprisals against Seoul for supporting Washington could. For this reason, we found that South Korean experts are far more worried about the risk of entrapment over Taiwan than their counterparts in Australia and Japan. As we discuss next, Beijing exerts powerful leverage over Seoul. The South Korean economy depends on access to the Chinese market, and Seoul needs Beijing's cooperation to address the North Korean threat. The risk of alienating China—including the specific threat that China would respond to a Taiwan crisis by encouraging North Korea to move against the South—looms large in the minds of South Korean security experts and the public.

In essence, the tradeoff between reputation and reliability is at its most acute in South Korea. Many interviewees did indicate that they "care" about Taiwan and view it as a proxy for American willingness to defend its other allies in the region. Nevertheless, most also recognized the inherent tension between reputation and reliability. Namely, while South Korean voters would likely question American resolve if Washington "abandons" Taipei, there was also broad acknowledgment that a US-led defense of Taiwan could weaken America's military, rendering it less capable of defending South Korea from a North Korean attack.

Taken together, these interrelated factors suggest that it would be unwise for the United States to defend Taiwan simply to burnish its reputation in South Korea's eyes. Even as recent public polls suggest that South Korean voters are increasingly aware both of Taiwan's predicament and the consequences of a war over its status, the interviews suggest that if China were to obtain political control over Taiwan, South Korea's most likely response would be closer to indifference than opposition. In fact, Seoul might be more likely than any other US ally in the region to feel relieved were the US to stay out of a war over Taiwan. The idea that Seoul might instead want Washington to risk a Pyrrhic victory or a costly defeat to defend Taiwan—either of which could limit the United States' ability to assist South Korea against North Korea—simply to uphold a reputation for resolve seems illogical.

A Methodological Note

All this being said, a note of methodological modesty is warranted at the outset. Of the three US allies that were closely examined over the course of this three-year project, South Korea proved the most difficult to "pin down" in terms of the degree to which it might reassess the credibility of US commitments in the wake of a cross-Strait invasion. Part of the challenge stemmed from a general reluctance among South Korean elites and experts to talk about Taiwan, particularly in comparison to their Australian and Japanese counterparts. This reluctance resulted in a considerably smaller "sample" from which to draw inferences. Indeed, this chapter contains fewer reflections from in-country experts than the ones from Japan or Australia, a gap that reflects the fact that Taiwan studies are not a major area of specialization among South Korean security experts. Although China is viewed as a matter of paramount importance, Taiwan is not.

Moreover, the experts who were willing to participate in interviews made clear that Seoul had only recently begun to think seriously about how it might want Washington to respond to a war over Taiwan. Several factors appear to have inhibited a more fulsome exploration of cross-Strait conflict scenarios within South Korean foreign policy and national security circles. For understandable reasons, South Korean officials and voters prioritize the more proximate and pressing threat of North Korea. As other scholars have also noted, the cumulative effect is that "neither

Korea's Taiwan policy nor a possible cross-Strait crisis appeared as mainstream policy concerns."[5] Concerns that even discussing Taiwan and a potential cross-Strait war might irritate Beijing also seem to have played a role. This type of apprehension was more pronounced early in the research period, which happened to coincide with the final year of the Moon administration. In comparison, by the end of this study, South Korean experts appeared more comfortable engaging in discussions about Taiwan scenarios.

What follows is the summary of the findings as they relate to particular aspects of the security challenges posed by Chinese aggression toward Taiwan, including the specific ramifications for South Korea and the potential impacts on its alliance with the United States. The discussion begins with how South Korea thinks about the risks and opportunities it faces in the Taiwan Strait and its perspectives on other regional partnerships. It then turns to South Korean views of the US alliance and plausible responses to the three basic scenarios in which a war over Taiwan might unfold. The section concludes by highlighting South Korea's domestic political environment, as the party in power is likely to have a far greater influence on Seoul's response to a Taiwan conflict than would be the case in either Australia or Japan.

How South Korea Thinks About China

China Looms Large as a Neighbor, Market, and Friend of the North

To understand how Seoul thinks about a potential cross-Strait war, it is useful to begin with its structurally inescapable connection to Beijing. Whereas geography bestowed Australia, Japan, and Taiwan with a maritime buffer that affords each a certain degree of freedom (and protection) from Chinese power, it locked the Korean Peninsula into a perpetual cultural, economic, and security relationship with China.[6] For centuries, Sinic influences shaped Korean language, culture, and politics. Nor did the peninsula's division in 1945 diminish China's gravitational pull, as Beijing continues to exercise an outsize impact on both Pyongyang and Seoul to the present day.

Two aspects of this multifaceted bilateral relationship are especially important for understanding how Seoul thinks about its options—and America's choices—in a cross-Strait contingency. The first is economic. South Korea depends on stable access to Chinese markets. Trade between the two countries increased by more than 600% between 1991 and 2018, to the point that South Korea trades more with China than with the United States and Japan combined.[7] China is South Korea's largest trading partner and is likely to remain so for the foreseeable future. In 2022, China was the destination for approximately a quarter of South Korean exports, with China and Hong Kong together accounting for about a third. These flows were more than double the volume of South Korea's trade with its next largest partner, the United States. Exports to China alone represent nearly 10 percent of South Korea's GDP.[8]

National security is the second critical facet of Seoul's relationship with Beijing. South Korea depends on China to address its top national security priority: North Korea. As a result, South Korean leaders have little choice but to pursue Chinese cooperation—or to at least avoid outright antagonism—to effectively navigate perilous inter-Korean relations. The interviewees were unanimous on this point: Seoul cannot "manage" Pyongyang without Beijing's help. Although domestic politics are discussed next, it suffices to say that even conservative South Korean governments, which tend to take a harder line toward North Korea and are more skeptical of Chinese intentions, have nevertheless been willing to work with Beijing when necessary. One South Korean academic put the matter succinctly, noting that even conservative President Park Geun-hye "stood shoulder to shoulder with Xi" when dealing with Pyongyang.

China Tries to Shape South Korean Perceptions...

The Chinese Communist Party has long sought to use its economic and security leverage to actively shape South Korean perceptions of China.

Several subject matter experts pointed out that Beijing is aggressively promoting a narrative of regional power transition, which juxtaposes a declining West against an ascendant China. One interviewee claimed that Beijing operates approximately twenty Confucius Institutes throughout South Korea.[9] While these institutions ostensibly exist to foster cultural exchange and understanding, scholars and policy analysts across the US political system have increasingly raised concerns that Confucius Institutes are little more than CCP-directed tools of soft power. In response to US political and law enforcement pressure in the United States, more than 100 of the 118 Confucius Institutes that once operated in the United States either closed or were in the process of closing between 2019 and 2022. Based on available information, it is reasonable to surmise that the Confucius Institutes in South Korea serve at least a dual function: promoting cultural exchange while also projecting Chinese soft power.

Beijing's perception and influence operations are amplified by the presence of Chinese citizens living and working in South Korea.[10] Chinese citizens comprise the largest group of non-Koreans residing in South Korea. As of late 2023, more than 600,000 of South Korea's nearly 1.5 million foreign residents were Chinese citizens.[11] To be sure, it is important not to overstate the impact that Chinese citizens have on South Korean public opinion. The total number of Chinese citizens living in South Korea represents just over one percent of the total population. Nevertheless, at least one interviewee suggested that because Chinese citizens are eligible to vote in local elections after three years of residence, they represent a potential avenue through which Beijing could exercise influence in local politics.[12]

...But it is Important Not to Overstate the Impact of Chinese Influence Operations

That said, it is important not to overstate the degree to which Beijing has successfully shaped South Korean politics to align with the Chinese Communist Party's preferences. If anything, China's efforts have either backfired or are overwhelmed by Xi's aggressive domestic, foreign, and economic policies. Public opinion polling is clear on this point: South Korean attitudes toward China are trending sharply negative, with nearly three-quarters of recent survey respondents expressing unfavorable views of Beijing.[13] This trend is especially pronounced among younger South Koreans.[14] The most significant declines appear to be a response to a combination of specific policy moves—such as Beijing's economic retaliation for Seoul's decision to host US missile defense installations (discussed next in greater detail) and Xi Jinping's draconian COVID-19 lockdowns[15]—and broader dissatisfaction with the perceived rise of authoritarianism and nationalism, coupled with economic and development policies that exacerbate environmental degradation.[16]

Public Opinion and THAAD: An Illustrative Case Study

Few episodes illustrate the extent to which Beijing's often ham-fisted overreactions have undermined or otherwise overwhelmed its efforts at swaying South Korean public opinion as clearly as the so-called "THAAD incident." Virtually every interviewee referenced the episode, identifying it as a major turning point in South Korean attitudes toward China.

The confrontation began in July 2016, when South Korea announced that it would host a single US Terminal High Altitude Air Defense (THAAD) missile battery near Seongju.[17] Washington and Seoul stated that the battery's purpose was to protect US and ROK military units on the peninsula from North Korean missile attacks.[18] Beijing strenuously objected to the move, claiming that the THAAD's advanced radar capabilities would give the United States greater visibility into Chinese airspace and potentially even allow US forces to track Chinese ground troop movements.[19] Washington proceeded with the deployment over China's objections, prompting Beijing to inflame anti-Korean sentiment among Chinese citizens. The result was a functional ban on Chinese tourism in Korea and on Chinese purchases of South Korean consumer goods. China also took selective action against South Korea's entertainment sector and targeted the Lotte Group,[20] because the THAAD system was to be placed on Lotte-owned land[21] The resulting losses to South Korea's economy totaled at least US$7.5 billion.[22]

South Korean public views of China quickly soured in the aftermath of the THAAD dispute. While some Korean voters had objected to the United States deploying the missile system, the majority viewed the THAAD deployment as a response to North Korean provocations—not as an attempt to contain China. As a result, many believed that Beijing was punishing them for a transgression they had not committed. Moreover, up until this point, many South Koreans assumed that Beijing shared their view that North Korean aggression was a major problem. China's willingness to punish South Korea over THAAD disabused them of that notion and revealed the extent to which Seoul and Beijing were misaligned in their approaches to Pyongyang.

Among the experts interviewed, the THAAD episode highlighted the asymmetries between the United States and Chinese toolkits. They pointed out that while Washington's decision to deploy THAAD represented a technical-military solution to a national security threat, Beijing responded with economic coercion. These experts noted that the United States lacked an economic countermeasure or mechanism to support—or otherwise shield—South Korean companies from Chinese economic compellence. The incident thus served as a wake-up call for how US–China competition could continue to play out on the Korean Peninsula, highlighting the need for Washington to develop tools to help protect the South Korean economy from similar Chinese efforts in the future.

How South Korea Thinks About Taiwan

Taiwan is Not a Priority

The fact that South Korean public opinion has turned sharply against China should not be taken to imply that South Koreans now embrace Taiwan or perceive a deep connection between Taiwan's security and their own. Instead, the interviewees conveyed a near-unanimous view that neither South Korean voters nor elites regard Taiwan as a top national security priority. As one source succinctly put it: "To the Korean public, Taiwan is not something they understand or would be willing to fight over. Taiwan is only interesting for the average Korean because the United States is involved there. If China invaded Taiwan and Taiwan became a part of China, I would bet South Korea would think nothing of it."

To be sure, not every interviewee framed the matter in such stark terms. Many South Korean experts were aware of, and sympathetic to, Taiwan's predicament. They recognize the historical, cultural, economic, and political parallels between their two nations. They also clearly prefer that China not control Taiwan. The stronger China grows, and the more it can project power beyond its borders, the more precarious South Korea's security situation appears. And they have an awareness of what Taiwan's annexation might mean for the regional and global economy, including the risk of restricted South Korean access to semiconductor chips (although several of the interviewees noted that Taiwanese and South Korean semiconductor fabrication plants are, in fact, direct competitors).

At the same time, South Korean experts routinely highlighted China's proximity to, and leverage over, their country. Many expressed a view that Taiwan's loss would be unlikely to directly threaten South Korea, whereas Chinese retaliation in response to a US-led defense of Taiwan almost certainly would. As discussed in greater detail next, the interviewees made clear that South Korean leaders are highly attuned to the risk of Chinese coercion and punishment in the event of a war over Taiwan's status, and that such dynamics are expected to shape whether—and how —Seoul responds. A public opinion poll conducted in late 2023 suggests that South Korean voters have a similar view to these practitioners. It found that, "while South Koreans are undoubtedly aware of the potential ramifications of a Chinese attack on Taiwan for South Korea, survey data suggests that many are reluctant to support direct Korean involvement in such a conflict."[23]

The most salient concern expressed by the interviewees revolved around whether and how Beijing might pressure Pyongyang to act. Many believed that China's relationship with North Korea would almost certainly be in play as both a carrot and a stick to induce South Korea to remain neutral, if not to actively support China. A robust US response that involved pressure on Seoul to participate could, in turn, lead China to encourage belligerent moves by North Korea. Some experts also raised the concern that China might deploy troops in a diversionary feint on the Korean Peninsula to distract from its main effort against Taiwan, although this was generally treated as a remote possibility. Many of the interviewees considered it far more likely that Beijing might prod or entice Pyongyang to provoke tensions in a way that would menace Seoul, distract Washington, and tie down US forces on the peninsula. Several noted that Beijing might need to do little more than offer tacit approval, as the Kim regime could opportunistically exploit US distraction, especially if the US Indo-Pacific Command began diverting resources and personnel away from US Forces Korea. Regardless of how such activity unfolded, these experts suggested that any North Korean activity could draw US attention away from Taiwan while also driving a wedge between Washington and Seoul.

The interviewees deemed economic coercion even more likely than actions involving North Korea. Chinese economic pressure has already proven effective against countries, like South Korea, that remain dependent on access to the Chinese market.[24] In a cross-Strait war scenario, Beijing's stakes could prompt a response that far exceeds the level of punishment imposed following the THAAD deployment.

Japan Matters Too

Although secondary to Seoul's economic and security ties to Beijing, Seoul's relationship with Tokyo remains a relevant and potentially fraught factor in assessing South Korea's options and actions in a Taiwan contingency. Washington's has long sought to transform its dual but largely separate alliances with Japan and South Korea into a genuine security "triangle." Unfortunately, until very recently, the realities of South Korea–Japan relations have prevented such a transformation, leaving the three trapped in a security "V," in which Seoul and Tokyo work closely with Washington but not with one another.

The relationship between South Korea and Japan remains freighted with history and shaped by domestic politics. For many South Koreans, the relationship is still tainted by Japan's actions during the Second World War and the perception that Tokyo has yet to fully apologize for its atrocities.[25] Relations reached a particularly low point in 2011, when these historical disputes led to a breakdown in regular exchanges between the two sides. Any hopes of pursuing a true trilateral security cooperation remained out of reach during President Moon Jae-in's progressive administration from 2017 to 2022, due both to his emphasis on pursuing peace with North Korea and his skepticism about the prospects for cooperation with Japan. That said, his conservative successor, President Yoon Suk-yeol, took significant steps to improve relations with Tokyo. He declined to make Japanese apologies a precondition for productive ties and re-engaged in shuttle diplomacy with Japanese Prime Minister Fumio Kishida.[26] The Biden administration nurtured this reproachment, hosting a key US–Japan–South Korea trilateral summit at Camp David in 2023.[27]

Most interviewees suggested that a more functional relationship with Japan is likely to remain possible under conservative South Korean administrations. From their perspective, South Korean presidential administrations that view the US alliance relationship as being essential to national security—an outlook currently more aligned with South Korea's conservative party—are also more inclined to pursue pragmatic forms of cooperation with Japan. Several of these experts also implied that, barring a major shift in South Korean politics, future progressive administrations will likely return to the cooler relationship with Japan that characterized the Moon administration. The dynamics of Korean domestic politics are addressed in greater detail in a subsequent section.

Several additional insights raised by the interviewees are also worth noting. First, while nearly all of these experts viewed improved relations between South Korea and Japan as beneficial, most also indicated that the prospects of an outright trilateral alliance remain dim. They suggested that explicit alignment with Japan and the United States against China would likely be perceived as too blunt a tool to gain broad support among South Korean voters.

Second, several interviewees noted that Washington's public calls for improved relations between Seoul and Tokyo are helpful to the extent that they make it easier for South Korean leaders to explain the need for greater cooperation to South Korean voters. These same experts also highlighted a number of uncontroversial ways for achieving "low-end" functional cooperation, such as rehearsing regional disaster responses. One expert also observed that multilateral groupings like the Quad help blunt the impression that South Korea is being asked—or pressured— to work exclusively with Japan. At the same time, the interviewees were skeptical that such low-end and informal efforts would ultimately produce higher-level security cooperation on contentious issues like defending Taiwan. In their view, achieving higher-level cooperation would require greater strategic convergence between Seoul and Tokyo. Accordingly, there remains a need for persistent communication from the United States to demonstrate to South Koreans that deeper trilateral cooperation—specifically on Taiwan-related issues—is in South Korea's interest and will yield tangible benefits for the South Korean public.

Third, notwithstanding the historical animosity between the two countries, Japan's response to a Chinese attack on Taiwan will also influence—and constrain—South Korea's actions. To be sure, Seoul will not base its decisions exclusively on Tokyo's choices. Nevertheless, if Japan permits US forces to conduct combat operations in support of Taiwan from its bases in Japan, provides non-combat support, or commits Japanese combat forces, it will become more difficult for Seoul to refrain from taking similar steps. Conversely, if Japan opts not to pursue one or more of these actions, such a decision would provide rhetorical and political cover for South Korea to do the same.

How South Korea Views the United States

Washington is Still Indispensable... but is Also Seen by Some as in Decline

The interviewees were unanimous: South Korea continues to depend on the United States for its security. If Seoul were suddenly unable to rely on Washington for support and protection against Pyongyang—which it still regards as its most important security threat—South Korean leaders would have no choice but to consider the extreme alternative of acquiring nuclear weapons. The interviewees also expressed a strong conviction that South Korean voters likewise favor maintaining a robust relationship with the United States. One expert cited polling data from 2021 indicating that 77 percent of South Koreans view the United States as both a friendlier and more reliable partner than China. Polling from 2022 echoed these findings, with China viewed more negatively than any other country (81 percent of respondents expressing a negative or very negative attitude), while the United States was viewed more positively than any other (slightly under 75 percent of respondents viewing it positively or very positively).[28]

That said, beneath the surface of this consensus, cracks appear to be forming. Multiple interviewees cautioned that high levels of elite and public support for the alliance should not be interpreted as evidence of unqualified and inalienable faith in US credibility. Many of the South Korean experts interviewed expressed concerns that the United States is experiencing a long-term decline. Several interviewees noted that the 2008 financial crisis continues to cast a long shadow over South Korean perceptions of both the United States and China. This view is particularly evident among the relatively small percentage of Koreans who believe their country's future lies more with China than with the United States (estimated by one analyst to comprise 5 to 10 percent of the Korean population). According to the interviewees, such individuals view Wall Street and Washington as responsible for the global economic collapse and interpret this as evidence that the American system is decadent, corrupt, and in decline. In contrast, they view China's response to the crisis as proof of its ability to build clean, efficient cities and keep its people fed.[29]

The term "power transitions" emerged repeatedly across the interviews. One academic traced South Korean interest in "power transition discourse" to 2008, suggesting that concerns over America's decline and China's rise became more prominent in South Korean analysis of regional security issues following the global financial crisis. Two post-crisis developments have further heightened interest in such shifts. The first was Xi Jinping's rise and demonstrable turn toward authoritarianism. The second was the first election of President Donald Trump, which some South Koreans viewed as parallel evidence of growing authoritarian tendencies within the United States. For South Koreans already inclined toward pro-China views, these developments reinforced their support for deepening South Korea's security and economic ties to China —or at least for finding a way to maintain a posture of neutrality in the event of a future US–China conflict. While only a small portion of South Korean voters hold such views, several interviewees noted that even among pro-US constituencies, there is growing discussion—and in some cases, reluctant acknowledgment—of the relative decline of US power and the corresponding rise in Chinese strength, particularly within Northeast Asia.

It is important to note that the experts who raised this issue still believe that, even in the absence of a strong US presence, the average South Korean voter would remain wary of closer ties with China. As one interviewee succinctly put it, "We would fall under their influence, but would we welcome it, with all the bullying it has entailed throughout history? Unlikely." This official also observed that Japan would be even less likely than South Korea to acquiesce to a more prominent Chinese role in regional affairs. Nonetheless, the interviews suggest there may be greater openness to a pro-China narrative in South Korea than in Japan or Australia. This finding is particularly noteworthy in the context of China's concerted efforts—conducted under the guidance of the CCP's United Front Work Department—aimed at shaping discourse and perceptions in South Korea and beyond.[30]

Elites Trust American Capability (For Now). It is American Resolve that Worries Them

In addition to expressing a unified view of Washington as an indispensable ally, the interviewees also overwhelmingly agreed that American capability is not in doubt, at least not in the short term.[31] Broadly speaking, South Koreans continue to assume that the US military maintains a clear lead over China in terms of technological capacity and warfighting prowess, although several interviewees urged Washington to take further steps to preserve its existing advantages in light of Beijing's concerted efforts to close the gap. That said, among those experts who approached the question from a longer-term perspective, divisions emerged.

A great deal of the disagreement appeared to hinge on how individual experts assessed the relative trajectories of US and Chinese power. Some interviewees viewed China's relative weakness over the past century as a historical anomaly. These experts tended to argue that US decline is already underway and that China will soon return to its "normal" place atop the regional hierarchy. Other interviewees contended that Washington will remain the most powerful actor in the region—albeit perhaps not as dominant as during the height of its "unipolar moment"— and that Beijing faces significant internal problems that will hinder its growth prospects. Interviewees who held this latter view generally suggested that the United States will maintain its dominance over regional security issues for the foreseeable future. It is important to note that the experts advancing this argument did not deny or discount China's eventual ascendence; rather, they emphasized was that it is still too early for South Korea to consider abandoning the US alliance in favor of forging closer ties with China.

Nonetheless, even if the United States' short-term capabilities are not in serious doubt, the interviewees expressed clear reservations about American resolve. One diplomat with experience serving in both the United States and China predicted that domestic politics may well lead the United States to retrench and "give up the Western Pacific" over the coming decades. This official also described conversations with Japanese analysts who harbor similar concerns about the possibility of US retrenchment.

The interviewees cited several incidents—both historical and recent —that have served to undermine their faith in US resolve. Several older experts pointed to the US withdrawal from the Vietnam War, with one specifically referencing the iconic image of the last helicopter leaving Saigon. In his words, "I couldn't believe the US would abandon an ally, and it really put the fear in me as a young kid." More than one interviewee also highlighted the much more recent but similarly chaotic withdrawal of US forces from Afghanistan as a disquieting example of the United States failing to follow through on a commitment, albeit not to a treaty ally.

Along similar lines, one source noted that Korean experts already associate the history of US engagement on Taiwan issues with diminished resolve. This expert argued that when Washington reformulated its military support for Taiwan while shifting diplomatic recognition to China, US officials assured their South Korean counterparts that US forces would remain on the peninsula. In practice, however, Washington still withdrew a ground division from South Korea. This interviewee interpreted the troop withdraw as an attempt to placate China regarding Taiwan and even linked it to South Korea's (ultimately abandoned) pursuit of an independent nuclear deterrent.[32] While this historical nuance is unlikely to play a major role in shaping broader public opinion, it may nonetheless influence how security practitioners draw parallels between US–Taiwan relations and the US–ROK alliance.

One interviewee made the point that Koreans understand the importance of US domestic political support for any international action. This source cited the aftermath of 9/11, when there was no ambiguity about US determination to pursue those responsible. This unity served as a signaling device, demonstrating US resolve and building Korean public support for joining the US-led coalition in Afghanistan. This interviewee suggested that a bipartisan show of unified resolve would be similarly important in the case of any action involving Taiwan. In their words, "You can't have large anti-war protests in Washington, DC, and still expect full Korean support."

When asked about whether and how Taiwan factors into South Korean assessments of US resolve, all the interviewees said that South Korean observers would closely watch how Washington responds—or fails to respond—to a conflict over Taiwan's status. One expert did suggest that the degree to which individual South Korean analysts link US action (or inaction) in a cross-Strait crisis to Washington's commitments to South Korea will depend largely on their familiarity with Taiwan issues. According to this interviewee, while US inaction would likely sow seeds of doubt among the relatively small number of South Korean national security professionals with a deep understanding of cross-Strait relations, most other policymakers would probably "shrug off the implications and simply go about doing their jobs."

How South Korea Thinks about US Options in a Cross-Strait Conflict

If Deterrence Falters, Washington Will be Damned if it Does and Damned if it Doesn't
The interviewees were unanimous in their view that any cross-Strait war would represent a worst-case scenario for Seoul. Their view can be summarized as follows: if China and America fight, no matter who wins, Korea loses. This is because South Korea would face the same fundamental problem, regardless of the outcome: it must still find a way to

coexist with China. Neither an American victory, an American defeat, nor a decision to remain on the sidelines can alter this inexorable challenge.

Making matters worse, if cross-Strait deterrence fails and China attacks, the interviewees suggested that Washington would face harsh criticism in South Korea no matter how it responds. A sizeable number of elites and voters would likely be dissatisfied if the United States defends Taiwan, while many others would be angered if the United States does nothing in response to an attack on its former ally. In essence, South Koreans would be angry with either US intervention or inaction—albeit for different reasons.

According to the interviewees, Washington will come under fire for being an unreliable ally if it opts to do nothing in the face of an overt attack on Taiwan. Critics of inaction will deride Washington for abandoning a vulnerable partner and will cite US inaction as evidence that that Seoul cannot trust Washington to show up on its behalf either—even to defend against an act of North Korean aggression.

Conversely, if the United States moves to defend Taiwan, most of the experts interviewed expect Washington to pressure Seoul to authorize the use of US bases, assets, and forces on the peninsula. Not only would such requests invite Chinese retaliation —or even preemption—against the Republic of Korea, they would also divert resources and attention away from the peninsula, rendering them unavailable for a North Korean contingency. And again: whether the United States wins or loses, South Korea will still have to coexist with China once the dust has settled. Thus, for many South Koreans, any US attempt to uphold its own credibility at the expense of regional stability will be deeply problematic.

Two additional findings are worth noting: First, of the two basic choices facing Washington in the event of a cross-Strait war, most of the Korean experts interviewed believed that intervention was far more likely than non-intervention. As a result, "abandoning" Taiwan would be more likely to catch South Korean leaders and voters off-guard than a decision to defend the island.

Second, when the interviewees were asked for a forced ranking of the worst outcomes, the response was consistent: from the South Korean perspective, the worst possible outcome of a cross-Strait war would be one in which the United States intervenes and suffers a decisive defeat. In this scenario, China would achieve its territorial and political aims while demonstrating its military prowess to the world. Seoul would have provoked Beijing's ire for having sided with Washington. And the United States, having suffered a clear-cut defeat, would no longer be able to shield South Korea from Chinese retaliation and predation or protect it from North Korean aggression.

Conversely, the least-worst of the undesirable scenarios according to all the interviewees is one in which the United States intervenes and achieves a decisive victory. This result would both enhance America's reputation for resolve and leave Beijing in a weakened position, at least temporarily. As one interviewee explained, in Korea's more than three-thousand-year history of interacting with China, "the only good China is a weak China."[33]

If Forced to Choose between Unpalatable Options, Many Might (Secretly) Prefer US Inaction

The majority of the interviewees candidly suggested that many South Koreans might be (quietly) relieved if the United States decides not to come to Taiwan's direct defense, even though this would inevitably undermine alliance confidence. As a matter of both treaty obligation and tradition, South Koreans generally understand that the alliance requires them to support the United States in its military ventures. Almost all of the interviewees pointed out that this is exactly what happened in Vietnam, Afghanistan, and Iraq. As such, US military action in Taiwan would force Seoul to take sides against China in a superpower conflict it would much prefer to avoid. As one former senior officer put it, "if the US did not intervene it would scare us, but I don't think we would mind not getting involved in a war."

Again, the experts interviewed fully expect that Beijing would pressure Seoul not to assist Washington. One expert went so far as to suggest that Beijing might even attempt to coerce Seoul into providing active support for China in such a conflict. This analyst pointed to the construction of a Chinese airport in Busan and Beijing's potential desire to use Busan as a logistics hub. The idea of South Korea succumbing to pressure to side actively with China was raised by only one source and appears to be an implausible edge case. Nonetheless, even if China did not pursue active South Korean support for its military effort, there is little reason to believe it would passively accept and acquiesce to Korean alignment with the United States without imposing some costs on the ROK. This threat looms large in the minds of South Korean security experts.

At the end of the day, according to the interviewed experts, peace and stability in the region are worth more to Seoul than a reinforced sense of US reputation for resolve. Inaction would also ensure that US forces on the Korean peninsula remain focused on, and prepared to deal with, Seoul's top security threat: Pyongyang. Thus, it bears emphasizing that at least from Seoul's vantage point, strengthening the perception of US resolve would be cold comfort given South Korea's dependence on China's economy, its need for Chinese cooperation to manage the North Korean threat, and its preference that the United States "keep its powder dry" to address the same.

Nuclear Dynamics

As highlighted in the introductory chapter, one of the unintended benefits of conducting these interviews over a three-year period was that it allowed for the capture of views both before and after Russia's re-invasion of Ukraine in February 2022. Even prior to that renewed conflict and Vladimir Putin's subsequent nuclear saber-rattling, South Korean experts acknowledged the possibility that a fight between the United States and China over the fate of Taiwan could escalate beyond conventional warfare. At the same time, consistent with the broader sense that Taiwan occupies only a limited place in Seoul's strategic consciousness, when interviewees discussed nuclear issues—whether in response to interview questions or by raising the topic themselves—they had little to say about US–China nuclear dynamics, instead tending to pivot quickly to South Korea's own internal nuclear debate.

Accordingly, the experts who were willing to discuss nuclear weapons made clear that if a fight over Taiwan ever sowed seeds of doubt in the credibility of the US alliance, South Korean leadership would very likely begin exploring or searching for alternate security guarantees. Several of the interviewees expressed a view that, when it comes to deterring North Korean aggression, nuclear weapons are the only viable alternative to a strong US–ROK alliance. In their assessment, Pyongyang has clearly and consistently demonstrated its belief that its most effective deterrent is the possession of nuclear weapons under its own control—and that this thinking likely extends to perceptions of South Korea as well. In other words, security experts in South Korea expect that Kim Jong Un engages in mirroring behavior and would likely project his own belief in the power of nuclear deterrence onto an analogous South Korean capability. The interviewees unanimously stated that the United States government does not appear to be seriously considering the possibility that South Korea could pursue nuclear armament or the downstream ramifications of such a move.

As discussed next, South Korean domestic politics and the party in power would play a role in any exploration of nuclear weapons. One interviewee estimated that approximately 70 percent of South Koreans are in favor of developing nuclear weapons. Recent public polling data corroborate this claim. A 2022 Chicago Council report found that 71 percent of South Korean respondents would support a domestic nuclear weapons program, compared to 56 percent who would favor the deployment of US nuclear weapons in South Korea.[34] Nevertheless, modern progressive administrations, such as that of President Moon Jae-in, have shown little appetite for pursuing such a course. Although war in the region could certainly shift this calculus, in the current political climate, the interviewees assessed that a conservative administration would be notably more likely to move in this direction than a progressive one.

What Might South Korea Do in Response to a Taiwan Crisis?

Again, because it would find itself "trapped" between two whales, Seoul —perhaps even more so than Tokyo or Canberra—prefers peace and stability in the Taiwan Strait over a conflict that forces it to choose sides. Uniquely among America's Pacific allies, the interviewees in South Korea suggested that if war comes to the Taiwan Strait, South Korean leaders would likely be less concerned with the ultimate outcome than with navigating the conflict and staying out of harm's way.

The interviews revealed several possible ways that South Koreans think their country might respond to a war over Taiwan. From Washington's perspective, the worst-case scenario would be one in which Seoul actively supports Beijing. Thankfully, bandwagoning appears to be a remote possibility. The interviewees—almost unanimously—deemed it unlikely, and public opinion polls, which portray a population that is highly distrustful of Beijing, reinforce its implausibility. Logically, it is also difficult to imagine how any South Korean administration could trust China immediately after it had demonstrated a willingness to use force against a neighbor to realize its ambitions. Suffice it to say, if South Korea were to provide overt support for China in a cross-Strait war, it would mean the functional termination of the US–ROK alliance.

In terms of more realistic possibilities, the interviewees suggested several potential approaches. At one extreme, Seoul might attempt to remain aloof from the conflict by declining to participate in combat operations, refraining from supporting non-combat operations, and denying US forces engaged in the fight access to US bases on South Korean soil. An intermediate stance would involve providing either tacit or overt approval for the United States to use forces and logistics capabilities based in South Korea, while ensuring that South Korean military forces played no role, either directly or indirectly. A third option would be to allow South Korean forces to assume a non-combat role, including the provision of logistical, humanitarian, and medical support for either the Taiwanese people, US forces, or both. At the opposite extreme, it is possible—although unlikely according to almost all interviewees—that Seoul might authorize its forces to participate in combat operations.

When the interviewed experts were asked to identify what they considered to be the best—or least bad—ways for South Korean involvement to take shape, they all expressed hesitance about South Korea participating directly in combat. One former military officer argued that the most useful option is to leave South Korean forces in place to "tie down" China's northern forces, which comprise approximately one-fifth of the PLA's total strength. This expert argued that the South Korean military lacks the combat capability to meaningfully alter the military balance in a cross-Strait war, but that the mere presence of South Korean troops on the Korean Peninsula, particularly if augmented by a continued US ground presence, will prevent Beijing from concentrating its own forces on the Taiwan theater of action. This expert also pointed out that the fight for Taiwan might be over before South Korean military units could arrive in force. They estimated that it would take at least a month, and potentially longer, to deploy even a limited number of special forces and light infantry units—capabilities that might be of limited utility in a primarily air and naval conflict.

In discussing the disposition of US forces and bases in Korea, one source observed that Seoul would seek to enable operational flexibility for the United States while also maintaining plausible deniability in its dealings with Beijing. For this reason, while the United States continues to reserve the right to use US troops for purposes other than a Korean Peninsula contingency, US and South Korean officials have never officially agreed on the details and parameters that would be acceptable. The current tacit understanding, as characterized by one former Korean military officer, is that any US forces based in Korea that depart the peninsula would not flow directly into an operational theater but would instead first redeploy to another US base (such as in Okinawa) for at least a day before moving onward. This source emphasized the importance of maintaining these sorts of useful fictions to give South Korean leaders the flexibility to navigate domestic political realities while managing their relationship with China.

Again, it bears repeating: the overall impression conveyed by the interviewees was one of hesitation and ambivalence regarding any South Korean involvement in military action against China. Even when asked about direct action, the sources uniformly averred and shifted the focus to ways South Korea could contribute to the effort without actually fighting China.

Domestic Politics Will Loom Large

One final point, underscored by the events surrounding President Yoon's short-lived declaration of martial law in late 2024, is worth keeping in mind: the interviewees made clear that domestic politics will loom large over Seoul's calculus—perhaps even more so than in Tokyo or Canberra.[35] These experts agreed that if forced to pick sides, any South Korean presidential administration would find itself torn between constituents who fear Chinese retaliation and those who seek to remain faithful to the US–ROK alliance. Ultimately, three factors in particular seem likely to influence whether Seoul decides to risk abandonment or entanglement.

The first and most obvious factor concerns which party occupies the Blue House when the conflict erupts.[36] All interviewees agreed that Seoul would be more likely to accede to Washington's requests if the conservative People Power Party (PPP) is in power than if the liberal Democratic Party of Korea (DPK) holds control. In general, the PPP and its voters tend to align more closely with Washington's leadership, creating more space for US–ROK cooperation under a PPP administration. A conservative administration is also more likely to place greater emphasis on Washington's commitment to alliance management and the maintenance of US credibility, even if doing so increases tensions with Beijing. The opposite dynamic would likely prevail if the DPK holds power. In fact, several interviewees suggested that some liberal South Korean politicians might view it as acceptable for the United States to sacrifice some of its credibility if doing so allows South Korea to maintain peace and stability on the Korean peninsula.

This basic contrast between the PPP and the DPK certainly held true during the Moon and Yoon administrations. President Moon Jae-in of the DPK led South Korea from 2017 to 2021, a period during which the country emphasized pursuing peace with North Korea and minimizing tensions with China. As a result, the Moon administration effectively reoriented South Korea toward China and away from the United States and Japan. South Korea's 2022 presidential election returned the PPP to power, with President Yoon Suk-yeol prevailing in the closest election in South Korean history. From Washington's perspective, Yoon's victory marked an improvement in bilateral relations. His constituency was generally more supportive of closer ties with the United States, meaning he faced fewer political consequences for improving relations with the United States than a DPK president might. Such partisan tendencies seem likely to hold so long as neither party undergoes a major realignment in the near future.[37]

Second, several experts suggested that demographics will also play a role in determining how the country responds to a Taiwan crisis. In particular, interviewees noted that South Korean attitudes and perceptions of the US alliance are heavily influenced by generational dynamics. When weighing the competing priorities of maintaining a tight relationship with Washington against avoiding antagonizing Beijing, older South Koreans—especially those with living memories of the Korean War—are generally more likely to emphasize the importance of the US–ROK alliance. Similarly, as one South Korean diplomat explained, if the United States remained on the sidelines as China attacked Taiwan, older South Koreans would be more likely to respond with deep concern. By contrast, interviewees expressed the view that younger Koreans might be less disturbed by US inaction in response to a crisis over Taiwan, and might even appreciate a US decision that avoids a conflict with China.

Culture is likely to serve as a third factor. Although some younger South Koreans view themselves as Western-oriented, others are more comfortable with the Confucian tradition. As one expert put it, "there are as many Koreans who can recite Three Kingdoms as the Bible." The CCP is actively cultivating this support base, engaging directly through its United Front in efforts to shape South Korean popular culture and attitudes in a manner that emphasizes historical connection. Such cultural affinity will inevitably affect public opinion, which will, in turn, be expressed politically through voter sentiment. Although the United States has enjoyed decades of support from South Koreans who feel deep gratitude for American involvement in the Korean War, the continuation of that affinity into the future cannot necessarily be assumed.

NOTES

1. For an overview of the unique aspects of this combined military relationship, see Park, "An Analysis and Lessons on South Korea's Attempt"; Botto, "Why Doesn't South Korea Have Full Control"; Chanlett-Avery, Campbell, and Arabia, *U.S.-South Korea Alliance*; Manyin et al., *U.S.-South Korea Alliance*, 18–27.
2. South Korea seems to be more concerned about being trapped in what Glenn Snyder refers to as the "alliance security dilemma" than either Australia or Japan. Whereas Snyder initially thought of entrapment as something only great powers worried about, more recent scholarship suggests that "junior" partners are also troubled by the prospect of being pulled into a fight. See Moller, "Domestic Politics, Threat Perceptions." Recall that we define abandonment as occurring when one ostensible ally fails to honor its commitment to support or defend the other; entanglement as when one ally feels compelled to enter an expensive and unnecessary conflict solely to uphold previous explicit commitments; and entrapment as a form of entanglement in which an ally deliberately provokes a conflict in order to draw the other into it.
3. For a succinct discussion of how this challenge plays out today, see Lee, "South Korea is Caught."
4. For a more extensive discussion of the US-ROK alliance and its origins, see Cha, *Powerplay*; Izumikawa, "Network Connections."
5. Lee and Liff, "Reassessing Seoul's 'One China' Policy," 746.
6. Kim, "By Any Other Name?"
7. Lee and Liff, "Reassessing Seoul's 'One China' Policy," 754.
8. The preceding data is from "South Korea Country Profile," (Observatory of Economic Complexity, October 12, 2023). https://oec.world/en/profile/country/kor; "South Korea / China," (Observatory of Economic Complexity, May 16, 2024). https://oec.world/en/profile/bilateral-country/kor/partner/chn
9. For a complete list of Confucius centers in South Korea (and around the world) as of late 2024, see "Confucius Institutes Around the World - 2024."
10. Of this number, 472,000 are ethnic Koreans with Chinese citizenship and 135,000 are ethnic Chinese with Chinese citizenship. See Yi, "Number of

Foreign Nationals in Korea"; Kang, "Number of Immigrants in S. Korea Rises."

11. This number is still considerably less than the pre-COVID total of 1.1 million. See Kim, "Number of foreigners in Korea up."

12. Regarding the Chinese Communist Party's specific efforts to influence South Korean public opinion on Taiwan, one interviewee noted that the South Korean press began to pay greater attention to Taiwan in late 2021. Another expert, however, alleged that Beijing has been paying South Korean journalists to avoid covering cross-Strait issues. While we include this observation for completeness, verifying its accuracy lies beyond the scope and resources of this project.

13. Cooper, "Biden's Asia Diplomacy is Still Incomplete"; Turcsanyi and Song, "South Koreans Have the Most Negative Views of China."

14. Dong and Kang, "How Should South Korea Respond."

15. Silver, Devlin, and Huang, *Unfavorable Views of China.*

16. Dong and Kang, "How Should South Korea Respond"; Turcsanyi and Song, "South Koreans Have the Most Negative Views of China."

17. For details on the THAAD missile defense system, see Feickert, *The Terminal High Altitude Air Defense (THAAD) System.*

18. U.S. Forces Korea, Office of Public Affairs Office, "ROK & U.S. Joint Statement."

19. Taylor, "Why China is so Mad About THAAD."

20. Lotte is South Korea's fifth largest multinational conglomerate. At the time of the THAAD deployment it operated approximately 100 retail stores within China.

21. Lim, *Chinese Economic Coercion.*

22. Kim, "When China and U.S. Spar."

23. Rich and Brueggemann, "South Korean Views."

24. United States Congress, House Committee on Rules, *Statement before the House Committee on Rules, "Examining China's Coercive Economic Tactics"*, 118th Congress.

25. Several experts noted that certain South Korean politicians are occasionally willing to seize upon and amplify such talking points, as Japan-bashing and emphasizing a narrative of historical victimization can offer electoral advantages.

26. Choe and Motoko, "Leaders of Japan and South Korea."

27. White House, "The Spirit of Camp David."

28. Turcsányi et al., "South Korean public opinion on the world."

29. Time constraints prevented us from asking these interviewees whether their views shifted as more information emerged about the impact and consequences of China's now well-documented COVID-19 lockdown protocols.

30. For an overview of United Front work in South Korea, see Hsiao, "A Preliminary Survey of PRC."

31. As defined in the introductory chapter, capability refers to an actor's ability to follow through on its threats and assurances.

32. For a detailed discussion of this episode as well as the link between US troop levels and South Korean perceptions of American credibility, see Fitzpatrick, *Asia's Latent Nuclear Powers*, 18–22; Lanoszka, *Atomic Assurance*, 110–131.

33. Several experts noted that the actual best-case conflict scenario would involve Washington abandoning Taipei, but Taiwanese forces nevertheless repelling a Chinese invasion on their own. Although the United States would lose some credibility for failing to intervene, this outcome would spare Seoul from having to choose between Beijing and Washington—even as the Chinese military suffers a humiliating defeat on the global stage. That said, consistent with the overarching approach introduced in chapter 1, this theoretically possible but practically implausible scenario is not explored in any real depth.

34. Dalton, Friedhoff, and Kim, *Thinking Nuclear*.

35. We submitted the final version of this manuscript as impeachment proceedings against President Yoon for declaring martial law on December 3, 2024, were getting underway.

36. While this observation may strike many readers as a truism, it is important to recall that Japan's Liberal Democratic Party exercised de facto one-party control over foreign policy for much of the country's modern history. Moreover, our conversations with experts in and on Japan did not suggest that domestic politics and voter preferences are likely to influence Japanese leaders' decision-making to the same degree as they might for their South Korean counterparts. As noted in chapter 2, one of our key findings is that Japanese foreign policy elites are well positioned to shape public opinion—particularly if Washington provides a plausible rationale for its actions (or inaction), reinforced by corresponding military moves.

37. The caveat to this statement is that, relative to the United States as a baseline, South Korea experiences more frequent emergence of new political parties, and party identification tends to be more fluid.

CHAPTER 4

AUSTRALIA

Australia presents the final case in this analysis. Unlike Seoul and Tokyo, Canberra benefits from a significantly greater geographic buffer in any potential conflict over Taiwan's status. Nevertheless, like the other two American allies examined, Australia suffers from a security paradox that will complicate both its choices in a Taiwan crisis and its responses to American action or inaction. Namely, the tighter its relationship with the United States becomes, the greater the threat it faces from China. At the same time, the higher the likelihood of conflict with China, the more Australia will need the United States. Meanwhile, the PRC remains an indispensable market, accounting for more than a quarter of Australia's total trade in goods and services with the world in 2023.[1] Put simply, Canberra, like Seoul and Tokyo, faces a difficult balancing act.

Across the board, Australian interviewees expressed the view that the United States does not fully appreciate the hard choices faced by Australia and the other Pacific allies. Alongside repeated assurances that Australia continues to value the alliance, these interviewees consistently indicated that Washington is taking Australia's support for granted, particularly with regard to the Taiwan issue. One source cautioned Washington policymakers to bear in mind that several of Australia's most vocal Taiwan hawks, however loud, are not broadly representative of the Australian public or political class. One expert offered this succinct summary:

> In Washington, both looking back over the last ten years and today, there is a very deep-seated failure to understand how complex the choices the countries in Asia face are. There are two things Americans don't fully understand. One, how much their allies in the region are afraid of making an economic enemy of China. And two, that allies' faith in America isn't as deep or as steadfast as Americans think they are. People in the region will pick the side that looks like it is going to prevail over the long haul. And American analysts have systematically underestimated Chinese power, which causes the US to underestimate in a systematic way how big the stick and how big the carrot is that China is waving at us in the region.

Thus, it may come as a surprise to some readers that when it came to the question of how Canberra thinks about Washington's options in a war over Taiwan, experts in Australia presented a uniformly pragmatic view, framed in realpolitik terms. As they explained it, any Chinese attack on Taiwan would unequivocally demonstrate that China is revanchist, thereby convincing Australians of the need for the US alliance. These experts were unanimous in their view that this dynamic would unfold regardless of whether Washington intervenes or remains on the sidelines. Provided that the United States retains a robust military presence in the region, none of the interviewees expect Canberra to fully acquiesce to Chinese regional hegemony in the Pacific. As such, even in the face of US inaction or an outright US defeat, the interviewees expect Australia would still double down on its own defense preparations, which would likely include a combination of purchasing additional US weaponry and recommitting to the US alliance.

What follows is the summary of the findings as they relate to particular aspects of the security challenges posed by Chinese aggression toward Taiwan, including the specific ramifications for Australia and the potential impacts on its alliance with the United States. The discussion begins with Australian perspectives on the Australia-US alliance followed by an examination of how Canberra's thinks about its other regional relationships. It concludes with a summary of the interviewees' views on how they believe Australia might react to various ways a war over Taiwan could unfold.

How Australia Views the United States

Mates, but Not Quite as Close as Washington Thinks
The interviews revealed a strong consensus that both policymakers and the Australian public view the United States positively and regard the Australia-US alliance as relevant and important. Recent Lowy Institute polling supports this view, reporting that as of 2024 "the vast majority of Australians (83%) say the alliance is 'very important' or 'fairly important' to Australia's security, steady from last year and five points below a record high of 87% in 2022."[2] Nonetheless, beneath this generally positive view, many experts expressed lingering doubts—concerns that they emphasized may not be well understood in Washington.

On the positive side, the United States remains generally trusted in Australia, though the interviewees also noted a generational shift at work whereby younger Australians, relative to their predecessors, tend to be more wary of US power and less trustful of US intentions. They suggest this shift is likely the result of several decades spent emphasizing Australia's status as a Pacific country with a close economic relationship with China. Politically, both major parties in Australia strongly support and back the alliance. The Morrison government emphasized the relationship more than most administrations since World War II, and the Albanese administration continued this support and focus, albeit with a different rhetorical tone. The defense experts among the interviewees also described a doubling down on the alliance in recent years, citing the 2018 celebration of "100 Years of Mateship," the enduring importance of the

Security Treaty between Australia, New Zealand, and the United States of America (ANZUS),[3] and the more recent announcement of AUKUS.[4]

At the same time, most of the experts interviewed also expressed some trepidation around the rhetorical focus on the alliance's profile. As one put it, "The more people talk about something, the more anxious they are about it." Several mentioned that the first Trump administration served as a reminder that even the friendliest alliance relationships carry a strong undercurrent of transactional utilitarianism.

The interviewees likewise agreed that the conventional view in Australia is that US credibility depends on its willingness to challenge China and confront Chinese aggression. Yet many of these same experts also indicated that this view has become outdated and does not hold up to intense scrutiny. Along these lines, one source posited that policymakers are more wedded to the idea that the United States will remain the strongest military power in the world than is the case among the voting public. In this expert's view, "If you argue to bureaucratic audiences in Canberra that the US might not be as militarily powerful, you get a lot of pushback. I think this speaks to the fact that, the more people have a professional stake in the outcome of the US–Australia relationship, the more impetus they have to psychologically sustain it."

Experts also acknowledged that the trilateral security partnership known as AUKUS was intended to signal a recommitment and deepening of the alliance, though some doubts persist. Furthermore, multiple interviewees characterized Australia as "gripping on to the United States more and more fervently" or "jumping up and down saying to Washington, 'We are at the front line of the new Cold War, so you cannot abandon us.'"

When asked how they assessed the American view of Taiwan, several experts expressed the belief that the defense of Taiwan remains in the US national interest, but that it is not a vital US interest. They noted, however, that this is probably the viewpoint of a minority of Australian experts who follow the issue closely, and they suggested that in Canberra overall there is a "rusted-on consensus that it is in America's interest to defend Taiwan, because if they don't it would be the end of the alliance system."

One interviewee warned against a failure of imagination, whereby American experts—even those with sophistication and experience—find it hard to conceive of China (or any country, for that matter) with an economy larger than America's and the ability to seriously challenge American dominance at sea. By contrast, according to this expert, the countries of the Western Pacific have no difficulty imagining a world in which China is this powerful, and it informs their thinking about the region, the US–Australia alliance, and Taiwan.

Strategic clarity? Yes please—for Canberra. No thanks—for Taipei

In addition to a desire for Washington to adopt a more realistic view of the hard choices its allies face, several experts also indicated that Canberra would benefit from greater clarity regarding US goals. To be clear, experts were not advocating an end to the policy of strategic ambiguity over Taiwan. This was one of the few areas where the interviewees were unanimous: despite the well-understood shortcomings of the policy, all agreed that it remains the least-bad option and should be maintained.

Unfortunately, one of those shortcomings is that, to maintain plausible ambiguity vis-à-vis China, the United States must also inject some uncertainty into the minds of its allies. Several interviewees noted that much of Australia's decision-making is based on what Washington wants, so the degree to which Australia lacks clarity regarding its ally's goals leads to suboptimal policy design.

Still, there was a clear consensus among Australian interviewees that strategic ambiguity vis-à-vis Taiwan creates optionality, space for negotiations, and room to maneuver. Given the strength of America's commitment to the region to date, interviewees offered no cons to maintaining the position. In other words, none believed that ambiguity diminished either allies' or China's perception that the United States could credibly engage in a conflict. As one said, "Australia would hate strategic clarity. The status quo is not static, and to maintain an uneasy peace you have to meet the aggressor as they up the ante. I don't have a preferred outcome for how I'd like to see things look in twenty years, but strategic clarity is unlikely to make Taiwan more safe."

Several sources also pointed out that strategic clarity could come in one of two forms: either a commitment to defend Taiwan, or outright abandonment. None of the interviewees favored the latter option. All believed that throwing Taiwan to the wolves would embolden Xi Jinping without providing any strategic benefits to the US or its allies. Meanwhile, interviewees indicated that the opposite option—shedding ambiguity in favor of a clear commitment—would increase risk by causing Xi Jinping to feel that his window of opportunity is closing.

Respondents also noted that the US policy of ambiguity is honest. They believe that, ex ante, Washington does not actually know how it will respond to a crisis because the response will depend on the facts and nature of the crisis at-hand. One characterized the US level of resolve not as a secret but rather a known unknown.

Multiple interviewees also acknowledged that, despite the name, strategic ambiguity is less a strategy than a tactic, in that it reflects an effort to prolong the status quo without specifying an intended end state. In terms of achievable goals, most interviewees offered some version of "the best realistic outcome is for each side to have a standoff until at some point one side grows too weak or both sides find this too costly," at which point negotiations could commence. On the other hand, they also acknowledged a fundamental problem with negotiations: unlike arms control or the South China Sea, Taiwan is not divisible, nor does it lend itself to the kinds of side payments and issue linkages that typically facilitate a negotiated settlement.[5] With this reality in mind, two interviewees suggested that the United States encourage Taiwan to begin seriously considering, when the time comes, how it can most effectively negotiate toward an outcome that, while unsatisfactory to all, would still allow it to exist in some form.

How Australia Views its Other Pacific Partnerships

Japan Above All

By far the most important regional player in the minds of the interviewees is Japan. Several emphasized that Japan is Australia's most trusted regional partner after New Zealand, that Canberra is fully committed to cooperation with Tokyo, and that Australia would welcome even higher levels of coordination and cooperation on matters such as maritime operations. Initiatives like the 2022 Japan-Australia Reciprocal Access Agreement, which establishes a legal framework for defense cooperation, are emblematic of this desire.[6] Indeed, one source noted that the close relationship between Australia and Japan is not sufficiently recognized in Washington.

Interviewees also unanimously agreed that in any Taiwan contingency, Japan will be by far the most important US ally in the region. That said, these experts disagreed significantly regarding how Japan would react to US action versus inaction, as well as how Japan's choices would shape Australia's. Opinions on these questions were widely divergent.

Interestingly, one important area of consensus among Australian interviewees was the belief that the United States may be overestimating Japanese resolve. One source advised, "Right at the heart of Japan's strategic culture is a pretty vivid sense of living next door to China and finding that fine line of where and how much to push." Another source noted that Japan's vulnerability to Chinese missile strikes necessitates caution, and for that reason Australia would not be surprised if Japan stayed out of the fight as long as China refrained from striking targets in Japan. At the same time, other interviewees suggested that US decisions around Taiwan could be the factor that determines Japan's reaction and its defense posture going forward: "A significant blow to US credibility— like a no-show over Taiwan—could nudge Japan over to a self-reliant defense policy rather easily."

Other players: South Korea and Indonesia

In discussing the regional alliance dynamics, interviewees expressed a consensus that South Korea does not feature significantly in Australian strategic thinking. As one expert put it:

> The general view of the Australian policy elite on Korea would be a wish that the Koreans would focus more on the wider region than they do. But for the Koreans this is just hard to do because of the magnetic pull of the North. So, we don't really have many expectations beyond talking to them and trying to involve them where and when we can.

Others echoed this sentiment, presenting a consensus that Canberra would welcome more constructive engagement by Seoul but is not counting on or even expecting it.

Finally, one interviewee noted that, for Australia, Indonesia remains one of the most important players in the region. Among the countries closest to Australia, Indonesia is the most powerful, and in a US–China confrontation, the degree to which Indonesia remained aloof or supported one side or the other would likely also factor into Australia's calculations. Sources explained that while Indonesia is less significant in this regard than Japan—and certainly far less so than the United States—its choices will still matter to Canberra, and indeed far more there than in Washington.

How Australia Views China

Increasing Consensus and Growing Concern

In the eyes of both the general public and security experts, Australia's relationship with China is characterized first by economic dependence, tempered in more recent years by an uneasy sense that China is becoming an increasingly dangerous partner. For several decades, Australia has recognized that China is both naturally its largest trading partner and the most important source of its future growth. As one interviewee put it,

Australia has been claiming for the last twenty years that we are Asian and are part of the Asian Century. The reason is because we've wanted to sell stuff to China. This has been a generational project. So, shifting that framing to China as a problem is a hard wake-up call. Australia and China also have very complementary economies, unlike the competitive economies between China and the US.

That said, Australian attitudes toward China have turned sharply negative in recent years. Many interviewees identified 2020 as a particularly noteworthy inflection point in Australian public and expert sentiment vis-à-vis China. They cited several inciting events that year. First was China's increasingly aggressive behavior toward Australia, including targeted punitive measures directed against the Australian economy.[7] These actions drew extensive media coverage, driving greater awareness among the Australian public. Additionally, concerns, particularly among younger Australians, about China's human rights violations have made it impossible for the Australian business community to offer the full-throated support of China that it had in the past. Indeed, a poll by the Lowy Institute found that the percentage of Australians who viewed China as more of a security threat than an economic partner had risen from 15 percent in 2015 to 53 percent in 2023 (and had reached 63 percent the year prior).[8]

According to the interviewees, Australia's resilience in the face of Chinese coercive economic policies is likewise relevant.[9] Although Chinese pressure tactics had an effect, they did not destroy the Australian economy. Interviewees suggested that Australia's economic fortitude and flexibility reduced the sense of existential dread that Australians had previously associated with Chinese economic threats.

A substantial shift in attitude toward China among voters and experts has occurred. Sizable majorities are now mistrustful of China. As one interviewee put it, "China has been doing everything it can to alienate populations in every country. Now with economic coercion, we are seeing negative attitudes on China sinking in deep. There is now no political room to make an argument that we need to come to terms with China." Or, as another described the situation: "It used to be true that elite opinion was evenly divided between the economic half and the security half. This division has not completely disappeared, but the economic argument has lost a lot of credibility. There has been a shift to a more critical view of China, based on the realization that in the end we didn't really have the choice between economics and security because of China's actions."

Several experts similarly noted that elite attitudes toward China have coalesced into two narrower, politically cross-cutting camps: China hawks and China realists. As one analyst put it, "The hawks think China is Nazi Germany. There are some who think the conquest of Taiwan would be an appetizer, not the dessert, and would be the start of a march north, south, or eastward." That same speaker referred to realists as those who: "see China as a rising power that may behave in ways we don't like, but that the attempt to change that behavior can cause even greater problems."

Belief that in Beijing, the Clock is Ticking
When asked follow-up questions about this so-called "hawk versus realist" divide, most interviewees used the opportunity to discuss each camp's assessment of Chinese intentions and capabilities. Regarding Beijing's intentions, the interviewees were unanimous on two points. First, all believed that China seeks to displace the United States as the primary power in the Western Pacific and that it is attempting to realize this ambition by increasing the cost of the American presence in the region and eroding Washington's credibility as an alliance partner.

Second, the interviewees all believed that Beijing feels a sense of urgency. One source stated, "If you talk to Japan, they will say that China has about a decade to establish a hegemonic position, a strategic order where they are at the center and they make the orders and rules, while the United States is preoccupied and before their population gets too old. So, I think we see a lot of pushing by China." Several other experts offered a more ominous framing, suggesting that Beijing is increasingly aware that time is no longer on its side, especially when it comes to Taiwan. Chinese leaders may therefore be more willing to press their luck when it comes to seeking a resolution to the "Taiwan problem". In one interviewee's words: "That doesn't mean we are specifically worried about an invasion of Taiwan per se, but rather that we now see Xi as a lot more unpredictable, more willing to use force, and not caring about international blowback." This viewpoint dovetails with observations that Xi may feel an imperative to resolve the Taiwan question during the remaining time he has available as China's leader.

Expert assessments differed when it came to Chinese capabilities. Some interviewees were confident that China already has the strength and geographic advantages it needs to press its advantage. As one interviewee put it, "If this were about American power in the Caribbean, then I would have a very different view. It's in China's backyard and it is unfolding in an era when China has the military and economic power to do something about it." The cogent summary of this viewpoint on defending Taiwan was: "The cost that China can impose on the US is now exceeding America's imperative to do so." However, other experts saw China as at risk of underestimating American resolve and overconfident based on capabilities that it has yet to fully develop or master. As one interviewee related when talking about the PLA Navy, "It's not a small thing to have an aircraft carrier battle group. But it takes a generation to turn that operational."

The interviewees did not express a consensus on whether they expect China to achieve its strategic aims, but many agreed that these goals are understandable and logically consistent. As one put it, "The CCP does see high stakes in Taiwan, but that doesn't make it insane. You can be unreasonable, but that doesn't make you irrational."

How Australia Views Taiwan[10]

Australians like Taiwan, When They Are Reminded it's Like Australia

When asked how much Taiwan matters to Australia, interviewees noted a divide between public and elite opinion. In characterizing Australian public sentiment toward Taiwan, interviewees unanimously expressed a version of the sentiment that while feelings are generally positive and warm, this favorability has its limits. Beyond the shared sense that Australia and Taiwan are island nations facing larger global threats, there is minimal awareness of Taiwan's specific challenges or their relevance to Australian security issues. As one respondent put it, "Australians will notice the similarities between Australia and Taiwan—democracy, population, economy size, on an island—but only when it's pointed out, usually by hawkish defense types." Or, as another interviewee stated, "The surfer crowd on the beach probably doesn't care. But if you couch it in terms of a vibrant democracy of 24 million people who live on an island, and then ask where people stand on supporting that island or standing with others to defend it against a threat, most would be committal to the defense of Taiwan."

More pointedly, interviewees almost uniformly indicated that, as one put it, "in the public eye, the issue is exclusively framed as a 'Would we go to war if the US does?'" Indeed, some suggested that polls showing hypothetical support for Taiwan are suspect, and that there is a danger of placing too much confidence in potential public support for an effort that many might not see as Australia's fight. One interviewee was especially forceful in making this point:

> Overwhelmingly, Australians care about Taiwan as a proxy or symbol of US commitment to the region. I get that Taiwan is an easy place to like and to want to help. But few Australians could even find Taiwan on a map. And no one in government would see

Taiwan as actually important to Australian security, aside from its importance as a decisive test of American commitment.

According to this viewpoint, Taiwan's security is not a vital Australian interest beyond serving as a bellwether for US credibility.

Defense Experts See Taiwan as a US Alliance Issue and a Regional One

The interviewees suggested that attitudes are more nuanced among defense and security experts. Nevertheless, several consensus viewpoints emerged from the interviews. First, Australian security experts are keen to remain close to the United States but are cautious on Taiwan— one interviewee characterized Australian policy as "reluctant"—because they take the threat from China seriously. This dynamic feeds into the aforementioned security paradox: as one interviewee put it, "closeness with the US brings greater threat with China, but greater likelihood of conflict with China means needing the US more."

However, Australia's dependency on the United States can lead to an overstatement of Australian resolve. Various security experts described an inclination toward virtue signaling and empty rhetoric. As one interviewee put it in a representative comment:

> If an Australian foreign policy leader gets a microphone shoved in his face and is asked: 'Is Taiwan important?' they will likely say 'Yes it is.' And certainly, there is more pressure coming from the United States to think about Taiwan contingencies and what to do in them. But I don't see Australia making policy moves at the Prime Ministerial level. From what I've seen the government has been very careful *not* to go beyond the positions that it formally holds on Taiwan.

Second, several experts stressed that the loudest Australian voices on this issue are not necessarily the most important. They emphasized that this point should be specifically communicated to the US policy audience, noting that in recent years several hawkish commentators have written extensively on why Australia needs to prepare for a military confrontation over Taiwan. However, several of the experts interviewed pointed out that, although these voices may seem prominent to a US audience due to their ability to attract attention, they are largely not influential or listened to within the Australian government.

In explaining why these hawks may hold as much weight domestically as they seem, one of the sources who made this point critiqued their line of argumentation:

> Nobody in Australia wants to see Taiwan fall under the PRC's control. But those who would advocate for Australia to join in a coalition to fight often rely on conjecture and domino intuition: If Taiwan falls, Indonesia falls, New Zealand falls, and Australia falls. The whole rhetoric of the First Island Chain. Personally, I think the whole idea that if Taiwan falls then Japan falls inexorably is specious reasoning.

Finally, multiple experts emphasized that Australia's defense thinking on Taiwan is closely linked to broader regional issues. One expert ran through the list:

> For the policy community, it's not just about Taiwan, it's about defense of Japan, access to the Pacific—China's ability to put submarine forces into the Pacific without the US seeing them—the nature of the democracy, and Chinese pride. Everyone thought we could ignore Taiwan for a while, but Xi has brought the issue forward and made it an issue of domestic pride and his Chinese Dream. More central to Australia though is Indonesia and Southeast Asia. But Taiwan is central because it's the place where the US can be tested.

In other words, while Australian elites might tend to think about a Taiwan contingency in terms of what it might reveal about US commitment, the fate of Taiwan is directly relevant to Japan and significant to Australia for its implications on Chinese power projection.

Nonetheless, the interviewees did not seem to view these concerns as constituting a matter of strategic national interest for Australia, and almost none emphasized the ideological dimensions of a conflict between the Communist Party-led China and Taiwan as a democracy. As one interviewee put it, "Imagine a sort of KMT-led government coming to some accommodation to One Country/Two Systems. That might have seemed plausible 10 years ago, and it wouldn't have concerned Australia very much, because the strategic implications are less important for us."

Australia's Sense of Taiwan's Defensive Posture
When asked to assess Taiwan's defensive preparations, the Australia experts did not generally express strong opinions on the matter. One interviewee explicitly noted that the Australian government has likely not reached a conclusion on the subject because Canberra's thinking on Taiwan is less developed than Washington's.

That said, the experts who did respond to this line of inquiry were clear in their view that Taiwan has not yet done enough to prepare for the possibility of war. They articulated a consensus vision for what effective preparation by Taiwan would look like: making the island as defensible as possible with the goals of deterring invasion and ensuring that even a successful outcome for China would come at a bitter cost. One expert urged Taiwan to transform itself into "the poison shrimp"—something that China might be able to consume but ultimately would be unable to digest (in contrast to what Beijing has succeeded in doing with Hong Kong). Australian analysts suggest that, to achieve this, Taiwan must be willing to reorient its force structure away from a traditional emphasis on large ships and tanks, while also strengthening the country's will and ability to maintain resolve. As to whether Taiwan would actually be willing and able to accomplish these objectives, the few analysts who expressed an opinion voiced their doubts.

The US Alliance and the Taiwan Question

Would Australia Fight for Taiwan? Maybe. But Not Definitely
When posed with the direct question of whether Australia would fight for Taiwan if the United States did, opinions among the analysts interviewed were decidedly mixed. All those consulted conceded that Washington would likely expect Australian forces to participate and that internal and external pressure to engage in combat operations would be significant. They anticipated the United States would view the decision as a test of Australia's resolve, particularly since, as multiple sources noted, Australia has intentionally cultivated a reputation as being America's most reliable ally. Indeed, one expert described it as a point of national pride that Australia has fought side by side with United States in every war since 1917.

At the same time, three-quarters of the interviewees also said the many public proclamations that Australia would have no choice but to fight are simply wrong. As a matter of both law and policy, Australia would indeed be able to choose whether to get involved at all, as well as calibrate its level of involvement.[11] Indeed, one Australian defense expert described the country as "the foremost advocate and practitioner of the art of token contributions." The question then becomes whether Australia's oft-stated willingness to stand by the United States reflects true intent, a tactical effort to bolster deterrence credibility, or mere cheap talk.

The interviewees did not frame the decision as one likely to be shaped significantly by direct Chinese coercion, though not for lack of effort on Beijing's part. The experts stated that they fully expect China to do everything in its power to pressure Australia to stay out of the conflict. They suggested that massive cyber-attacks, aggressive economic pressure, curtailed access to Chinese markets, and even hostage diplomacy targeting Australians living in China could all be "on the table." However, they went on to mention that, unless the United States is seen to be the force driving the initiation of the conflict, these measures alone would be unlikely to peel Australia away from the United States. One source related this to the national character of Australia: "The more you try and coerce Australians not to do something, the more likely they are to do it. If we have to go in with one arm behind our backs, we still go in swinging."

Nonetheless, opinions remained mixed, with one source interviewed assessing the most likely outcome as one in which Canberra decides not to fight. This analysis was based on the view that when push comes to shove, Australia and the United States fundamentally diverge on the underlying stakes:

> When the price and cost become real, and Australians realize they don't have to do this, they may well contemplate not doing it. My gut feel is that Australia would or might go away on this one, and that Australia is so adamant that it won't abandon the US because it wants deterrence to work. There is a real divergence of interests in extremis, because I think America really would fight over Taiwan.

In the interest of thoroughness, these Australian interviewees were also asked the converse question: Would Australia defend Taiwan if the United States did not intervene in the fight? On this point, experts were unanimous and emphatic in their responses: there is no scenario in which Australia would fight China over Taiwan if the United States remained on the sidelines. As one source succinctly put it: "Absolutely not. No way. Ever."

No Consensus on How Abandoning Taiwan Might Affect the Alliance

As was the case with Japanese and South Korean interviewees, the experts in Australia were uncomfortable contemplating the two worst-case scenarios—that is, Washington opts not to defend Taiwan against invasion, or the United States intervenes and loses. However, once their initial discomfort was past, it was possible to explore these taboo topics.

There was little consensus when these experts were asked what it would mean for the Australia-US alliance if the Unites States abandoned Taiwan in the face of Chinese invasion, though Australia was the only place where several interviewees flatly dismissed questions about US non-intervention as impossible, or at least so highly improbable as to be unworthy of even hypothetical contemplation. One interviewee stated definitively: "It is unambiguously clear that the US would get involved." Another suggested that under any traditional Democrat or Republican administration, US involvement would be a given, but that a second Trump administration or something similar would force a reassessment of the possibility of non-intervention, along with many other questions.[12]

Two interviewees suggested that it would be worse for the United States to stay away than to lose, predicting that a decision by Washington not to aid Taiwan would irrevocably destroy US credibility in the minds of Australian decisionmakers. In their view, such a choice would confirm Australia's deepest suspicions that the US security umbrella does not provide the protection they believed it did. They predicted widespread disillusionment and anxiety among policymakers, along with significant public concern. As one put it, "The Australian strategic imagination has been dominated by having a great power able to keep the threats from Asia at bay. In this scenario people would think the alliance isn't worth the paper it was printed on." These experts emphasized that beneath Australia's self-perception as "ally number one" lies a sense of insecurity as a small, distant country. To provide historical context, one source recalled the reaction to the 1969 enunciation of the Nixon Doctrine: "In Australia, there was a sense of being given a death warrant. Nixon was saying Asian allies need to stand on their own two feet. But Australia can't defend this continent."

These interviewees also discussed the psychological effects of US non-intervention. One noted that not intervening would be experienced as more of a shock than losing, given that non-intervention would occur suddenly, whereas losing—like in Vietnam or Afghanistan—unfolds gradually, losing its shock value by the end. Another source noted that not intervening would be harder to reconcile with the Australian mentality, whereas "the other option—we gave it a go and it didn't work out—is a much more Australian vibe."

These strident voices notwithstanding, a larger number of those interviewed suggested that while a US no-show would trigger howls of despair and gnashing of teeth in Australia, it would also bring "lots of secret sighs of relief. Not everyone will say that. But not everyone really does want to fight a war over Taiwan against an adversary that has a major balance of resolve in its favor and is willing to go to the mat." The experts who held this view indicated that there are many Australians whose commitment to a free Taiwan does not necessarily extend to defending that freedom with their own lives. Some would take solace in a US decision to spare the region and the world from the horrors of great power war. These experts further suggested that Australia's ultimate response would depend heavily on the regional order that emerges after the conflict, particularly the future direction of the US commitment to the region.

Similar to the insights provided by Japanese and South Korean experts, several analysts noted that as long as the United States does not retreat all the way back to its own shores, Washington will retain significant force projection capabilities in the region. Additionally, some experts emphasize that even without US involvement, the complexity and risks of a large-scale invasion over water mean that an easy Chinese victory is not assured. A fight that leaves China bloodied and weakened would deplete Beijing's capabilities while further damaging its reputation.

A US defeat? Bad. But not Necessarily Alliance-Ending Bad
Every interviewee agreed that a US loss over Taiwan would be devastating, with enormous consequences for the region. However, only two experts were convinced it would necessarily constitute a worst-case scenario

for the existence of the alliance. One described their reaction to a defeat scenario as follows:

> The US cannot afford to lose. It's better not to engage. Once you lose, credibility is destroyed across the Indo-Pacific. It's not some discretionary war in someplace like Afghanistan. Empires lose wars all the time, but they lose wars on the periphery where it doesn't matter. Taiwan would be a direct confrontation between a rising power and the established power. It's central to the future strategic architecture of the region. So, a confrontation where there's a defeat sends a signal throughout the Indo-Pacific that the US is not capable of responding to an emerging power, and everyone would look to other options.

A different source also predicted that a military loss of this kind would be more traumatic than the US losses in Iraq and Afghanistan. However, this source acknowledged that this reaction would not be purely rational or logical, "given how often the US has failed to achieve its strategic objectives." Nonetheless, this expert predicted that a loss over Taiwan would carry greater emotional weight because it could be "bigger, faster, and more telegenic. Endless raids in Afghanistan or convoys in Iraq have a different kind of impact in the US and Australia than the loss of an aircraft carrier would."

By the logic of these two experts, defeat would leave Washington with fewer options than if it had not engaged in the first place. They predicted that this outcome would also lead to even more hedging by countries already on the fence, such as India.

Only one source made a firm prediction about the likely US reaction to a defeat, essentially suggesting that a true US defeat is impossible:

> I don't think that if the US was pushed back, it would stay out. I think it becomes too hard for the fight not to become drawn out. Either nuclear escalation, or the US fights its way back in. I don't think hegemons go quietly into the night. The US will see its whole position in Asia hanging in the balance, and it would

be angry and vengeful. It would want revenge. It would react –
emotions would be very high.

Most experts, however, presented a more nuanced view of Australia's
reaction to a US defeat. They highlighted several factors that would
complicate the situation, including the strength of Australian public
sentiment regarding whether the United States had been right to join the
conflict, the historical precedent of alliance persistence following other
wars fought and lost, the US domestic reaction, and whether China's
victory was decisive and swift or protracted and costly.

One source suggested that even a defeat in Taiwan might not necessarily
lead America's allies to conclude that the United States lacked the
capabilities to defend Australia or Japan. As this source put it, "Defending
Taiwan is bloody hard, China has the homefield advantage, and it's not
a guarantee that America could use Japanese bases. So, there would be
an acknowledgment of how difficult the US military challenge was."
This expert predicted that reactions would ultimately depend on public
sentiment regarding whether the United States should have intervened
in the first place. If the general consensus was that the US had been
wrong to intervene, the focus would be on the judgment error rather
than a demonstration of lacking capabilities. Conversely, if the public
deemed the US engagement justified, the analogy would be to the good
doctor who did all they could but still lost the patient.

As referenced earlier, several sources drew comfort from history,
noting that a loss over Taiwan would not be the first time the United
States has failed to achieve its military objectives. As one expert expressed
with a crude metaphor, "Look at the resilience of the alliance system
after Vietnam. America was humiliated in Vietnam, and Iraq is a strategic
failure, and yet the alliance system survives. There has been a view in
the US policy community that US credibility is like virginity: once you
lose it you can never get it back. But US credibility survives."

Several experts delved further into the hypothetical scenarios
surrounding the question, concluding that Australia's reaction would

depend on how the conflict unfolded, how much military strength the United States and China had at their disposal at the end, and what actions each side took next. These experts generally agreed that a quick Chinese victory would signal the end of American hegemony and the dawn of a new security era in the Indo-Pacific. However, in a different and more likely scenario, they suggested that a protracted fight would still benefit the United States, regardless of the ultimate outcome:

> We could end up with a US that has lost some hegemony in the Pacific, but a China that is toothless and is trying to hold onto Taiwan because that's all that's left for it to focus on. US credibility would remain, but there would be a spike in Australian defense spending. And it would bring about a [repeat of the] 1942 discussion of the British as a defender of Australian security, looking at the question: if the US can't defend us, who can. We would have a complete look at our security framework.

Meanwhile—echoing the question of whether a true US defeat is even possible—another source pointed out that contemplating a US defeat calls into question not only capabilities but the entire US commitment to the region, since it assumes a loss after which the United States does not return to the fight. This expert predicted this would set the stage for

> A very acrimonious debate in the entire region about balancing vs. band-wagoning. They won't use those terms. Those who don't want to balance will say we need a new regional construct of arms control and mediation with China as a major stakeholder. They won't say we need a new order and pay tribute to Beijing and supplicate. They won't put it in those terms. And to be clear: there are some Australians who right now think that's what the country needs to do.

This source also suggested, without prompting, that some in Australia would respond by pushing hard for nuclear weapons, discussed further next.

Several interviewees suggested that ultimately the result would depend on the reaction in the United States. There was a clear understanding that a defeat would be a traumatic moment for the United States in terms of its sense of self, and all eyes would be on US domestic politics to gauge what would happen next. One source quoted Dean Acheson (possibly apocryphally) as saying, "80% of foreign policy is having the domestic ability to have that policy." In other words, would the United States view the loss as stemming from a reluctance to fully commit? Did the public perceive it as a close fight? The source went on: "You could see that, if Washington does a NSC 68 redux and rearms and takes things very seriously, you would be in a very different place than if the US questions why it intervened in the first place. So, the US reaction will be quite important in shaping Australian perception of what it all means."

Finally, some Australian experts noted that the reaction to events in Taiwan could be a self-inflicted wound in terms of US credibility. One interviewee was explicit on this point, advising that the time has come for the United States to step back from the position it has held since 1949—that Taiwan is a litmus test for American commitment to Asian security. As this expert put it, "It is a test the US is not likely to be able to pass. But America now finds itself in a position where its capacity and willingness [to defend Taiwan] have become the key test of American ability to stay in East Asia. But I don't think America's position in East Asia would be devastated by the loss of Taiwan, except for the fact that America makes a big deal that Taiwan is such a test!"

Any Chinese Attack Drives Australia toward the United States, No Matter How Washington Responds

Asking interviewees to force-rank the worst-case scenarios yielded no consensus. Two interviewees indicated that a US decision not to intervene would be the worst possible outcome, worse even than if the United States fought and lost. By contrast, about a third of the interviewees suggested that Australia might be relieved at being spared the prospect of a war with China. Meanwhile, several sources also stated or implied that it would be equally damaging for the United States to lose as it would be not to intervene at all.

Interestingly, given this lack of concurrence, the most important finding from the interviews was a broad, realpolitik consensus that Chinese aggression against Taiwan would solidify regional opposition to China. This shift would, in turn, drive regional allies closer to the United States, regardless of what the United States had or had not done during the conflict itself. Sources anticipate that Washington would make this argument and that Australia would ultimately be receptive to it. As one interviewee put it:

> Allies and partners might not trust the US as much. But the US can play hardball and say, "OK, you don't trust us. But now China is unambiguously the predator. Do you want Gucci kit to stand up against the predator? Or do you want to try to go it alone?" So, I think as long as the US stays in the region as a pole to facilitate balancing, then the allies will take that option to form an arsenal of democracy... or rather an arsenal of non-Chinese hegemony.

Another expressed: "A crappy alliance still beats no alliance, so I don't think that we would do a de Gaulle or something like that. But I think the perception shifts from 'we need the alliance because of the US presence in Asia' to 'we need the alliance so we can get American tech so we can be ready to do it alone.'" Viewed in this light, Australia would become even more dependent on US arms sales if it were forced to confront China alone.

What Does Australia Expect if China Loses? Round Two

In addition to discussing the difficult downstream effects of various worst-case scenarios, interviewees were also asked to discuss what it might mean for the region if China's ambitions in Taiwan were thwarted. These experts were unanimous in their belief that Beijing's ambitions to control Taiwan would persist even after a defeat. As observed elsewhere in the interviews, multiple Australian sources also expressed their strongly held belief that decisively losing Taiwan would lead to a political crisis that could ultimately end CCP rule. If they are correct—or, equally importantly in the current political context—if Xi Jinping shares this conclusion, failure for China is not an option. The question then becomes, what happens next?

Every source interviewed in Australia agreed that, following a loss, China would immediately begin planning to reverse the setback. One expert compared this to the aftermath of the 1996 Cross Strait Crisis, in which the United States "won," prompting China to back off temporarily before strengthening its anti-access and area-denial maritime and air capabilities, which it now employs to reshape the conditions of a conflict.

Furthermore, as another expert explained, a US victory would result in China becoming "systematically, permanently, and deeply opposed to the United States and any Western role in the Pacific." This opposition would unfold within a geographic context that continues to favor China while disadvantaging the United States.

In other words, in a conflict over Taiwan's status, no expert consulted believes that the United States and its allies can secure a decisive, long-term victory over China under CCP rule. The best-case scenario, according to the Australians interviewed, would be a return to the status quo ante, but with the full expectation that all parties would then prepare for round two. As one expert put it, "If China loses, it will spend the next 50 years rebuilding to try and take Taiwan again."

Nuclear Issues

In general, the interviewees presented a nearly unanimous consensus that neither the Australian government nor the Australian public is seriously considering the prospect or ramifications of nuclear use in a war over Taiwan. As one source put it, "the defense department here really does not have a bench of people who spend a lot of time thinking about this issue. I think this is changing now and we are starting to think about it.

But it is really early days, and if you talk to people about escalation and escalation management, you largely get blank faces."

Moreover, several interviewees suggested that the United States government is similarly not taking this possibility seriously enough. This criticism extended to US leadership across the political spectrum. One source pointed out forcefully: "What strikes me is that every time a senior American leader wants to explain to Asians why the US is ready to sustain its position in Asia it boils down to, 'America is a Pacific power; America has economic interests; microchips'.... *But none of it articulates a compelling reason to risk nuclear war.*"

One expert, who has written extensively on the subject, expressed the belief that the nuclear dimension of the US–China military rivalry is generally underemphasized and that the United States tends to exaggerate the extent to which its numerical advantage in nuclear weapons will deter China from considering the use of its own. This source believes China is unlikely to initiate a conflict at the nuclear level but would be willing to escalate to it gradually. Another source mentioned that, in a Taiwan conflict, Canberra would likely monitor potential escalation triggers, such as one side targeting the other's nuclear assets (which this source characterized as a stupid move) or whether the CCP felt its existence was threatened.

Another source emphasized that the United States would not necessarily be able to control escalation. This source pointed to the fog of war and the possibility that a conflict could involve long-range strikes into China. In the face of strikes against targets within China, Beijing might not know exactly which of its own assets are being targeted. Colocation and shared command-and-control systems across Chinese conventional and nuclear missile forces could complicate matters considerably (a phenomenon sometimes called entanglement).[13] This interviewee noted that the risks of entanglement—and possible Chinese first use—will be higher if a conflict occurs within the next five to ten years, before China has a sufficiently large nuclear arsenal to be confident in its ability to absorb a first strike while maintaining survivable nuclear capability. If this expert is correct, a counterintuitive dynamic emerges: As China's nuclear arsenal grows, stability might actually increase because China will be less vulnerable to having its arsenal attritted through conventional US attacks.

In exploring the Chinese defeat scenario, one source also cautioned that, because the CCP cannot accept a loss and must at least fight to a stalemate, being thrown back across the Strait could induce Beijing to reach for its nuclear option. China's long-range strike capabilities allow it to credibly threaten US bases and military assets in the region, as well as domestic US targets. This gives China the option of launching a demonstration nuclear strike to suggest to Washington that worse is coming, which could, of course, lead to escalation rather than de-escalation. The grim picture emerges that, if the CCP believes that it will face a domestic coup if it de-escalates, nuclear escalation becomes a rational option.

Questions about nuclear issues led some interviewees to raise the pivotal question of whether the United States has the conventional capabilities it needs for a Taiwan fight. As one interviewee put it, the United States needs to "stop talking about building new forces required to win a conventional war and actually start doing it. This means stopping the building of aircraft carriers and other big ships." This source implored the United States to define what would count as winning in Taiwan (i.e., what would convince China to stop fighting), articulate a credible strategy to achieve that victory, and then build the forces to pursue that strategy.

To conclude the nuclear discussion, all interviewees were asked whether various potential outcomes might change Australian thinking on its own need for an independent nuclear deterrent. One interviewee believes that if Australia lost faith in US credibility and capability and wanted to preserve its middle-power ability to independently deter foreign aggression, it would need to develop its own minimal nuclear deterrent. Other sources acknowledged the logic behind pursuing nuclear weapons, but claimed this argument would find no traction in Canberra because no serious constituency is open to making the necessary spending trade-offs. According to several experts, the issue would be framed by opponents as taking money from social programs to pay for nuclear weapons, which no politician could ultimately support. Nonetheless, several sources noted that if there were a Taiwan conflict and the United States either did not show up or showed up and lost badly, Australia would likely become more open to discussing the possibility of developing an independent nuclear capability.

Gray-Zone Provocations

Finally, the interviewees were asked about the risks of provocative activity short of war. The interviewees agreed unanimously that concerns about the gray-zone threat are overstated. In fact, Australian sources, as a group, paid far less attention to gray-zone provocations in the Taiwan Strait than their Japanese or South Korean counterparts. This is perhaps understandable, given that Australia is less immediately affected by Chinese physical provocations and territorial claims. Still, several sources pointed out that any conflict in the gray zone is, by definition, an event short of war and that Australia would be likely to welcome it—or at least tolerate it—given the far worse alternative.

More than one expert also expressed skepticism that anything short of a full-scale military conflict could ever achieve Beijing's aims. Given how much Taiwan has to lose, they deem it unlikely that the people of Taiwan would give up in response to cyber-attacks alone, or even naval blockades or aggressive Chinese activity in outlying islands (which would, by our definition, be considered acts of war rather than gray-zone tactics).

Several sources responded to questions about the gray zone by describing scenarios in which they believe the lack of a strong US response could lead to a loss of credibility. One such scenario involved China establishing naval bases in Indonesia, Vanuatu, or Papua New Guinea. However, this scenario is not directly related to Taiwan, and the source who suggested it immediately dismissed it as highly unlikely. Another expert suggested that a naval blockade preventing foreign military vessels from crossing the Nine Dash Line, or a full naval and air blockade of Taiwan that diverted trade intended for Taiwan to China would constitute red lines that would necessitate a US response.

One interviewee suggested that China might seize an island with Taiwanese forces on it, forcing or encouraging Taiwan to deploy its naval forces quickly, only to see them destroyed. This would be a blow to Taiwanese morale, and according to this source might cause the US to question intervening once Taiwan's navy had already been depleted. Again, however, this would clearly be an act of war rather than a gray-zone tactic. Nonetheless, it was illustrative that so many of the interviewees, when asked specifically about gray-zone issues, responded in terms of military operations such as blockades and island grabs.

The highest-risk scenarios that the interviewees posited involved moves by Beijing to throttle Taiwan's economy, but to do so in a manner that fell short of any specific US red lines and thereby muddled the justification for US and allied intervention. China's experience in Hong Kong was pointed out as instructive here, in that Beijing has achieved functional political control without prompting a US response. However, the analogy obviously breaks down quickly, given that Hong Kong had previously and peacefully been incorporated into Chinese territory, whereas Taiwan has not. Moreover, several sources who discussed this possibility concluded that the ultimate result would be to drive the United States and Taiwan closer, strengthening the resolve of America's Pacific allies. They believe Xi Jinping likely sees the same dynamic and suggested that this makes China's choices even more stark by introducing an expectation that time and US deterrence are not on Beijing's side.

NOTES

1. Australia, Department of Foreign Affairs and Trade, *China Country Brief.*
2. Neelam, *Lowy Institute Poll 2024.*
3. Australia. Department of External Affairs. *Security Treaty between Australia, New Zealand and the United States of America (ANZUS).*
4. AUKUS is a trilateral security partnership between the United States, the United Kingdom, and Australia. Announced in September 2021, its primary aim is to support Australia in designing and building a small fleet of nuclear-powered attack submarines. It also facilitates collaborative development of other advanced defense capabilities—including artificial intelligence, undersea warfare, and hypersonic weaponry, among others. For a detailed overview of the agreement and related debates, see Nicastro, *AUKUS Pillar 2 (Advanced Capabilities).*
5. For a deeper theoretical exploration of the problem created by so-called issue indivisibility, see Fearon, "Rationalist Explanations for War." For a direct application to Taiwan, see Kastner, *War and Peace in the Taiwan Strait.*
6. Japan, Ministry of Foreign Affairs, *Japan-Australia Reciprocal Access Agreement, 2022.*
7. Needham, "Australia Rejects Chinese."
8. Neelam, *Lowy Institute Poll 2024.*
9. Herscovitch, "Australia's Answer"; McGregor, *Chinese Coercion, Australian Resilience.*
10. For an overview of the political, economic, and people-to-people aspects of the Australia-Taiwan relationship, see Australia, Department of Foreign Affairs and Trade, "Australia-Taiwan Relationship."
11. See, for example, Hurst, "Australia has 'Absolutely Not' Committed." For an overview of Canberra's official policies regarding Taiwan, see Australia, Department of Foreign Affairs and Trade, "Australia-Taiwan Relationship."
12. This interview took place during the Biden administration, before Donald Trump's second presidential run and eventual victory.
13. Talmadge, "Would China Go Nuclear?"; Posen, *Inadvertent Escalation*; Acton, "Escalation through Entanglement."

CONCLUSION

REPUTATION MATTERS, RELIABILITY MATTERS MORE

The goal of this study was to determine whether Taiwan serves as a bellwether for American credibility in East Asia. Do Australia, Japan, and South Korea view it as the proverbial canary in the coal mine such that its fate will reveal much about how and whether the United States might defend them? Or do they assume that Taiwan is sui generis and therefore unlikely to reveal much about what America might do for them if they come under attack? The preceding chapters lay out the findings in detail, and a brief recap of the topline findings follows.

Taiwan is Not a Linchpin Holding the Rest of America's Alliances in East Asia Together
Most of the experts interviewed agreed that allies' assessments of the value of maintaining their alliances with the United States are unlikely to hinge on whether Washington defends Taipei. Rather, the extent to which Tokyo, Seoul, and Canberra continue to have faith in Washington's security commitments will depend much more on whether, once the

dust settles, the United States retains sufficient military power to defend what each of them values most.

As discussed throughout the book, in terms of the Taiwan question, while reputation matters, reliability matters more. Japan, South Korea, and Australia all expect that the United States will defend Taiwan. All three prefer that Washington honor its commitments, implicit or otherwise. And all three would be shocked if Washington remained on the sidelines. However, they also recognize the difficulty of winning any conflict over Taiwan, acknowledging that victory would come at a high cost. Therefore, the three allies appear to be fundamentally pragmatic in their assessments. If they had to choose between an exhausted patron with a rock solid reputation burnished by defending Taiwan and a patron with a diminished reputation but the military capability to defend them, most of the interviewees—though by no means all—reluctantly favored the latter.

No Matter the US Response, An Attack on Taiwan Drives the Allies Closer to the United States

The vast majority of those interviewed expressed a surprisingly realpolitik stance regarding Taiwan. Australia, Japan, and South Korea view the Taiwan issue differently, shaped by their respective geographic proximity, cultural, and historical connections to the island, and unique security concerns. While none of these nations wants China to control Taiwan, the harsh reality is that Taiwan's fate is of secondary (or even tertiary) concern to Tokyo, Seoul, and Canberra, particularly if a US-led defense of Taiwan compromises Washington's ability to defend them thereafter. Intentional signaling and rhetoric notwithstanding, Japan, South, Korea, and Australia, according to the interviewees, care more about America's ability and willingness to protect them than Washington's demonstration of commitment to Taiwan. As much as all three would be dismayed if Washington abandons Taipei, they also acknowledge that the United States remains the "only game in town" capable of standing up to a revanchist China.

The conclusion consistently voiced by experts across all three countries—most strongly in Japan and Australia—was that any war started by China will push them closer to the United States. Their embrace of the alliance may be eager and enthusiastic, or reluctant and marked by well-founded doubts, but in either case, it will be driven by their real security needs. As long as the United States does not voluntarily choose to withdraw entirely from Asia, a clear majority of interviewees believe that stronger alliances will inevitably result from any conflict. If China attacks its neighbor, the US alliance network will only grow more robust in the aftermath.

Japan Cares the Most About Taiwan and Is the Most Skeptical of Coexistence with Xi

In Japan, both elites and voters share the general perception that a threat to Taiwan's status is a threat to Japan's security. While various factors contribute to this view, the most significant is geographic proximity. As a result, concerns about America's reputation and reliability overlap more in Tokyo than in Seoul or Canberra. Many of the interviewees said that preventing China from controlling Taiwan is a Japanese national security priority. Thus, defending Taiwan to uphold a reputation for resolve could also burnish perceptions of the United States as a reliable ally. Moreover, Japanese experts are generally more skeptical than their counterparts in South Korea or Australia about the possibility of coexistence with Xi Jinping.

Nonetheless, despite these sentiments, it was clear from the interviews that reliability matters more to Japan than reputation. The experts largely agreed that if Washington cannot win quickly and without depending on direct support from the Japan Self-Defense Forces, it should keep its powder dry. They also believe that if Washington allows Taipei to fall without a fight, it must do so in a way that maintains—and likely expands—its military footprint in Japan and the wider Indo-Pacific. They emphasized that US policymakers must thoroughly communicate their intentions and provide their Japanese counterparts with a compelling narrative to explain and justify American inaction. Pro-alliance elites in Tokyo will play an important role in maintaining the alliance and will need a narrative to sell to frightened and wary voters.

South Korea Feels Most Trapped and is Therefore Most Eager to Avoid Conflict

South Korea is in a far more complicated position than Japan or Australia. Being much farther from the Taiwan Strait, Seoul does not perceive Taiwan's loss as fundamentally altering its security environment. However, a prolonged conflict over Taiwan's status could devastate the global economy, provoke Chinese coercion or retaliation, and enable North Korean predation, all while risking US exhaustion. In other words, it would indisputably make South Korea less secure and less prosperous. For obvious reasons therefore, interviewees in South Korea expressed a much stronger desire for accommodation with China compared to Japan or Australia. Provided that Washington remains a security guarantor against North Korea and protects the South Korean economy against Chinese retaliation, Seoul might (secretly) breathe a sigh of relief if the US refrains from engaging in a war over Taiwan. This would be even more true if a progressive administration holds the Blue House at the time.

Australia is Least Worried about Taiwan and Xi, and Canberra is Still Committed to the US Alliance

When it comes to the US–Australia relationship, interviewees indicated that Washington might be placing more weight on its history and camaraderie with Canberra than is warranted. While the two nations are indeed "mates," experts in Australia were notably unsentimental about the choices they would face if Beijing attacks Taiwan. Although the Australian public holds Taiwan in high regard, neither voters nor elites see its fate as a core national interest. Once again, geography matters. Rightly or wrongly, the sources interviewed expressed a strong sense of security derived from the distance between China and themselves, with virtually none suggesting that a Chinese takeover of Taiwan would have significant strategic consequences for Australia. However, they do believe that a Chinese attack on Taiwan would underscore Australia's increased reliance on the United States. Regardless of whether US forces defend Taiwan, as long as America does not retreat from the Indo-Pacific, suffer a major defeat, or experience a debilitating Pyrrhic victory, Canberra will be compelled to stand by Washington's side.

Alternative Explanations and Critiques

This study aims to accurately represent the full range of views encountered during a multi-year research process. While the interpretation presented here provides a considered synthesis of these diverse—and at times contradictory—perspectives, complex issues often allow for multiple, equally plausible interpretations. Taiwan, furthermore, has long functioned as a sort of Rorschach test in American politics and security studies. Thus, it is appropriate to consider at least three alternative perspectives on how Australia, Japan, and South Korea view Taiwan and the reputational stakes for the United States in a cross-Strait conflict.

Allies are Concealing their True Views Because They Do Not Want to Admit They Might Bandwagon

One possible critique of this analysis is that the interviewees, as a group, may have been strategically dissembling, claiming they would have to rely on the United States while avoiding the uncomfortable truth that bandwagoning with China remains a potential option. While it is often unwise to take any interview entirely at face value, this critique can be countered with a simple question: if the United States is not going to listen to its most trusted allies, then to whom should it be listening? A principal motivation behind this project was the belief that much of Washington's discourse on Taiwan is based on deductive theorizing rather than direct engagement with allies and subject matter experts in the region. Ignoring or discounting these regional perspectives only reinforces the paternalistic, "father knows best" approach for which US foreign policy is often—and rightly—criticized by friends and allies.

This critique also contains a logical inconsistency: if Australia, Japan, and South Korea genuinely feared that they might need to bandwagon with Beijing—a prospect that is understandably distasteful given the obvious drawbacks to joining an adversary's coalition—then it would be illogical to remain silent about these concerns. From a rational bargaining standpoint, one would expect multiple interviewees to acknowledge bandwagoning as a real possibility in order to warn Washington that it must defend Taiwan to prevent Beijing from gaining the upper hand. To borrow a concept from Dr. Strangelove: Just as it makes no sense to keep a doomsday machine secret if the goal is deterrence, it would be equally irrational to remain silent about the risk of bandwagoning if the goal is to compel the United States to fight for its reputation. Arguing that interviewees' statements on this matter are unreliable reverses the fundamental bargaining logic of alliance communication.

Finally, returning to a central theme in this study, suggesting that allies want the US to fight for Taiwan to prevent bandwagoning implies that those allies believe the US will win decisively. If bandwagoning is a genuine possibility, then a US defeat would almost certainly increase the likelihood of this undesirable outcome, far more than if the US simply refrains from engaging.

Allies Might Not Care about US Reputation Now... But They Will When It Is Gone

A variation on the preceding critique suggests that while the interviewees were sincere in their statements, they might be inaccurate in predicting how their countries would respond. According to this logic, it may be reasonable to claim now that reputation isn't crucial, but once the United States reveals itself as irresolute, the resulting spiral of recriminations could lead to catastrophic, alliance-breaking consequences. As discussed throughout this book, the views expressed by the interviewees were not unanimous—some believed that US reputational failures would have major consequences. However, it is important to give credentialed experts the benefit of the doubt rather than systematically questioning their understanding of their own area of expertise.

"You're gonna miss me when I'm gone" may resonate as an understandable sentiment for US planners dealing with the costs and frustrations of maintaining America's reputation for resolve. However, this reflects the frustrations of the aggrieved and has no place in rigorous international relations analysis. The most reliable inputs for analysis are the statements of regional experts who have a vested interest in the outcome. Discounting these voices undermines the quality of analysis and decision-making.

Downplaying Taiwan's Reputational Significance Will Undermine Cross-Strait Deterrence

A final critique expected from proponents of deterrence is that downplaying the significance of America's reputational commitment to Taiwan could weaken Washington's ability to deter China from attacking. This argument represents not an alternative explanation for the findings, but rather a critique of the policy implications that follow from them. The logic is straightforward: deterrence depends on convincing Beijing that that America will defend Taiwan. Therefore, the greater the reputational stakes for the United States, the easier it will be for Washington to convince the world—and especially Beijing—that it will commit blood and treasure over Taiwan in order to uphold the credibility of its other commitments. This is an argument frequently advanced by US policy elites regarding the importance of defending Taiwan.[1]

It bears repeating a point first raised in the introduction: the goal was never to downplay the importance of reputation in relation to the United States and Taiwan. Again, the authors' initial hypothesis—and, to be candid, shared preference—was that, if Washington abandons Taipei, the reputational damage would strike a fatal blow to America's network of Pacific alliances. Such a finding would certainly make deterring Beijing a more straightforward task.

In other words, in response to critics who argue that this study's findings make deterrence harder: we agree. Stating that reputation matters makes for an intuitively compelling narrative, and narratives undeniably play an important role in the formulation and execution of national security policy.[2] Therefore, the idea that US allies in Asia might prioritize reliability over reputation (at least in a war over Taiwan's status) certainly challenges Washington's current approach to cross-Strait deterrence.

That said, a robust and resilient deterrent posture must ultimately be grounded in hard facts. The interviews with experts in the region suggest that the current realities are already undermining a reputation-based rationale.

Therefore, critics should not shoot the messenger. Shedding light on a potential complication does not create the challenge, just as ignoring an inconvenient problem cannot make it disappear. If the findings of this study are accurate, it would be naïve to assume that Beijing is unaware of these matters or is not already incorporating them into its own war plans. Ultimately, the idea that reliability matters more than reputation may prove more controversial in Washington than in Beijing, Canberra, Seoul, or Tokyo.

It is also worth considering the costs and risks associated with linking the defense of Taiwan to the credibility of America's commitments elsewhere in the region. The most concerning drawback is the creation of a self-fulfilling prophecy. In essence, the more that high-ranking US officials publicly declare that the credibility of America's position in Asia demands a full-throated military defense of Taiwan (if that is not actually the case), the more American, Australian, Japanese, and Korean voters might begin to view it that way, thereby painting Washington into a corner. It would certainly not be the first time in history that strategically advantageous rhetoric used by foreign policy elites became entrenched as a widely held shibboleth.[3]

Some US strategists will see this self-fulfilling prophecy as a "feature," not a "bug," because it helps the United States "tie its own hands." However, preemptively eliminating a viable course of action that a future US president might need or want to pursue is problematic. As much as it would be personally disheartening to see a president abandon Taiwan in a moment of crisis, the fact is that every presidential administration since 1979 has deemed it strategically necessary—if not politically expedient—to keep that option open. Washington could easily come to regret using reputation to bind itself to Taiwan. One such example would be if Washington were to convince itself and others that Taiwan is the linchpin of the rest of the US-led alliance system, and China then attacked Taiwan beleiving it had the upper hand militarily (a distinct possibility if Washington continues to underinvest in hard military power). If Washington then realizes that it cannot win quickly or decisively, it will find that it has deliberately created for itself the worst possible scenario: one in which all remaining options—abandonment, defeat, and Pyrrhic victory—lead to the collapse of its alliance network in Asia.

Policy Implications

The following set of practical recommendations emerges from the core findings of this study, providing guidance for future policy and strategic decision-making.

Reliability Should Carry More Weight than Reputation in Washington's Calculus

The most important finding of this study is that American credibility in the Asia-Pacific region does not rest solely—or even primarily—on whether Washington defends Taiwan to uphold its reputation for resolve. Instead, the credibility of Washington's extended deterrence commitments depends on tangible (and costly) US military capabilities. When it comes to critical decisions, Australia, Japan, and South Korea prioritize Washington's ability to protect their own interests over its demonstrated willingness to defend others.

This is not to suggest that reputation is meaningless or that reputational concerns should be disregarded. Washington will face significant criticism if it is perceived as "abandoning" Taipei. Experts in and on all three countries made it clear that they would expect the United States to uphold its reputation by defending Taiwan, even without an explicit security guarantee and even at the risk of outright defeat. Indeed, when pressed, more than one interviewee indicated that a dead patron is better than an unreliable one.

The key point is that reliability should be prioritized over reputation in the minds of American decision makers. A Chinese attack on Taiwan will undoubtedly cement Beijing's image as an expansionist predator. At that point, for Tokyo, Seoul, and Canberra, any alternatives to the US alliance are all worse options. They can align with China and acquiesce to Beijing's regional hegemony, which none are likely to desire, particularly given the deeply concerning precedents set by China's crackdown on Hong Kong, genocide in Xinjiang, and (in this scenario) invasion of Taiwan. They can each attempt to oppose China alone, but none is strong enough to do so. Or they could attempt to form a coalition against China without the United States, which would still not present a sufficiently strong front. The only viable option to prevent full-scale Chinese dominance in the region is continued active engagement by the United States. Even if these countries focus on their own armament, as is likely in the event of a Chinese victory over Taiwan, they will remain dependent on the United States to supply the necessary weapons.

Fundamentally, unless the United States voluntarily relinquishes its position as a Pacific power, the more aggressive Beijing becomes, the more it will drive its neighbors toward Washington. Defending Taiwan and achieving a quick victory would leave Washington in a position to reciprocate, but so would abandoning Taiwan without retreating from the broader region. A defeat or Pyrrhic victory—particularly if either one results in a diminished US military presence in the broader region—will not. While Tokyo, Seoul, and Canberra clearly prefer a swift US-led victory to Taiwan's abandonment, either outcome would be far preferable (according to most of the experts interviewed for this study) than a world in which the United States is too exhausted or too defeated to defend them. In essence, even if America's reputation is severely damaged, Japan, South Korea, and Australia will still (reluctantly) have no choice but to stay aligned with the United States. However, if America's reliability is compromised, bandwagoning with China will become an uncomfortably plausible alternative for all three.

A Deterrence Posture Built upon Military Capability Remains the Best Possible Option

The conclusion that naturally follows is that the optimal scenario for Washington is one in which neither it nor its allies are compelled to choose between reputation and reliability. All plausible outcomes of a Chinese attack on Taiwan are significantly worse for the United States and its allies—and, of course, for Taiwan itself—than any version of the current status quo. If Xi Jinping's stated ambitions regarding Taiwan are to be taken seriously, deterrence remains the only realistic strategy to prevent Beijing from placing Washington, Tokyo, Seoul, and Canberra in an untenable position. Therefore, Washington should spare no effort —and be willing to accept significant risks—to enhance cross-Strait deterrence. This should remain Washington's top policy priority vis-à-vis Beijing for the foreseeable future.

But Credible Deterrence Won't Be Cheap

US planners should also avoid deluding themselves—or the American people—into believing there is a simple or cost-free way to deter Xi and the Chinese Communist Party. China is, after all, no "paper tiger." Proximity, capability, and determination all work in Beijing's favor, and its decades-long investments in military modernization render any claims that Washington could achieve a quick and easy victory over China highly questionable. Credible deterrence will depend instead on a sustained willingness to bear significant financial costs, accept the uncomfortable risks of miscalculation or escalation, and encourage allies to do the same.[4] Without a meaningful commitment to such investments, a combination of symbolic gestures, rhetorical policy shifts, and high-ranking visits will likely inflame Beijing rather than deter it. Washington must also prepare the American public and its allies for the costs they will all bear to strengthen collective military power and the willingness to put it to use.

If a War for Taiwan Does Break Out, It Won't Be Short ...

Many interviewees pointed to the war in Ukraine as evidence that modern states have immense staying power. We agree. Washington must disabuse itself of any illusions that a conflict with China could be won swiftly. If Xi Jinping orders an attack on Taiwan, there are only three ways it could end quickly: the United States remains on the sidelines and the PLA rapidly overruns Taiwan's defenses; US forces are defeated quickly and Washington "throws in the towel"; or the war escalates to nuclear. (Even in this third, nightmare scenario, there is no guarantee that a nuclear war will be short). Xi is well aware that an outright defeat could mean the end of his rule. It follows that he will pay any price and bear any burden to prevail.

And the Risk of Nuclear Escalation Will be Real

A surprising number of experts raised and discussed the specter of nuclear war and nuclear proliferation. While not every interview touched on these topics, they were mentioned voluntarily and frequently enough to make clear that many US allies view these risks as real and believe the United States is not paying enough attention to them. Japanese experts were the most consistent in bringing up these topics. They are concerned that China might use nuclear rhetoric and threats to exploit Japan's historical fears, pressuring the country to remain on the sidelines. At the very least, Washington should be prepared for nuclear saber-rattling early in a conflict. Moreover, China's rapid nuclear modernization efforts suggest that Beijing may be taking nuclear escalation risks more seriously than

Washington is. Given that China considers Taiwan part of its homeland, and that Xi cannot afford to lose a war over Taiwan, the balance of nuclear resolve may well lie in Beijing's favor.

The consensus among the experts interviewed points to a need for the United States to place greater focus on nuclear deterrence in relation to China. The existing intellectual framework, strategy, doctrine, and force structures were all developed for a conflict between two adversaries whose thinking was rooted in the Western canon of political and military philosophy. The emergence of China as a nuclear peer competitor transforms the Cold War nuclear deterrent diode into a triangle, introducing a party that grounds its approach to deterrence in a different strategic tradition and corpus of thought. As one expert put it, "The European theater was a relatively simple: one team, NATO, against one enemy, Warsaw Pact." By contrast, the Indo-Pacific, is more complex, with multiple nuclear-armed states (China and North Korea, as well as India and Pakistan), multiple potential adversaries, and differing threat perceptions of these potential adversaries among the US allies. Another expert recommended that analysts undertake a deeper study of Chinese nuclear strategy to better prepare the publics in Japan—and potentially South Korea as well—to handle such coercion. These complex factors, coupled with the relative lesser focus compared to the European theater, warrant greater attention from US nuclear planners.

From An Alliance Maintenance Perspective, the US Should Prioritize Real Military Power Over Symbols and Focus on General Capabilities over Narrowly Optimized Ones

US defense officials increasingly refer to the Indo-Pacific as the priority theater, China as the pacing threat, and Taiwan as the pacing scenario.[5] The first two statements are undoubtedly reassuring for US allies in the region to hear. Given how many of the interviewees appeared enthusiastic about any efforts to enhance the perceived credibility of US support, it is likewise safe to conclude that US efforts to demonstrate or improve its commitment to the region writ large will be pushing on an open door as far as most Australian, Japanese, and South Korean security experts are concerned.

At the same time, the topline finding of this study is that US allies in the region prioritize Washington's ability to defend them over its willingness to protect Taiwan. As such, optimizing the US military for a Taiwan conflict might prove suboptimal, in that the more training, positioning, planning, posture, and capabilities are narrowly tailored to protect Taipei, the less trust Canberra, Seoul, and Tokyo will place in Washington's reliability.

Unless Taiwan is unequivocally the highest-risk issue in the region, Washington should avoid public declarations prioritizing Taiwan's defense over other plausible conflicts and contingencies (such as the reignition of the Korean conflict or a military confrontation in the South China Sea). US defense planners should also be cautious about prepositioning any units, equipment, or munitions on Taiwan that cannot be easily displaced or replaced should US forces be needed elsewhere in the Indo-Pacific, or if Taiwan is attacked and the US president opts not to defend the island.

Instead, Washington should focus on "multi-use" posture and capabilities. This refers to units, platforms, and weapons that could be employed either to defend Taiwan (if China attacks and the president orders US forces to intervene) or to address a range of plausible regional contingencies. Options include an increased emphasis on long-range missiles (along with the supporting infrastructure to facilitate targeting and guidance), long-range uncrewed weapons, and the expansion of the US military footprint in Japan, South Korea, other Pacific islands such as Guam, and, to a lesser degree, Australia.

Low-Hanging Fruit
Again, if reliability matters more than reputation, it is imperative that Washington takes every possible step to strengthen its military posture in the region. However, doing so will require time, especially given the

political, economic, and industrial challenges that will hinder the rapid expansion of the US defense industrial base, as well as the Department of Defense and its budget.[6] Fortunately, the interviews with the experts revealed a number of practical, low-cost, and immediate steps Washington can implement in the meantime, many of which focus on improving communication and regional coordination.

Foster More Coordination and Conversation Among Allies

As Washington seeks to transition its network of Indo-Pacific alliances from a hub-and-spoke system to one functioning more like a lattice, it must make every effort to avoid the bilateral stove-piping of information. Interviewees from all three countries consistently urged Washington to improve its communication, particularly regarding changes in one part of the US-led regional network that could affect others. For example, AUKUS remains a contentious issue for Japanese security elites. Several Japanese sources stated Tokyo was not adequately consulted before Washington announced the new security cooperation arrangement with Canberra and London. Japan was left unprepared and feeling sidelined. As one source said, "You have to make sure you talk to the regional friends and partners first. The goal should be a loose but close network to deal with Chinese expansion."

Similarly, interviewees emphasized the interconnected nature of security issues in Northeast Asia. One expert highlighted the importance of the US leadership role in this context: "Cross Straits issues are only one issue brought up by Chinese advances in the region. Strategically it makes more sense to talk about all the first island chain issues together. It's good that the Biden administration was in the mood to talk to everyone in the region, from Australia to Southeast Asia. The US is the only country that is able to bring in all the relevant countries. All the relevant parties in the region want to talk about the issues, but Japan cannot convene these sorts of meetings."

Do More to Explain Why Taiwan Matters and Why the Risk of War is Real

The experts consulted acknowledged that their elected leaders could do more to convince voters of the importance of fighting for Taiwan. However, they also emphasized that Washington must take a more active role in explaining this need, both to its own citizens and to the publics in its allied countries. Instead of assuming that US allies and their populations share a common understanding of the stakes, the risks, or the solutions—which they do not—US policymakers must proactively communicate *to the citizens of its allied countries* why Taiwan matters and why the risk of war is real. This will be especially critical in South Korea and Australia, where dire warnings from Washington are competing against Beijing's messages of economic interdependence and, in South Korea's case, geographic and cultural proximity. Several experts recommended that Washington facilitate a series of Track II dialogues, as well as bilateral, trilateral, and multilateral conferences, to address Taiwan's significance to the relevant partners. These efforts should aim to enhance deterrence by conveying to Beijing that each party in the alliance has its own independent and specific stake in Taiwan's political independence and territorial integrity.

If War Does Come to the Taiwan Strait, be Ready and Able to Explain US Actions (or Inaction)

Domestic politics in each country will play a significant role in any crisis regarding Taiwan's status. In any conflict over Taiwan, there will be domestic political constituencies in each country who are already skeptical of the United States, and their voices will be amplified by Chinese information warfare efforts. A US abandonment of Taiwan or defeat by China would strengthen arguments—particularly prevalent among political progressives and communities hosting US bases—that the US alliance is more trouble than it is worth. Pro-US national security experts in Canberra, Seoul, and Tokyo will be crucial thought leaders in either scenario, and US engagement will be essential to help them garner support within their own countries for maintaining the alliances in challenging times.

The United States Should be Ready to Fight... But for the Right Reasons

Nothing outlined in the preceding pages implies that Washington should abandon Taipei, either now or in the earliest moments of a crisis. It is important to emphasize: *there are compelling reasons to defend Taiwan.* These include upholding a rules-based order, protecting a flourishing liberal democracy, maintaining a vital economic partnership, safeguarding global supply chains, preventing a competitor from gaining a critical strategic advantage, and defusing nuclear proliferation risks. Individually and collectively, these considerations indicate that preserving the status quo in the Taiwan Strait is in the US national interest.

Ultimately, the goal is to convey that US allies may neither want nor need Washington to add reputation to the already robust list of justifications for defending Taiwan. It must be acknowledged that reputation is an inherently difficult concept to measure. It is rooted in collective perception and can be invoked, leveraged, and even weaponized to shape both public opinion and elite behavior. Yet even if scientific precision is elusive, true understanding remains possible. The well-considered views, thoughts, and opinions summarized earlier paint a clear picture of a network of allies that is eager for active US involvement in the Indo-Pacific but also painfully aware that their benefactor is spread thin. They believe that a genuine American withdrawal from Asia is a potentially existential risk, and that this danger is even greater for them than the risk of losing Taiwan. This consensus view does not make Taiwan unworthy of protection. However, it does suggest that any sound justifications for defending the island must rest on firmer foundations than the need to uphold America's reputation as a resolute ally. The most important conclusion remains that a war over Taiwan would be catastrophic. Preventing such a war will be worth a high price indeed.

NOTES

1. Sullivan, *A Test of Will*, 14–15; Santoro and Cossa, *The World After Taiwan's Fall*; Cunningham, *The American Case for Taiwan*, 7–9; Belloc-chi, "The Strategic Importance of Taiwan," 72–76; Gordon, Mullen, and Sacks, *U.S.-Taiwan Relations in a New Era: Responding to a More Assertive China*, 9–10.

2. Krebs, *Narrative and the Making of US National Security*.

3. Snyder, *Myths of Empire*.

4. Fearon, "Signaling Foreign Policy Interests"; Pottinger and Turpin, "The Myth of Accidental War"; Kanapathy, "Countering China's Use of Force."; Hunzeker, Wu, and Marom, "A New Military Culture for Taiwan."; Newsham, "Japan as the 'Swing Vote'"; Pettyjohn, "Spiking the Problem"; Dougherty, "Don't Trust the Process."

5. Campbell, Lawrence, and Arabia, *Taiwan Defense Issues for Congress*, 1.

6. On human capital constraints, see Bensahel and Barno, "Addressing the U.S. Military Recruiting Crisis"; Quiroz, "The U.S. Military's Personnel Crisis"; Spoehr and Handy, *The Looming National Security Crisis*. On the defense industrial base, see Nicastro, *The U.S. Defense Industrial Base*; Decker and Sheinbaum, "Shining a Light"; Jones, *Empty Bins*; Salisbury, "The Sinking Submarine Industrial Base"; Smith, "Manufacturing is a War Now." On the national debt, see Hensarling, "Debt and Inflation Threaten US Security"; Bloomberg, "US Fiscal 2025 Defense Budget"; Committee for a Responsible Federal Budget. "Interest Costs."

BIBLIOGRAPHY

ABC News. "Full Transcript of ABC News' George Stephanopoulos Interview with President Joe Biden." *ABC News.* August 19, 2021. https://abcnews.go.com/Politics/full-transcript-abc-news-george-stephanopoulos-interview-president/story?id=79535643.

Acton, James. "Escalation through Entanglement: How the Vulnerability of Command-and-Control Systems Raises the Risks of an Inadvertent Nuclear War." *International Security* 43, no. 1: 56–99. https://doi.org/ https://doi.org/10.1162/isec_a_00320.

Allen, Susan H. ""Time Bombs: Estimating the Duration of Coercive Bombing Campaigns."" *Journal of Conflict Resolution* 51, no. 1 (2007): 112–133. https://doi.org/https://doi.org/10.1177/0022002706296153.

———, and Carla Martinez Machain. "Understanding the Impact of Air Power." *Conflict Management and Peace Science* 36, no. 5 (2019): 545–558. https://doi.org/10.1177/073889421668.

Alperovitch, Dmitri. "Taiwan Is the New Berlin: A Cold War Lesson for America's Contest with China." *Foreign Affairs.* https://www.foreignaffairs.com/taiwan/taiwan-new-berlin-china-cold-war-dmitri-alperovitch

Ashley, Ryan, "Japan's Revolution on Taiwan Affairs." *War on the Rocks.* https://warontherocks.com/2021/11/japans-revolution-on-taiwan-affairs/.

Australia, Department of External Affairs. *Security Treaty between Australia, New Zealand and the United States of America (ANZUS).* Canberra: Australian Government Publishing Service, 1951.

Australia, Department of Foreign Affairs and Trade. "Australia-Taiwan Relationship." https://www.dfat.gov.au/geo/taiwan/australia-taiwan-relationship#:~:text=The%20Australian%20Government%20strongly%20supports,people%2Dto%2Dpeople%20links.

Australia, Department of Foreign Affairs and Trade. *China Country Brief.* May 2024, updated June 21, 2024. https://www.dfat.gov.au/geo/china/china-country-brief#:~:text=sister%2Dcity%20relationships.-,Trade%20and%20investment,in%202023%2C%20totalling%20%24326.9%20billion.

Babbage, Ross. *The Next Major War: Can the Us and Its Allies Win against China?* Amherst, NY: Cambria Press, 2023.

Bak, Daehee. "Alliance Proximity and Effectiveness of Extended Deterrence." *International interactions* 44, no. 1 (2018): 107–131. https://doi.org/10.1080/03050629.2017.1320995.

Beckley, Michael. "The Myth of Entangling Alliances: Reassessing the Security Risks of U.S. Defense Pacts." *International Security* 39, no. 4 (2015): 7–48. https://doi.org/10.1162/ISEC_a_00197.

Bellocchi, Luke P. "The Strategic Importance of Taiwan to the United States and Its Allies: Part One." *Parameters* 53, no. 2 (2023): 61–77. https://doi.org/doi:10.55540/0031-1723.3223.

Bensahel, Nora, and David Barno, "Addressing the U.S. Military Recruiting Crisis." *War on the Rocks.* March 10, 2023. https://warontherocks.com/2023/03/addressing-the-u-s-military-recruiting-crisis/.

Bercaw, Ryan C. "Yes, Taiwan Will Defend Taiwan." *The Diplomat*, May 18, 2024. https://thediplomat.com/2024/05/yes-japan-will-defend-taiwan/.

Biddle, Stephen, and Ivan Oelrich. "Future Warfare in the Western Pacific: Chinese Antiaccess/Area Denial, U.S. Airsea Battle, and Command of the Commons in East Asia." *International Security* 41, no. 1 (2016): 7–48. https://doi.org/10.1162/ISEC_a_00249.

Blechman, Barry M., and Stephen S. Kaplan. *Force without War: U.S. Ared Forces as a Political Instrument.* Washington, DC: The Brookings Institution, 1978.

Bloomberg. "Japan Sees China-Taiwan Friction as Threat to Its Security." *Bloomberg*, June 24, 2021. https://www.bloomberg.com/news/articles/2021-06-24/japan-sees-china-taiwan-friction-as-threat-to-its-security.

———. "US Fiscal 2025 Defense Budget Constrained by Law, Inflation." *Bloomberg*, June 26, 2024. https://www.bloomberg.com/professional/

insights/markets/us-fiscal-2025-defense-budget-constrained-by-law-inflation/#:~:text=US%20defense%20discretionary%20spending%20is,terms%2C%20given%20consensus%20for%20inflation.

Blumenthal, Dan, Frederick W. Kagan, Jonathan Baumel, Cindy Chen, Francis de Beixedon, Logan Rank, and Alexis Turek. *From Coercion to Capitulation: How China Can Take Taiwan without a War.* American Enterprise Institute, 2024. http://www.jstor.org/stable/resrep59832.

Bolton, John. *The Room Where It Happened: A White House Memoir.* New York, NY: Simon and Schuster, 2020.

Bosco, Joseph. "Taiwan and Strategic Security." *The Diplomat*, May 15, 2015. https://thediplomat.com/2015/05/taiwan-and-strategic-security.

Botto, Kathryn, "Why Doesn't South Korea Have Full Control over Its Military?," *Commentary.* Carnegie Endowment for International Peace, August 21, 2019. https://carnegieendowment.org/posts/2019/08/why-doesnt-south-korea-have-full-control-over-its-military?lang=en.

Brodie, Bernard. *Strategy in the Missile Age.* Princeton, NJ: Princeton University Press, 1959.

Campbell, Caitlin, Susan V. Lawrence, and Christina L. Arabia. *Taiwan Defense Issues for Congress.* Washington, DC: U.S. Library of Congress, Congressional Research Service, 2024.

Cancian, Mark F., Matthew Cancian, and Eric Heginbotham. *The First Battle of the Next War: Wargaming a Chinese Invasion of Taiwan.* Center for Strategic and International Studies, January 2023.

Caverley, Jonathan D. "The Taiwan Fallacy: American Power Does Not Hinge on a Single Island." *Foreign Affairs*, August 7, 2024. https://www.foreignaffairs.com/taiwan/taiwan-fallacy.

Central News Agency. "Xi Prefers 'Peaceful' Unification of Taiwan: Us Official." *Focus Taiwan*, May 5, 2023. https://focustaiwan.tw/cross-strait/202305050005.

Cha, Victor. *Powerplay: The Origins of the American Alliance System in Asia.* Princeton, NJ: Princeton University Press, 2016. doi:10.1515/9781400883431.

Chamberlin, Dianne Pfundstein. *Cheap Threats: Why the United States Struggles to Coerce Weak States.* Washington, DC: Georgetown University Press, 2016.

Chanlett-Avery, Emma, Caitlin Campbell, and Christina L. Arabia. *U.S.-South Korea Alliance: Issues for Congress.* Washington, D.C.: U.S. Library of Congress, Congressional Research Service, 2023.

Chen, Kelvin. "Taiwan, Japan Ruling Parties to Hold Defense Meeting Later This Month." *Taiwan News*, February 7, 2023. https://www.taiwannews.com.tw/en/news/4802869.

Choe, Sang-Hun, and Rich Motoko. "Leaders of Japan and South Korea Vow to Deepen Ties." *The New York Times*, May 7, 2023. https://www.nytimes.com/2023/05/07/world/asia/south-korea-japan-summit-apology.html.

Chong, Ja Ian, and Todd H. Hall. "The Lessons of 1914 for East Asia Today: Missing the Trees for the Forest." *International Security* 39, no. 1 (Summer 2014): 7–43. http://www.jstor.org/stable/24480543.

Christensen, Thomas J., and Jack Snyder. "Chain Gangs and Passed Bucks: Predicting Alliance Patterns in Multipolarity." *International Organization* 44, no. 2 (1990): 137–168. https://doi.org/10.1017/S0020818300035232.

Chung, Jake. "Japan to Build Munitions Depots Close to Taiwan." *Taipei Times*, September 8, 2022. https://www.taipeitimes.com/News/front/archives/2022/09/08/2003784951.

Clinton, William J., and Zemin Jiang. *China-Us Joint Statement.*

Colby, Elbridge. "Against the Great Powers: Reflections on Balancing Nuclear and Conventional Power." *Texas National Security Review* 2, no. 1 (November 2018): 144–152. http://dx.doi.org/10.26153/tsw/864.

———. "Why Protecting Taiwan Really Matters to the U.S." *Time*, October 11, 2022. https://time.com/6221072/why-protecting-taiwan-really-matters-to-the-u-s/.

———, and Jim Mitre, "Why the Pentagon Should Focus on Taiwan," *War on the Rocks*, October 7, 2020. https://warontherocks.com/2020/10/why-the-pentagon-should-focus-on-taiwan/.

Committee for a Responsible Federal Budget. "Interest Costs Just Surpassed Defense and Medicare." https://www.crfb.org/blogs/interest-costs-just-surpassed-defense-and-medicare#:~:text=In%20the%20first%20seven%20months,totaled%20%243.9%20trillion%20thus%20far.

Committee on Rules. *Statement before the House Committee on Rules, "Examining China's Coercive Economic Tactics."* 118th Congress.

"Confucius Institutes around the World - 2024." Dig Mandarin, Updated October 12, 2024, 2024, https://www.digmandarin.com/confucius-institutes-around-the-world.html.

Cooper, Zack, "Biden's Asia Diplomacy Is Still Incomplete," *War on the Rocks*, August 23, 2023. https://warontherocks.com/2023/08/bidens-asia-diplomacy-is-still-incomplete/

———, and Christopher B. Johnston. "Getting U.S.-Japanese Command and Control Right." *War on the Rocks*, June 28, 2023. https://warontherocks.com/2023/06/getting-u-s-japanese-command-and-control-right/.

Copeland, Dale C. "Do Reputations Matter?" *Security Studies* 7, no. 1 (1997): 33–71. https://doi.org/10.1080/09636419708429333.

Copp, Tara. "'It Failed Miserably': After Wargaming Loss, Joint Chiefs Are Overhauling How the US Military Will Fight." *Defense One*, July 26, 2021. https://www.defenseone.com/policy/2021/07/it-failed-miserably-after-wargaming-loss-joint-chiefs-are-overhauling-how-us-military-will-fight/184050/.

Crescenzi, Mark J. C., Jacob D. Kathman, Stephen B. Long, and Andrew P. Enterline. "Reliability, Reputation, and Alliance Formation." *International Studies Quarterly* 56, no. 2 (2012): 259–274. https://doi.org/10.1111/j.1468-2478.2011.00711.x.

Culver, John, "The Unfinished Chinese Civil War," *The Interpreter*. The Lowy Institute, September 30, 2020. https://www.lowyinstitute.org/the-interpreter/unfinished-chinese-civil-war.

Cunningham, Fiona S., and M. Taylor Fravel. "Assuring Assured Retaliation: China's Nuclear Posture and U.S.-China Strategic Stability." *International security* 40, no. 2 (2015): 7–50. https://doi.org/10.1162/ISEC_a_00215.

Cunningham, Michael. *The American Case for Taiwan*. The Heritage Foundation, March 27, 2024.

Dalton, Toby, Karl Friedhoff, and Lami Kim. *Thinking Nuclear: South Korean Attitudes on Nuclear Weapons*. Chicago Council on Global Affairs, February 2022. https://globalaffairs.org/sites/default/files/20 22-02/Korea%20Nuclear%20Report%20PDF.pdf.

Decker, Jeff, and Noah Sheinbaum. "Shining a Light on the Defense Department's Industrial Base Problems." *Texas National Security Review* 7, no. 1 (Winter 2023/2024): 75–88. https://doi.org/10.26153 /tsw/50673.

DeLisle, Jacques. "The Taiwan Relations Act at 40: A Troubled but Durable Legal Framework for U.S. Policy." *Asia Policy* 14, no. 4 (2019): 35–42. https://doi.org/10.1353/asp.2019.0057.

Dong, Gyu Lee, and Chungku Kang, "How Should South Korea Respond to Youths' Worsening Perception of China?" *Issue Briefs*. The Asan Institute for Policy Studies, November 10, 2023. https://en.asaninst.org/contents/how-should-south-korea-respond-to-youths-worsening-perception-of-china/.

Dougherty, Chris, "Don't Trust the Process: Moving from Words to Actions on the Indo-Pacific Posture," *War on the Rocks*, February 23, 2022., https://warontherocks.com/2022/02/dont-trust-the-process-moving-from-words-to-actions-on-the-indo-pacific-posture/.

Easton, Ian. *The Chinese Invasion Threat*. Arlington, VA: Project 2049, 2017.

Edelstein, David M. , and Joshua R. Itzkowitz Shifrinson. "It's a Trap! Security Commitments and the Risks of Entrapment." In *Us Grand Strategy in the 21st Century: The Case for Restraint*, edited by A. Trevor Thrall and Benjamin H. Friedman, 19–41. New York, NY: Routledge, 2018.

Fearon, James D. "Rationalist Explanations for War." *International Organization* 49, no. 3 (Summer 1995): 379–414. https://doi.org/http:/ /www.jstor.org/stable/2706903.

———. "Signaling Foreign Policy Interests: Tying Hands Versus Sinking Costs." *The Journal of Conflict Resolution* 41, no. 1 (1997): 68–90. https://doi.org/10.1177/0022002797041001004.

Feickert, Andrew. *The Terminal High Altitude Air Defense (Thaad) System.* Washington, DC: U.S. Library of Congress, Congressional Research Service, 2024.

Feng, John. "China Officials Share Viral Video Calling for Atomic Bombing of Japan." *Newsweek*, July 14, 2021. https://www.newsweek.com/china-officials-share-viral-video-calling-atomic-bombing-japan-exception-theory-1609586.

Ferreira, Gustavo F., and Jamie A. Critelli. "Taiwan's Food Resiliency— or Not—in a Conflict with China." *Parameters* 53, no. 2 (2023): 39–60. https://doi.org/doi:10.55540/0031-1723.3222.

Fitzpatrick, Mark. *Asia's Latent Nuclear Powers: Japan, South Korea, and Taiwan.* London: Routledge, 2016.

Freedman, Lawrence. *Deterrence.* Cambridge, UK: Polity Press, 2004.

———. "Going Nuclear." *Comment is Freed*, September 20, 2022, https://samf.substack.com/p/going-nuclear.

Friedberg, Aaron L. "Will We Abandon Taiwan?" *Commentary*, May 2000, 26–31.

Galic, Mirna, and Frank Aum, "What's Behind Japan and South Korea's Latest Attempt to Mend Ties?" *Analysis. United States Institute of Peace*, March 21, 2023. https://www.usip.org/publications/2023/03/whats-behind-japan-and-south-koreas-latest-attempt-mend-ties.

Gartzke, Erik, and Jon R. Lindsay. *Elements of Deterrence: Strategy, Technology, and Complexity in Global Politics.* Oxford: Oxford University Press, 2024.

Geddes, Alistair, Charlie Parker, and Sam Scott. "When the Snowball Fails to Roll and the Use of 'Horizontal' Networking in Qualitative Social Research." *International Journal of Social Research Methodology* 21, no. 3 (2018): 347–358. https://doi.org/10.1080/13645579.2017.1406219.

Giarra, Paul S. "Time to Recalibrate: The Navy Needs Tactical Nuclear Weapons . . . Again." *Proceedings* 149, no. 7 (July 2023). https://

www.usni.org/magazines/proceedings/2023/july/time-recalibrate-navy-needs-tactical-nuclear-weapons-again.

Glaser, Charles L. "U.S.-China Grand Bargain? The Hard Choice between Military Competition and Accommodation." *International Security* 39, no. 4 (Spring 2015): 49–90. https://doi.org/doi.org/10.1162/ISEC_a_00199.

Goldstein, Steven M. *The United States and the Republic of China, 1949–1978: Suspicious Allies.* Walter H. Shorenstein Asia-Pacific Research Center. February 1, 2000. https://aparc.fsi.stanford.edu/publications/united_states_and_the_republic_of_china_19491978_suspicious_allies_the.

Gordon, Susan M., Michael G. Mullen, and David Sacks. *U.S.-Taiwan Relations in a New Era: Responding to a More Assertive China.* Council on Foreign Relations, 2023.

Haas, Richard, and David Sacks. "To Keep the Peace, Make Clear to China That Force Won't Stand." *Foreign Affairs.* https://www.foreignaffairs.com/articles/united-states/american-support-taiwan-must-be-unambiguous.

Heath, Timothy R., Sale Lilly, and Eugeniu Han. *Can Taiwan Resist a Large-Scale Military Attack by China? Assessing Strengths and Vulnerabilities in a Potential Conflict.* Rand Corporation, 2023.

Henry, Iain D. *Reliability and Alliance Interdependence: The United States and Its Allies in Asia, 1949–1969.* Cornell Studies in Security Affairs. Ithaca, NY: Cornell University Press, 2022. doi:10.1515/9781501763052.

———. "What Allies Want: Reconsidering Loyalty, Reliability, and Alliance Interdependence." *International Security* 44, no. 4 (2020): 45–83. https://doi.org/10.1162/isec_a_00375.

Hensarling, Jeb. "Debt and Inflation Threaten Us Security." *The Wall Street Journal,* Febuary 22, 2022. https://www.wsj.com/articles/debt-and-inflation-threaten-us-security-jerome-powell-supply-chain-federal-reserve-russia-china-defense-spending-11645565624.

Hernandez, Javier C. "China Suspends Diplomatic Contact with Taiwan." *The New York Times*, June 25, 2016. https://www.nytimes.com/2016/06/26/world/asia/china-suspends-diplomatic-contact-with-taiwan.html.

Herscovitch, Benjamin, "Australia's Answer to China's Coercive Challenge." *Commentary*. The Royal United Services Institute, August 18, 2021. https://rusi.org/explore-our-research/publications/commentary/australias-answer-chinas-coercive-challenge.

Hornung, Jeffrey W., and Christopher B. Johnstone. "Japan's Strategic Shift Is Significant, but Implementation Hurdles Await." *War on the Rocks*, January 27, 2023. https://warontherocks.com/2023/01/japans-strategic-shift-is-significant-but-implementation-hurdles-await/.

Horowitz, Michael C., Paul Poast, and Allan C. Stam. "Domestic Signaling of Commitment Credibility: Military Recruitment and Alliance Formation." *The Journal of Conflict Resolution* 61, no. 8 (2017): 1682–1710. https://doi.org/10.1177/0022002715612576.

Horowitz, Michael C., and Dan Reiter. "When Does Aerial Bombing Work?: Quantitative Empirical Tests, 1917–1999." *Journal of Conflict Resolution* 45, no. 2: 147–173. https://doi.org/10.1177/0022002701045002001.

Hsiao, Russell. "A Preliminary Survey of PRC United Front Activities in South Korea." *China Brief* 23, no. 7 (April 14, 2023). Jamestown Foundation. https://jamestown.org/program/a-preliminary-survey-of-prc-united-front-activities-in-south-korea/.

Huang, Christine, and Laura Clancy. "Taiwan Seen More Favorably Than Not across 24 Countries." *Short Reads*. Pew Research Center, August 11, 2023, https://www.pewresearch.org/short-reads/2023/08/11/taiwan-seen-more-favorably-than-not-across-24-countries/#:~:text=Attitudes%20toward%20Taiwan%20are%20most,report%20favorable%20views%20of%20Taiwan.

Hunzeker, Michael A., and Alexander Lanoszka. *A Question of Time: Enhancing Taiwan's Conventional Deterrence Posture.* Arlington, VA: Center for Security Policy Studies, 2018.

Hunzeker, Michael A., Enoch Wu, and Kobi Marom. "A New Military Culture for Taiwan." In *The Boiling Moat: Urgent Steps to Defend Tai-*

wan, edited by Matt Pottinger, 61–82. Stanford, CA: Hoover Institution Press, 2024.

Hunzeker, Michael Allen, and Alexander Lanoszka. "Landpower and American Credibility." *Parameters* 45, no. 4 (2015): 17. https://doi.org/10.55540/0031-1723.2983.

Hurst, Daniel. "Australia Has 'Absolutely Not' Committed to Join Us in Event of War over Taiwan, Marles Says." *The Guardian*, March 18, 2023. https://www.theguardian.com/world/2023/mar/19/australia-has-absolutely-not-committed-to-join-us-in-event-of-war-over-taiwan-marles-says.

Ikenberry, G. John. *After Victory: Institutions, Strategic Restraint, and the Rebuilding of Order after Major Wars*. Princeton, NJ: Princeton University Press, 2019.

Izumikawa, Yasuhiro. "Network Connections and the Emergence of the Hub-and-Spokes Alliance System in East Asia." *International Security* 45, no. 2: 7–50. https://doi.org/https://doi.org/10.1162/isec_a_00389.

Japan, Ministry of Foreign Affairs. *Treaty of Mutual Cooperation and Security between Japan and the United States*, 1960.

Japan, Ministry of Foreign Affairs. *Japan-Australia Reciprocal Access Agreement*, 2022.

———. "Japan-China Economic Relationship and China's Economy." 2023. https://www.mofa.go.jp/files/100540401.pdf.

Jervis, Robert, Keren Yarhi-Milo, and Don Casler. "Redefining the Debate over Reputation and Credibility in International Security: Promises and Limits of New Scholarship." *World Politics* 73, no. 1 (January 2021): 167–203.

Jestrab, Marek. *A Maritime Blockade of Taiwan by the People's Republic of China: A Strategy to Defeat Fear and Coercion*. The Atlantic Council of the United States. Washington, DC: December 2023. https://www.atlanticcouncil.org/wp-content/uploads/2023/12/strategy-paper_naval-blockade-of-Taiwan.pdf.

Johnson, Jesse C., Brett Ashley Leeds, and Ahra Wu. "Capability, Credibility, and Extended General Deterrence." *International*

Interactions 41, no. 2 (2015): 309–336. https://doi.org/10.1080/03050 629.2015.982115.

Jones, Seth G. *Empty Bins in a Wartime Environment: The Challenge to the U.S. Defense Industrial Base.* Center for Strategic and International Studies, January 23, 2023. https://www.csis.org/analysis/empty-bins-wartime-environment-challenge-us-defense-industrial-base.

Kanapathy, Ivan. "Countering China's Gray-Zone Activities." In *The Boiling Moat: Urgent Steps to Defend Taiwan,* edited by Matt Pottinger, 105–127. Stanford, CA: Hoover Institution Press, 2024.

———. "Countering China's Use of Force." In *The Boiling Moat: Urgent Steps to Defend Taiwan,* edited by Matt Pottinger. Stanford, CA: Hoover Institution Press, 2024.

Kaneko, Kaori , Yukiko Toyoda, Yukiko Kelly, and Sakura Murakami. "Exclusive: Japan Elevates Taiwan Security Ties in Move Likely to Rile China." *Reuters,* September 13, 2023. https://www.reuters.com/world/asia-pacific/japan-elevates-taiwan-security-ties-move-likely-rile-china-2023-09-12/.

Kang, Yoon-seung. "Number of Immigrants in S. Korea Rises Some 10 Pct in 2023." *Yonghap News Agency,* December 18, 2023. https://en.yna.co.kr/view/AEN20231218002200320023.

Kastner, Scott L. *War and Peace in the Taiwan Strait.* New York, NY: Columbia University Press, 2022.

Kelly, Laura. "Xi Rejects Us Offer to Set up Military Crisis Hotline, Blinken Says." *The Hill,* June 19. 2023. https://thehill.com/policy/international/4056697-xi-rejects-us-offer-to-set-up-military-crisis-hotline-blinken-says/

Kerr, George H. *Formosa Betrayed.* Boston, MA: Houghton Mifflin, 1965. https://archive.org/details/formosabetrayed00kerr/page/n9/mode/2 up.

Khan, Sulmaan Wasif. *The Struggle for Taiwan: A History of America, China, and the Island Caught Between.* New York, NY: Basic Books, 2024.

Kim, D.G., Joshua Byun, and Jiyoung Ko. "Remember Kabul? Reputation, Strategic Contexts, and American Credibility after the Afghanistant

Withdrawal." *Contemporary Security Policy* 45, no. 2: 265–297. https://doi.org/https://doi.org/10.1080/13523260.2023.2253406.

Kim, Tongfi, "By Any Other Name? The Camp David Summit, Us-Japan-South Korea Trilateral Security Cooperation and Military Alliances," *CSDS Policy Brief. Centre for Security, Diplomacy, and Strategy*, January 22, 2024. https://csds.vub.be/publication/by-any-other-name-the-camp-david-summit-us-japan-south-korea-trilateral-security-cooperation-and-military-alliances/.

———. "Why Alliances Entangle but Seldom Entrap States." *Security Studies* 20, no. 3 (2011): 350–377. https://doi.org/10.1080/09636412.2011.599201.

Kim, Victoria. "When China and U.S. Spar, It's South Korea That Gets Punched." *Los Angeles Times*, November 20, 2020. https://www.latimes.com/world-nation/story/2020-11-19/south-korea-china-beijing-economy-thaad-missile-interceptor.

Kim, Yon-se. "Number of Foreigners in Korea up for 1st Time in 20 Months." *The Korea Herald*, September 26, 2021. http://www.koreaherald.com/view.php?ud=20210926000093.

Kine, Phelim. "'Spiral into Crisis': The US-China Military Hotline Is Dangerously Broken." *Politico*, September 1, 2021. https://www.politico.com/news/2021/09/01/us-china-military-hotline-508140.

Koda, Yoji. "The Sun Also Rises." In *The Boiling Moat: Urgent Steps to Defend Taiwan*, edited by Matt Pottinger, 201–210. Stanford, CA: Hoover Institution Press, 2024.

Krebs, Ronald R. *Narrative and the Making of Us National Security*. Cambridge, UK: Cambridge University Press, 2015.

Kuo, Raymond. *Contests of Initiative: Countering China's Gray Zone Strategy in the East and South China Seas*. Washington, DC: Westphalia Press, 2020.

Kuo, Raymond C. *Following the Leader: International Order, Alliance Strategies, and Emulation*. 1st ed. Palo Alto, CA: Stanford University Press, 2021.

Kuo, Raymond, Christian Curriden, Cortez A. Cooper III, Joan Chang, Jackson Smith, and Ivana Ke. *Simulating Chinese Gray Zone Coercion of Taiwan: Identifying Redlines and Escalation Pathways.* Rand, June 22, 2023). https://www.rand.org/pubs/conf_proceedings/CFA2065-1.html.

Kwan, Rhoda. "China Begins Live-Fire Military Drills around Taiwan." *NBC News,* August 4, 2022. https://www.nbcnews.com/news/world/china-begins-live-fire-drills-taiwan-pelosi-visit-rcna41461.

Lanoszka, Alexander. *Atomic Assurance: The Alliance Politics of Nuclear Proliferation.* Ithaca, NY: Cornell University Press, 2018.

———. *Military Alliances in the Twenty-First Century.* Cambridge: Polity, 2022.

———. "Russian Hybrid Warfare and Extended Deterrence in Eastern Europe." *International Affairs* 92, no. 1 (2016): 175–195. https://doi.org/10.1111/1468-2346.12509.

Lee, Chaewon, and Adam P. Liff. "Reassessing Seoul's 'One China' Policy: South Korea-Taiwan 'Unofficial' Relations after 30 Years (1992 – 2022)." *Journal of Contemporary China* 32, no. 143 (2023): 745–764. https://doi.org/https://doi.org/10.1080/10670564.2022.2113959.

Lee, Chung Min, "South Korea Is Caught between China and the United States," *Q&A. Carnegie Endowment for International Peace,* October 21, 2020. https://carnegieendowment.org/posts/2020/10/south-korea-is-caught-between-china-and-the-united-states?lang=en.

Lee, Hsi-Min, and Michael A. Hunzeker. "The View of Ukraine from Taiwan: Get Real About Territorial Defense." *War on the Rocks,* March 15, 2022. https://warontherocks.com/2022/03/the-view-of-ukraine-from-taiwan-get-real-about-territorial-defense/.

Leeds, Brett Ashley. "Alliance Treaty Obligations and Provisions (Atop) Codebook." (August 9, 2023). http://www.atopdata.org/uploads/6/9/1/3/69134503/atop_5_1_codebook.pdf.

———, and Sezi Anac. "Alliance Institutionalization and Alliance Performance." *International Interactions* 31, no. 3 (2005): 183–202. https://doi.org/10.1080/03050620500294135.

———, Michaela Mattes, and Jeremy S. Vogel. "Interests, Institutions, and the Reliability of International Commitments." *American Journal of*

Political Science 53, no. 2 (2009): 461–476. https://doi.org/10.1111/j. 1540-5907.2009.00381.x.

———, Andrew G. Long, and Sara McLaughlin Mitchell. "Reevaluating Alliance Reliability: Specific Threats, Specific Promises." *The Journal of Conflict Resolution* 44, no. 5 (2000): 686–699. https://doi.org/10.1 177/0022002700044005006.

———, and Burcu Savun. "Terminating Alliances: Why Do States Abrogate Agreements?" *The Journal of Politics* 69, no. 4 (2007): 1118–1132. https://doi.org/10.1111/j.1468-2508.2007.00612.x.

Lehmann, Todd C. "Projecting Credibility: Alliance Commitments, Limited Security Partnerships, and International Crisis Responses." Working Paper. 2019.

LeVeck, Brad L., and Neil Narang. "How International Reputation Matters: Revisiting Alliance Violations in Context." *International Interactions* 43, no. 5 (2017). https://doi.org/10.1080/03050629.2017.1237818.

Li, Lauly, and Cheng Ting-Fan. "How Taiwan Became the Indispensable Economy." *Financial Times*, May 30, 2023. https://ig.ft.com/taiwan-economy/.

Liff, Adam P., "No, Japan Is Not Planning to 'Double Its Defense Budget," *Brookings Commentary*. The Brookings Institution, May 22, 2023, https://www.brookings.edu/articles/no-japan-is-not-planning-to-double-its-defense-budget/.

———. "The U.S.-Japan Alliance and Taiwan." *Asia Policy* 17, no. 3 (July 2022): 125–160. https://adampliff.com/wp-content/uploads/2023/01/liff2022_asiapolicy_us-japan-alliance-taiwan.pdf.

Lim, Darren. *Chinese Economic Coercion during the Thaad Dispute.* The Asan Institute for Policy Studies, December 28, 2019. https://theasanforum.org/chinese-economic-coercion-during-the-thaad-dispute/.

Logan, David C. "Chinese Views of Strategic Stability: Implications for US-China Relations." *International Security* 49, no. 2 (Fall 2024): 56–96. https://doi.org/https://doi.org/10.1162/isec_a_00495.

Lohman, Walter, and Frank Jannuzi. "Preserve America's Strategic Autonomy in the Taiwan Strait." *War on the Rocks*, October 29, 2020.

https://warontherocks.com/2020/10/preserve-americas-strategic-autonomy-in-the-taiwan-strait/.

Lupton, Danielle L. *Reputation for Resolve: How Leaders Signal Determination in International Politics*. Ithaca, NY: Cornell University Press, 2020. doi:10.7591/j.ctvq2w564.

Madhani, Aamer. "Us, Japan, South Korea to Announce Deeper Defense Cooperation at Camp David Summit." Associated Press, August 14, 2023. https://apnews.com/article/biden-yoon-kishida-camp-david-missile-defense-f3ce58da383f2255ee479624645db542.

Mahadzir, Dzirhan. "China Targets Taiwan in Major Military Exercise, Pentagon Condemns 'Irresponsible' Action." USNI News, October 14, 2024. https://news.usni.org/2024/10/14/china-targets-taiwan-in-major-military-exercise-pentagon-condemns-irresponsible-action.

Mai, Jun, Amber Wang, and Wendy Wu. "Mainland China Kicks Off Pla Blockade around Taiwan, 3 Days after William Lai Speech." *South China Morning Post*, May 23, 2024. https://www.scmp.com/news/china/military/article/3263719/mainland-chinese-forces-begin-military-exercises-around-taiwan-3-days-after-lai-speech.

Manyin, Mark E. , Caitlin Campbell, Emma Chanlett-Avery, Mary Beth D. Niktin, and Brock R. Williams. *U.S.-South Korea Alliance: Issues for Congress*. Washington, DC: U.S. Library of Congress, Congressional Research Service, 2024.

Mattes, Michaela. "Reputation, Symmetry, and Alliance Design." *International Organization* 66, no. 4 (2012): 679–707. https://doi.org/10.1017/S002081831200029X.

Mazarr, Michael J. *Mastering the Gray Zone: Understanding a Changing Era of Conflict*. Carlisle Barracks, PA: United States Army War College Press, 2015.

McGregor, Richard. *Chinese Coercion, Australian Resilience*. Lowy Institution, October 2022. https://www.lowyinstitute.org/publications/chinese-coercion-australian-resilience.

McManus, Roseanne W., and Mark David Nieman. "Identifying the Level of Major Power Support Signaled for Protégés: A Latent Measure

Approach." *Journal of Peace Research* 56, no. 3 (2019): 364–378. https://doi.org/10.1177/0022343318808842.

McManus, Roseanne W., and Keren Yarhi-Milo. "The Logic of "Offstage" Signaling: Domestic Politics, Regime Type, and Major Power-Protégé Relations." *International Organization* 71, no. 4 (2017): 701–733. https://doi.org/10.1017/S0020818317000297.

Mearsheimer, John J. *Conventional Deterrence*. Ithaca, NY: Cornell University Press, 1983.

———. "Say Goodbye to Taiwan." *The National Interest*, February 25, 2014. https://nationalinterest.org/article/say-goodbye-taiwan-9931.

Menendez, Bob. "This Is How the Us Will Stand with Taiwan." *The New York Times*, August 3, 2022. https://www.nytimes.com/2022/08/03/opinion/taiwan-us-defense-china.html.

Mercer, Jonathan. *Reputation and International Politics*. Ithaca, NY: Cornell University Press, 1996.

Metz, Rachel, and Erik Sand. "Defending Taiwan: But...What Are the Costs?" *The Washington Quarterly* 46, no. 4 (Winter 2023): 65–81. https://doi.org/https://doi.org/10.1080/0163660X.2023.2285165.

Moller, Sara Bjerg. "Domestic Politics, Threat Perceptions, and the Alliance Security Dilemma: The Case of South Korea, 1993–2020." *Asian Security* 18, no. 2: 119–137. https://doi.org/doi:10.1080/14799855.2021.1984231.

Montgomery, Evan, and Julian Ouellet. "American Defense Planning in the Shadow of Protracted War." *War on the Rocks*, November 18, 2024. https://warontherocks.com/2024/11/american-defense-planning-in-the-shadow-of-protracted-war/.

Morrow, James D. "Arms Versus Allies: Trade-Offs in the Search for Security." *International Organization* 47, no. 2 (1993): 207–233. https://doi.org/10.1017/S0020818300027922.

———. "Capabilities, Uncertainty, and Resolve: A Limited Information Model of Crisis Bargaining." *American Journal of Political Science* 33, no. 4 (1989): 941–972. https://doi.org/10.2307/2111116.

"Mutual Defense Treaty between the United States and the Republic of China." 1954. https://avalon.law.yale.edu/20th_century/chin001.asp.

Nakada, Ayako. "Aso: Fighting in Taiwan Strait Could Force Sdf to Defend Japan." *The Asahi Shimbun*, January 12, 2024. https://www.asahi.com/ajw/articles/15109484.

Narang, Vipin. *Nuclear Strategy in the Modern Era: Regional Powers and International Conflict.* Princeton, NJ: Princeton University Press, 2014.

National Defense Strategy (Provisional Translation as of December 28, 2022). 2022.

National Security Strategy of Japan (Provisional English Translation). 2022.

Needham, Kirsty. "Australia Rejects Chinese 'Economic Coercion' Threat Amid Planned Coronavirus Probe." *Reuters*, April 27, 2020. https://www.reuters.com/article/world/australia-rejects-chinese-economic-coercion-threat-amid-planned-coronavirus-prob-idUSKCN2290XW/.

Neelam, Ryan. *Lowy Institute Poll 2024: Understanding Australian Attitudes toward the World.* Lowy Institute, June 2024. https://poll.lowyinstitute.org/files/lowyinsitutepoll-2024.pdf.

Nemoto, Ryo, and Natsumi Iawata. "74% in Japan Support Engagement in Taiwan Strait: Nikkei Poll." *Nikkei Asia*, April 26, 2021. https://asia.nikkei.com/Politics/International-relations/74-in-Japan-support-engagement-in-Taiwan-Strait-Nikkei-poll.

Newsham, Grant. "Japan as the 'Swing Vote.'" In *The Boiling Moat: Urgent Steps to Defend Taiwan*, edited by Matt Pottinger, 187–200. Stanford, CA: Hoover Institution Press, 2024.

Nicastro, Luke A. *Aukus Pillar 2 (Advanced Capabilities): Background and Issues for Congress.* Washington, DC: U.S. Library of Congress, Congressional Research Service, 2024.

———. *The U.S. Defense Industrial Base: Background and Issues for Congress.* Washington, DC: U.S. Library of Congress, Congressional Research Service, 2023.

"Number of Residents from Japan Living in Taiwan from 2013–2022." *Statista*, 2024. https://www.statista.com/statistics/1080654/japan-number-japanese-residents-taiwan/.

Office of the Secretary of Defense. *Military and Security Developments Involving the People's Republic of China, 2022.* U.S. Department of Defense. https://media.defense.gov/2022/Nov/29/2003122279/-1/-1/1/2022-MILITARY-AND-SECURITY-DEVELOPMENTS-INVOLVING-THE-PEOPLES-REPUBLIC-OF-CHINA.PDF.

Pape, Robert A. *Bombing to Win : Air Power and Coercion in War.* Ithaca, NY: Cornell University Press, 1996.

Park, Hwee-rhak. "An Analysis and Lessons on South Korea's Attempt and Postponement of the Opcon Transition from the Rok-U.S. Combined Forces Command." *The Korean Journal of Defense Analysis* 27, no. 3 (September 2015): 347–363.

Park, Ju-min. "Japan Official, Calling Taiwan 'Red Line,' Urges Biden to 'Be Strong.'" *Reuters*, December 25, 2020. https://www.reuters.com/article/japan-usa-taiwan-china-idINKBN29001T.

President Joe Biden: The 2022 60 Minutes Interview, Aired September 18, 2022, on CBS. https://www.cbsnews.com/news/president-joe-biden-60-minutes-interview-transcript-2022-09-18/.

Pettyjohn, Stacie L. "Spiking the Problem: Developing a Resilient Posture in the Indo-Pacific with Passive Defenses." *War on the Rocks*, January 10, 2022. https://warontherocks.com/2022/01/spiking-the-problem-developing-a-resilient-posture-in-the-indo-pacific-with-passive-defenses/.

———. "War with China: Five Scenarios." *Survival* 64, no. 1: 57–66. https://doi.org/10.1080/00396338.2022.2032960.

———, Becca Wasser, and Chris Dougherty. *Dangerous Straits: Wargaming a Future Conflict over Taiwan.* Center for a New American Security, June 15, 2022). https://www.cnas.org/publications/reports/dangerous-straits-wargaming-a-future-conflict-over-taiwans.

Pietrucha, Mike. "Amateur Hour Part I: The Chinese Invasion of Taiwan." *War on the Rocks*, May 18, 2022. https://warontherocks.com/2022/05/amateur-hour-part-i-the-chinese-invasion-of-taiwan/.

Porter, Patrick, and Michael J. Mazarr. *Countering China's Adventurism over Taiwan: A Third Way.* Lowy Institute, May 2021. https://www.lowyinstitute.org/publications/countering-china-s-adventurism-over-taiwan-third-way-0#heading-2537.

Posen, Barry R. *Inadvertent Escalation.* Ithaca, NY: Cornell University Press, 1991.

———. "Pull Back: The Case for a Less Activist Foreign Policy." *Foreign Affairs* 92, no. 1 (January/February 2013): 116–128.

———. *Restraint: A New Foundation for Us Grand Strategy.* Ithaca, NY: Cornell University Press, 2014.

Post, Abigail. "Flying to Fail: Costly Signals and Air Power in Crisis Bargaining." *Journal of Conflict Resolution* 63, no. 4 (2019): 869–895. https://doi.org/10.1177/0022002718777043.

Pottinger, Matt, ed. *The Boiling Moat: Urgent Steps to Defend Taiwan.* Stanford, CA: Hoover Institution Press, 2024.

Pottinger, Matt, and Matthew Turpin. "The Myth of Accidental War." In *The Boiling Moat: Urgent Steps to Defend Taiwan*, edited by Matt Pottinger, 43–58. Stanford, CA: Hoover Institution Press, 2024.

Press, Daryl Grayson. *Calculating Credibility: How Leaders Assess Military Threats.* Ithaca, N.Y: Cornell University Press, 2005.

Quinn, Jimmy. "Biden Says, for Fourth Time, U.S. Would Send Troops to Defend Taiwan from Chinese Invasion." *The National Review*, September 18, 2022. https://www.nationalreview.com/corner/biden-says-u-s-would-send-troops-to-defend-taiwan-from-chinese-invasion-for-fourth-time/

Quiroz, Juan. "The U.S. Military's Personnel Crisis." *Foreign Affairs* , January 5, 2024. https://www.foreignaffairs.com/united-states/us-militarys-personnel-crisis.

Rachman, Gideon. "Why Taiwan Matters to the World." *Financial Times*, April 10, 2023. https://www.ft.com/content/11b82a88-57ae-44b1-8368-864f42ffac7f

Ratner, Ely S. Statement by Ely S. Ratner, Assistant Secretary of Defense for Indo-Pacific Security Affairs, Office of the Secretary of Defense, before the Committee on Foreign Relations, United States Senate, 117th Congress, December 8, 2021.

———. Statement by Ely S. Ratner, Assistant Secretary of Defense for Indo-Pacific Security Affairs, Office of the Secretary of Defense, before the House Armed Services Committee, 118th Congress, September 19, 2023.

Rehman, Iskander. *Planning for Protraction: A Historically Informed Approach to Great-Power War and Sino-Us Competition.* London, UK: The International Institute for Strategic Studies, 2023.

Republic of China (Taiwan). Ministry of National Defense. *Guofang Xiaoxi* 國防消息 [Defense News]. https://www.mnd.gov.tw/PublishTable. aspx?Types=%E5%8D%B3%E6%99%82%E8%BB%8D%E4%BA%8B%E5 %8B%95%E6%85%8B&title=%E5%9C%8B%E9%98%B2%E6%B6%88%E6 %81%AF.

Reuters. "China Trying to 'Normalise' Military Drills near Taiwan: Island's Top Security Official." *Reuters*, March 10, 2024. https://www.reuters. com/world/asia-pacific/china-trying-normalise-military-drills-near-taiwan-islands-top-security-official-2024-03-11/.

———. "China's Xi Says Political Solution for Taiwan Can't Wait Forever." October 16, 2013. https://www.reuters.com/article/us-asia-apec-china-taiwan/chinas-xi-says-political-solution-for-taiwan-cant-wait-forever-idUSBRE99503Q20131006/.

———. "US and Japan Draw up Joint Military Plan in Case of Taiwan Emergency – Report." *The Gaurdian*, December 23, 2021. https:// www.theguardian.com/world/2021/dec/24/us-and-japan-draw-up-joint-military-plan-in-case-of-taiwan-emergency-report

Rich, Timothy, and Carolyn Brueggemann. "South Korean Views on Cross-Strait Tensions." *Global Taiwan Brief* 9, no. 1 (2024): 13–15. https://globaltaiwan.org/wp-content/uploads/2024/01/GTB-Vol-9-Issue-1.pdf.

Rigger, Shelley. "The Taiwan Relations Act: Past, Present, Future." *Asia Policy* 14, no. 4 (2019): 11–17. https://doi.org/10.1353/asp.2019.0061.

Rittenhouse Green, Brendan, and Caitlin Talmadge. "Then What? Assessing the Military Implications of Chinese Control of Taiwan."

International Security 47, no. 1: 7–45. https://doi.org/https://doi.org/
10.1162/isec_a_00437.

Robert, Blackwill D., and Philip Zelikow. *The United States, China, and Taiwan: A Strategy to Prevent War.* Council on Foreign Relations, February 2021. https://www-jstor-org.mutex.gmu.edu/stable/resrep2
8673?sid=primo.

Rogin, Josh. *Chaos under Heaven: Trump, Xi, and the Battle for the Twenty-First Century.* Boston: Houghton Mifflin Harcourt, 2021.

Ross, Joseph. "What's Missing from Japan's Defense Buildup?" *The Diplomat,* April 4, 2024. https://thediplomat.com/2024/04/whats-missing-from-japans-defense-buildup/.

Russett, Bruce M. "An Empirical Typology of International Military Alliances." *Midwest Journal of Political Science* 15, no. 2 (1971): 262–289. https://doi.org/10.2307/2110272.

Sacks, David, and Jennifer Hillman. "The Time Is Now for a Trade Deal with Taiwan." *Asia Unbound.* Council on Foreign Relations, June 14, 2021. https://www.cfr.org/blog/time-now-trade-deal-taiwan.

Salisbury, Emma. "The Sinking Submarine Industrial Base." *War on the Rocks,* October 26, 2023. https://warontherocks.com/2023/10/the-sinking-submarine-industrial-base/.

Santoro, David, and Ralph Cossa, eds. *The World after Taiwan's Fall* Vol. 23, Issues & Insights, vol. 2: Pacific Forum, 2023.

Schelling, Thomas C. *Arms and Influence.* New Haven, CT: Yale University Press, 1966.

———. *The Strategy of Conflict.* New York, NY: Oxford University Press, 1963.

Sechser, Todd S. "Reputations and Signaling in Coercive Bargaining." *Journal of Conflict Resolution* 62, no. 2 (2018): 318–345. https://doi.org/10.1177/0022002716652687.

Sechser, Todd S., and Matthew Fuhrmann. *Nuclear Weapons and Coercive Diplomacy.* Cambridge: Cambridge University Press, 2017.

Shattuck, Thomas J., and Benjamin Lewis. *Breaking the Barrier: Four Years of PRC Military Activity around Taiwan.* Foreign Policy

Research Institute, October 9, 2024. https://www.fpri.org/article/2024/10/breaking-the-barrier-four-years-of-prc-military-activity-around-taiwan/.

Shelbourne, Mallory. "Davidson: China Could Try to Take Control of Taiwan in 'Next Six Years.'" *USNI News*, March 9, 2021. https://news.usni.org/2021/03/09/davidson-china-could-try-to-take-control-of-taiwan-in-next-six-years.

Silver, Laura , Kat Devlin, and Christine Huang. *Unfavorable Views of China Reach Historic Highs in Many Countries.* Pew Research Center, October 6, 2020. https://www.pewresearch.org/global/2020/10/06/unfavorable-views-of-china-reach-historic-highs-in-many-countries/?utm_content=bufferc0664&utm_medium=social&utm_source=twitter.com&utm_campaign=buffer.

Smith, Noah. "Manufacturing Is a War Now, and the Democracies Are Losing." *Noahpinion*, December 4, 2024. https://www.noahpinion.blog/p/manufacturing-is-a-war-now.

Snyder, Glenn H. *Deterrence and Defense: Toward a Theory of National Security.* Princeton, NJ: Princeton University Press, 1961.

———. "Deterrence and Power." *The Journal of Conflict Resolution* 4, no. 2: 163–178. https://www.jstor.org/stable/172650.

———. "The Security Dilemma in Alliance Politics." *World Politics* 36, no. 4 (1984): 461–495. https://doi.org/10.2307/2010183.

Snyder, Jack. *Myths of Empire: Domestic Politics and International Ambition.* Ithaca, NY: Cornell University Press, 1991.

"South Korea / China." Observatory of Economic Complexity, May 16, 2024. https://oec.world/en/profile/bilateral-country/kor/partner/chn

"South Korea Country Profile." Observatory of Economic Complexity, October 12, 2023. https://oec.world/en/profile/country/kor.

Spoehr, Thomas, and Bridget Handy. *The Looming National Security Crisis: Young Americans Unable to Serve in the Military.* The Heritage Foundation, February 13, 2018. https://www.heritage.org/sites/default/files/2018-02/BG3282.pdf.

Steinberg, James, and Michael E. O'Hanlon. *Strategic Reassurance and Resolve: U.S.-China Relations in the Twenty-First Century.* Princeton, NJ: Princeton University Press, 2014.

Stokes, Jacob. *Atomic Strait: How China's Nuclear Buildup Shapes Security Dynamics with Taiwan and the United States.* Center for a New American Security, February 7, 2023. https://www.cnas.org/publications/reports/atomic-strait-how-chinas-nuclear-buildup-shapes-security-dynamics-with-taiwan-and-the-united-states.

Sullivan, Dan. "A Test of Will: Why Taiwan Matters." Speech, Hudson Institute, Washington, DC, February 22, 2024. https://www.hudson.org/events/test-will-why-taiwan-matters-dan-sullivan.

Sweeney, Mike. "How Militarily Useful Would Taiwan Be to China?" Defense Priorities, February 22, 2024. https://www.defensepriorities.org/explainers/how-militarily-useful-would-taiwan-be-to-china.

———. "Why a Taiwan Conflict Could Go Nuclear." Defense Priorities, March 4, 2021 2021. https://www.defensepriorities.org/explainers/why-a-taiwan-conflict-could-go-nuclear.

Swenson-Wright, John. *Unequal Allies? United States Security and Alliance Policy toward Japan, 1945–1960.* Stanford, CA: Stanford University Press, 2005.

Taiwan Relations Act. Public Law 96–8, 93 Stat. 14 (1979).

Talmadge, Caitlin. "Would China Go Nuclear?: Assessing the Risk of Chinese Nuclear Escalation in a Conventional War with the United States." *International security* 41, no. 4 (2017): 50–92. https://doi.org/10.1162/ISEC_a_00274.

Tang, Shiping. "Reputation, Cult of Reputation, and International Conflict." *Security Studies* 14, no. 1 (2005): 34–62. https://doi.org/10.1080/09636410591001474.

Taylor, Adam. "Why China Is So Mad About Thaad, a Missile Defense System Aimed at Deterring North Korea." *The Washington Post,,* March 7, 2017. https://www.washingtonpost.com/news/worldviews/wp/2017/03/07/why-china-is-so-mad-about-thaad-a-missile-defense-system-aimed-at-deterring-north-korea/.

Tingley, Dustin H., and Barbara F. Walter. "The Effect of Repeated Play on Reputation Building: An Experimental Approach." *International Organization* 65, no. 2 (2011): 343–365. https://doi.org/10.1017/S002 0818311000026.

Truman, Harry S. *Memoirs by Harry S. Truman: Years of Trial and Hope.* 2 vols. Vol. II, New York, NY: Doubleday, 1956.

———. "Statement by the President, Truman on Korea." June 27, 1950. Wilson Center Digital Archive, November 8, 2024. https:// digitalarchive.wilsoncenter.org/document/statement-president-truman-korea.

Trung, Nguyen Thanh. "How China's Coast Guard Law Has Changed the Regional Security Structure." Asia Maritime Transparency Initiative, April 12, 2021, https://amti.csis.org/how-chinas-coast-guard-law-has-changed-the-regional-security-structure/#:~:text=China's%20newly %20passed%20coast%20guard,operations%20in%20the%20waters%20 under.

Tsuneo, Watanabe. "What's New in Japan's Three Strategic Documents." Center for Strategic and International Studies, February 13, 2023. https://www.csis.org/analysis/whats-new-japans-three-strategic-documents.

Tucker, Nancy Bernkpf, and Bonnie Glaser. "Should the United States Abandon Taiwan?" *The Washington Quarterly* 34, no. 4 (Fall 2011 2011): 23–37. https://doi.org/DOI: 10.1080/0163660X.2011.609128.

Turcsanyi, Richard Q., and Esther E. Song. "South Koreans Have the Most Negative Views of China. Why?" *The Diplomat*, December 24, 2022. https://thediplomat.com/2022/12/south-koreans-have-the-worlds-most-negative-views-of-china-why/.

Turcsányi, Richard Q., Klára Dubravčíková, Su-Jeong Kang, James Iocovozzi, Matej Šimalčík, and Lucia Husenicová. *South Korean Public Opinion on the World in Times of Global Turmoil.* Central European Institute of Asian Studies, September 2022. https://ceias. eu/wp-content/uploads/2022/09/Korean-poll-finaldraft-adjustments-3-1_rqt-1-2.pdf.

U.S. Department of Commerce. *Taiwan – Cybersecurity.* Country Commercial Guides. Washington, DC: International Trade Administration. Last modified August 8, 2023. https://www.trade. gov/country-commercial-guides/taiwan-cybersecurity.

U.S. Department of State. "U.S.-Japan Joint Press Statement." news release, March 16, 2021, https://www.state.gov/u-s-japan-joint-press-statement/

U.S. Forces Korea, Office of Public Affairs. "ROK & U.S. Joint Statement: ROK-U.S. Alliance Agrees to Deploy THAAD." News release, July 7, 2016. https://www.usfk.mil/Media/Newsroom/News/Article/831175/ rok-us-joint-statement-rok-us-alliance-agrees-to-deploy-thaad/.

Webster, Joseph, "Does Taiwan's Massive Reliance on Energy Imports Put Its Security at Risk?" *The Atlanticist.* The Atlantic Council of the United States, July 7, 2023. https://www.atlanticcouncil.org/blogs/ new-atlanticist/does-taiwans-massive-reliance-on-energy-imports-put-its-security-at-risk/.

Welch, Jennifer, Jenny Leonard, Maeva Cousin, Gerard DiPippo, and Tom Orlik. "Xi, Biden and the $10 Trillion Cost of War over Taiwan." *Bloomberg,* January 8, 2024. https://www.bloomberg.com/news/ features/2024-01-09/if-china-invades-taiwan-it-would-cost-world-economy-10-trillion.

Welch, Jennifer, Jenny Leonard, Maeva Cousin, Gerard DiPippo, and Gerard Orlik. "Xi, Bide, and the $10 Trillion Cost of War over Taiwan." *Bloomberg,* January 8, 2024. https://www.bloomberg.com/news/ features/2024-01-09/if-china-invades-taiwan-it-would-cost-world-economy-10-trillion?embedded-checkout=true.

Welsh, Sophie, "How Did the Japanese Public React to the Us Withdrawal Decision from the Afghanistan Crisis?" Weatherhead Program on US-Japan Relations, February 14, 2022. https://us-japan.wcfia.harvard. edu/blog-2-14-2022.

White House, The. *Readout of President Joe Biden's Meeting with Prime Minister Anthony Albanese of Australia,* 2022.

———. "Remarks by President Biden after Marine One Arrival." News release, October 5, 2021, https://www.whitehouse.gov/briefing-room/speeches-remarks/2021/10/06/remarks-by-president-biden-after-marine-one-arrival-6/.

———. "Remarks by President Biden and Prime Minister Kishida Fumio of Japan in Joint Press Conference." News release, May 23, 2022, https://www.whitehouse.gov/briefing-room/speeches-remarks/2022/05/23/remarks-by-president-biden-and-prime-minister-fumio-kishida-of-japan-in-joint-press-conference/.

———. "The Spirit of Camp David: Joint Statement of Japan, the Republic of Korea, and the United States." News release, August 8, 2023, https://www.whitehouse.gov/briefing-room/statements-releases/2023/08/18/the-spirit-of-camp-david-joint-statement-of-japan-the-republic-of-korea-and-the-united-states/.———. *U.S.-Japan Joint Leaders' Statement, "U.S.-Japan Global Partnership for a New Era"*, 2021.

———. *U.S.-Rok Leaders' Joint Statement*, 2021.

World Population Review. "Taiwan Population 2024." World Population Review. https://worldpopulationreview.com/countries/taiwan-population.

Wu, Sarah. "Bridge Dilemma Captures Divide over China in Taiwan Elections." *Reuters*, January 10, 2024. https://www.reuters.com/world/asia-pacific/bridge-dilemma-captures-divide-over-china-taiwan-elections-2024-01-09/.

Xi, Jinping, "Yishiweijian kaichuangweilai maitoukugan yongyiqianxing" 以史为鉴、开创未来、埋头苦干、勇毅前行 [Take history as a mirror, open up the future; bury oneself in hard work, and move forward with courage and resolve]. *Qiushi*, January 1, 2021, https://archive.ph/3kxGX.

Xinhuanet. "Full Text: Speech by Xi Jinping at a Ceremony Marking the Centenary of the Communist Party of China." July 1, 2021. http://www.xinhuanet.com/english/special/2021-07/01/c_1310038244.htm.

Xinhuanet. "Xinhua Headlines: Xi Says "China Must Be, Will Be Reunified" as Key Anniversary Marked." January 2, 2019. http://www.xinhuanet.com/english/2019-01/02/c_137714898.htm.

Yarhi-Milo, Keren. *Who Fights for Reputation: The Psychology of Leaders in International Conflict*. Princeton, NJ: Princeton University Press, 2018. doi:10.23943/9781400889983.

Yarhi-Milo, Keren, Alexander Lanoszka, and Zack Cooper. "To Arm or to Ally? The Patron's Dilemma and the Strategic Logic of Arms Transfers and Alliances." *International Security* 41, no. 2 (2016): 90–139. https://doi.org/10.1162/ISEC_a_00250.

Yi, Whan-woo. "Number of Foreign Nationals in Korea Rises to Record High of 1.43 Mil." *The Korea Times*, December 12, 2023. https://www.koreatimes.co.kr/www/biz/2024/06/602_365339.html.

Yu, Miles Maochun, "Five Reasons Why Taiwan Should Lie within the Defense Umbrella of the United States." *Hoover Institution*, June 30, 2021, https://www.hoover.org/research/five-reasons-why-taiwan-should-lie-within-defense-umbrella-united-states.

INDEX

ABOUT THE AUTHORS

Michael A. Hunzeker is an Associate Professor at George Mason University's Schar School of Policy and Government, where he serves as the Director of the Program Faculty in Government and International Affairs and the Associate Director of the Center for Security Policy Studies. His research focuses on military strategy, defense reform, deterrence, and cross-Strait security issues.

Mark A. Christopher is a nonresident fellow at the Atlantic Council's Global China Hub. He holds a bachelors degree from the Georgetown School of Foreign Service and an MPA from the Princeton School of Public and International Affairs. His writing has appeared in *Foreign Affairs*, *Foreign Policy*, the Jamestown Foundation's *China Brief*, *Defense One*, and the *Wall Street Journal*.

CAMBRIA RAPID COMMUNICATIONS IN CONFLICT AND SECURITY SERIES

General Editor: Thomas G. Mahnken
(Founding Editor: Geoffrey R. H. Burn)

This series provides policymakers, practitioners, analysts, and academics with in-depth analysis of fast-moving topics requiring urgent yet informed debate. Since its launch in October 2015, the RCCS series has published the following volumes:

- *A New Strategy for Complex Warfare: Combined Effects in East Asia* by Thomas A. Drohan

- *US National Security: New Threats, Old Realities* by Paul R. Viotti

- *Security Forces in African States: Cases and Assessment* edited by Paul Shemella and Nicholas Tomb

- *Trust and Distrust in Sino-American Relations: Challenge and Opportunity* by Steve Chan

- *The Gathering Pacific Storm: Emerging US-China Strategic Competition in Defense Technological and Industrial Development* edited by Tai Ming Cheung and Thomas G. Mahnken

- *Military Strategy for the 21st Century: People, Connectivity, and Competition* by Charles Cleveland, Benjamin Jensen, Susan Bryant, and Arnel David

- *Ensuring National Government Stability After US Counterinsurgency Operations: The Critical Measure of Success* by Dallas E. Shaw Jr.

- *Reassessing U.S. Nuclear Strategy* by David W. Kearn, Jr.

- *Deglobalization and International Security* by T. X. Hammes

- *American Foreign Policy and National Security* by Paul R. Viotti

- *Make America First Again: Grand Strategy Analysis and the Trump Administration* by Jacob Shively
- *Learning from Russia's Recent Wars: Why, Where, and When Russia Might Strike Next* by Neal G. Jesse
- *Restoring Thucydides: Testing Familiar Lessons and Deriving New Ones* by Andrew R. Novo and Jay M. Parker
- *Net Assessment and Military Strategy: Retrospective and Prospective Essays* edited by Thomas G. Mahnken, with an introduction by Andrew W. Marshall
- *Deterrence by Denial: Theory and Practice* edited by Alex S. Wilner and Andreas Wenger
- *Negotiating the New START Treaty* by Rose Gottemoeller
- *Party, Politics, and the Post-9/11 Army* by Heidi A. Urben
- *Resourcing the National Security Enterprise: Connecting the Ends and Means of US National Security* edited by Susan Bryant and Mark Troutman
- *Subcontinent Adrift: Strategic Futures of South Asia* by Feroz Hassan Khan
- *The Next Major War: Can the US and its Allies Win Against China?* by Ross Babbage
- *Warrior Diplomats: Civil Affairs Forces on the Front Lines* edited by Arnel David, Sean Acosta, and Nicholas Krohley
- *Russia and the Changing Character of Conflict* by Tracey German
- *Planning War with a Nuclear China: US Military Strategy and Mainland Strikes* by John Speed Meyers
- *Winning Without Fighting: Irregular Warfare and Strategic Competition in the 21st Century* by Rebecca Patterson, Susan Bryant, Ken Gleiman, and Mark Troutman
- *US Coercive Diplomacy and the Global Order: A Critical Analysis of Post–Cold War Strategies* by Richard Outzen
- *America's Taiwan Dilemma: Allies' Reactions and the Stakes for US Reputation* by Michael A. Hunzeker and Mark A. Christopher

www.ingramcontent.com/pod-product-compliance
Lightning Source LLC
Chambersburg PA
CBHW052001270326
41929CB00015B/2742